Bookstagram

IDEAS AND PROMPTS FOR
BOOKISH CONTENT ON INSTAGRAM

100 WAYS

Engagement

BOOKSTAGRAM 100 WAYS: ENGAGEMENT

ASTURIAN HOUSE PRESS

Bookstagram

IDEAS AND PROMPTS FOR
BOOKISH CONTENT ON INSTAGRAM

100 WAYS

Engagement

asturian
HOUSE PRESS

CONTENTS

THIS BOOK SERIES

A BOOK SERIES OF IDEAS AND PROMPTS FOR BOOKISH CONTENT ON INSTAGRAM

Welcome to the enchanting world of Bookstagram, where literature comes alive through the lens of creativity and passion. In the vast expanse of this virtual bookish community, countless stories find their way into the hearts of readers, thanks to the dedicated bookstagrammers who curate captivating content. If you have stumbled upon this book series, "Bookstagram 100 Ways," consider yourself fortunate to have discovered a wellspring of ideas and prompts that will elevate your bookish endeavors on Instagram.

Before we embark on this exciting journey, let us clarify the essence of this book series. It was meticulously prepared as a reference, carefully crafted to inspire and guide you in your quest to create engaging bookish content on Instagram. However, you need not follow a linear path and read it cover to cover. Instead, treat this book as a treasure trove, and explore the table of contents to find concepts that pique your interest and resonate with your unique style.

Each bookstagrammer brings a distinctive literary taste, and not all the ideas presented here will be applicable to everyone. Embrace your individuality and let your creativity thrive as you tailor these concepts to suit your preferences, interests, and vision.

"Bookstagram 100 Ways" is a compilation of existing ideas that thrive within the vibrant Bookstagram community. We want to emphasize that none of these ideas are originally ours; rather, they have been thoughtfully collected in this guide to support both new and seasoned bookstagrammers in their quest to connect remarkable stories with eager readers.

While we encourage you to draw inspiration from these prompts, remember that they should serve as a springboard for your imagination. The true essence of Bookstagram lies in authenticity and innovation. Feel free to expand upon these ideas, infuse them with your personal touch, and let your creative prowess shine through.

We are well aware that there exists an endless sea of possibilities and ideas within the Bookstagram universe. However, to avoid overwhelming you, we have carefully selected 100 of the most common and popular concepts. Think of these as sparks that ignite your creative fire, propelling you to explore the boundless potential of bookish expression.

This is not a "how-to" book that lays down rigid rules and instructions. Instead, it is a guide designed to inspire and empower you to experiment, evolve, and invent new ways to celebrate literature. While we plan to create "how-to" content in the future, we acknowledge the brilliance of numerous creative souls who have already mastered these ideas and more. We wholeheartedly encourage you to seek inspiration from other bookstagrammers, for this community thrives on support, collaboration, and admiration.

In essence, consider these books as "field guides" in the captivating realm of Bookstagram. They open the doors to a world where books transcend their physical forms and take on a life of their own, captivating the hearts of readers from all corners of the globe. So, whether you are a seasoned bookstagrammer seeking fresh inspiration or a newcomer eager to embark on a magical journey, we invite you to immerse yourself in "Bookstagram 100 Ways." May it fuel your creativity, kindle your passion for literature, and lead you to create something extraordinary in the enchanting world of Bookstagram.

- Asturian House Press Team

OTHER BOOKS IN THIS SERIES:

Bookstagram 100 Ways: Reels (Vol. 1)

Bookstagram 100 Ways: Engagement (Vol. 2)

Bookstagram 100 Ways: Carousels (Vol. 3)

Bookstagram 100 Ways: Lives (Vol. 4)

Bookstagram 100 Ways: Stories (Vol. 5)

BOOKSTAGRAM100WAYS

Scan or Click to Connect!

BOOKSTAGRAM 100 WAYS: ENGAGEMENT

IDEAS AND PROMPTS FOR ENGAGING YOUR BOOKSTAGRAM AUDIENCE

Welcome to the enchanting universe of Bookstagram, where the love for books transcends the boundaries of space and time, uniting book lovers and bookstagrammers in a vibrant community of literary passion. If you hold this book in your hands, consider yourself on the brink of embarking on an exciting journey into the art of captivating your bookstagram audience.

Within the pages of "Bookstagram 100 Ways: Engagement," we present a captivating collection of 100 diverse and delightful ways to connect with your bookstagram followers. Our goal is to empower you with a myriad of ideas and prompts to enrich your bookish content on Instagram and to forge meaningful connections with fellow book enthusiasts.

As you flip through these pages, you will find a treasure trove of creative approaches, each designed to spark intrigue, foster conversations, and ignite the flames of passion for reading. We invite you to immerse yourself in these ideas, to explore the depths of your imagination, and to adapt them to suit your unique voice and style.

From creative photo challenges that transport books to new dimensions, to interactive story polls that invite your audience to choose their own literary adventures, "Bookstagram 100 Ways: Engagement" covers a wide spectrum of strategies. Dive into the world of bookish quizzes, thought-provoking discussions, behind-the-scenes glimpses, and so much more – all carefully curated to captivate your audience and keep them eagerly awaiting your next post.

We recognize that every bookstagrammer is a storyteller in their own right, weaving tales of literary fascination through visuals, captions, and shared experiences. As you explore these engagement ideas, remember that each one is a blank canvas awaiting your creative strokes. Let your personality shine through, and breathe life into these concepts with your unique flair, transforming them into captivating experiences for your followers.

In a world overflowing with digital content, we understand the importance of fostering genuine connections with your bookstagram audience. These 100 ways to engage are more than mere strategies; they are gateways to forming lasting relationships built on shared love for literature.

Whether you're a seasoned bookstagrammer seeking fresh inspiration or a newcomer eager to make your mark, "Bookstagram 100 Ways: Engagement" is your companion on this thrilling quest. Embrace the possibilities, experiment fearlessly, and let your passion for books guide you as you traverse the wondrous landscape of bookish content on Instagram.

As you absorb the essence of each idea, remember that Bookstagram is a community of kindred spirits, eager to cheer you on, collaborate, and celebrate your literary explorations. Join us as we embark on this exciting adventure together, discovering the joy of engagement and the power of stories to unite us all. Let "Bookstagram 100 Ways: Engagement" be your gateway to cultivating an enchanting bookstagram journey that leaves a lasting imprint on the hearts of your audience.

ONE
WEEKLY BOOK CHALLENGES:
EXPLORING LITERATURE THROUGH THEMES AND GENRES

THE CONCEPT EXPLAINED:

At its core, the concept of weekly book challenges revolves around the idea of creating a shared reading experience within the bookstagram community. Bookstagrammers, who are influential figures on Instagram known for their captivating book-related content, initiate these challenges to foster a sense of community and ignite excitement for reading. Every week, a new theme or genre is announced, setting the tone for the reading journey ahead.

Embracing Themes:

Themes provide a thematic framework for the reading challenge. They can range from specific emotions, historical periods, diverse cultures, seasons, or even abstract concepts. For example, a theme might be "Summer Escapes," encouraging followers to read books set during the summer or with a strong focus on vacations and travel. Another theme could be "Books that Made You Cry," prompting readers to explore poignant and emotionally charged narratives.

By delving into books that align with the chosen theme, followers not only broaden their literary horizons but also discover new perspectives, settings, and characters that they might have otherwise overlooked.

Exploring Genres:

On the other hand, genre-based challenges focus on the style and form of the books. Popular genres include fantasy, mystery, romance, science fiction, historical fiction, non-fiction, and many more. Each week, the booksta-grammer announces a particular genre as the focal point, encouraging followers to delve into the diverse worlds and storytelling techniques that each genre offers.

For instance, during a science fiction-themed week, followers might immerse themselves in futuristic societies, advanced technology, and space exploration. Conversely, a historical fiction-themed week could lead them to explore the past through well-researched narratives, reliving significant events and uncovering lesser-known stories.

Creating a Community of Readers:

The beauty of the weekly book challenges lies in their ability to create a sense of community and shared enthu-siasm for reading. As followers participate in the chal-lenge, they engage with one another, sharing their book selections, thoughts, and recommendations. This interac-tivity fosters meaningful discussions and connections, as individuals with diverse backgrounds and interests come together to celebrate their love for books.

The bookstagrammer, acting as a facilitator and host, plays a pivotal role in this community-building process. By sharing their own book choices, insights, and reflections on the theme or genre, they provide a focal point for discussions and encourage followers to share their own unique perspectives.

Encouraging Reading Diversity:

One of the significant advantages of weekly book challenges is their ability to promote reading diversity. By exploring different themes and genres, followers are encouraged to step outside their comfort zones and read books they might not have considered before. This exposure to various styles and subjects broadens their literary palate and encourages an open-minded approach to reading.

Moreover, the challenges provide an excellent opportunity for bookstagrammers to highlight diverse authors, underrepresented voices, and marginalized perspectives. Themes centered around diversity, social issues, and inclusion can serve as a platform to amplify and celebrate the richness of literature from diverse backgrounds.

IN CONCLUSION:

The concept of weekly book challenges has evolved into a cherished tradition in the bookstagram community. By embracing themes and genres, followers embark on a literary adventure that not only enriches their reading experiences but also creates a sense of belonging and camaraderie. As bookstagrammers continue to curate these challenges, they fuel the collective passion for reading and inspire their followers to cherish the world of literature, one theme or genre at a time.

TWO
"GUESS THE BOOK" QUIZZES:
UNVEILING LITERARY PUZZLES

THE CONCEPT EXPLAINED:

"Guess the Book" quizzes are a captivating form of book-related content in which the bookstagrammer or host presents followers with visual or textual puzzles related to books. The primary goal is to create an enjoyable and interactive experience for the community while fostering a sense of literary camaraderie. By engaging followers in a game-like format, these quizzes add an element of fun and excitement to the bookstagram feed, encouraging followers to participate actively.

Blurry Cover Images:

One variant of the "Guess the Book" quiz involves using deliberately blurry or obscured cover images of well-known books. The challenge for followers is to decipher the book's identity based on the limited visual cues provided. To make it more engaging, the level of blurriness can vary, ranging from subtle obscurity to complete distortion, requiring varying degrees of familiarity with the book's cover design.

This form of the quiz not only tests the readers' visual memory but also prompts them to draw connections between partial visual information and the books they might have encountered before.

Mysterious Excerpts:

Another exciting version of the "Guess the Book" quiz features intriguing excerpts from various books. The chosen passages can be thought-provoking lines, pivotal moments, or even obscure descriptions that capture the essence of the story. However, the excerpts often exclude any explicit reference to the book's title or author, challenging the followers to rely solely on their knowledge of literature to identify the source.

This textual approach appeals to readers who have a keen eye for memorable quotes and are well-versed in the narrative styles of different authors.

Promoting Active Reading Engagement:

The "Guess the Book" quizzes go beyond mere entertainment; they also promote active reading engagement among followers. As participants strive to identify books based on blurred covers or excerpts, they tend to reflect on their reading experiences, drawing upon their memories of books they have read in the past. This process not only reinforces their literary knowledge but also kindles their desire to explore more books to improve their chances of success in future quizzes.

Moreover, participants are likely to engage in discussions with fellow followers, sharing their interpretations of excerpts or comparing their bookish insights. This social interaction fosters a sense of community and encourages a healthy exchange of reading recommendations.

Encouraging Curiosity and Discovery:

The allure of the "Guess the Book" quizzes lies in the element of mystery and surprise. As followers encounter blurry covers or intriguing excerpts, they are driven by curiosity to unlock the hidden answers. This sense of curiosity can inspire them to seek out new books and authors they may not have encountered previously.

Additionally, the quizzes provide an opportunity for bookstagrammers to feature a diverse range of books from various genres, time periods, and cultures. In turn, this exposure to a broad spectrum of literature motivates followers to broaden their reading preferences and explore beyond their comfort zones.

Interactive and Inclusive:

The interactive nature of "Guess the Book" quizzes contributes to an inclusive atmosphere within the bookstagram community. Readers of all ages and backgrounds can participate and enjoy the challenge, regardless of their reading experience or the number of books they have read. The quizzes celebrate the joy of reading itself and encourage followers to appreciate the beauty of storytelling.

IN CONCLUSION:

"Guess the Book" quizzes, with their blend of creativity and interactivity, have become a captivating fixture in the bookstagram landscape. By challenging followers to identify books based on blurry covers or enigmatic excerpts, these quizzes ignite curiosity, encourage active reading engagement, and foster a sense of community among literature enthusiasts. As the bookstagram community continues to thrive, these quizzes will undoubtedly remain an exciting and cherished tradition, inspiring readers to delve deeper into the world of literature while having fun along the way.

THREE
COLLABORATIVE BOOK RECOMMENDATIONS:
UNITING BOOKSTAGRAMMERS THROUGH SHARED READING EXPERIENCES

THE CONCEPT EXPLAINED:

Collaborative book recommendations on bookstagram are a form of crowdsourcing literary expertise. The bookstagrammer, acting as a host or facilitator, proposes a particular topic or theme for which they seek book recommendations. This theme could be broad, such as "Timeless Classics," "Fantasy Worlds," or "Books that Made You Cry," or more niche, such as "Books set in Japan" or "Female Sci-Fi Authors."

Followers are then encouraged to participate actively by commenting on the post or sending direct messages with their recommended books that align with the chosen theme. The host compiles these suggestions into a comprehensive list, either in the form of a post, story highlights, or a blog post, sharing the collective wisdom and literary tastes of the bookstagram community.

Fostering a Sense of Community:

Collaborative book recommendations create a powerful sense of community among bookstagrammers. As participants share their favorite books, they not only celebrate their individual reading preferences but also gain insight into the diverse tastes and interests of fellow readers. This collaborative effort fosters a feeling of camaraderie and shared passion for books, forging connections among followers who might have otherwise been strangers.

The bookstagrammer, in turn, plays a crucial role in nurturing this community spirit by acknowledging and celebrating each participant's contribution, making followers feel valued and appreciated for their input.

Expanding Literary Horizons:

One of the significant advantages of collaborative book recommendations is the opportunity for readers to expand their literary horizons. By exploring books based on a specific theme, readers are exposed to titles they might not have encountered through traditional reading channels. This exposure to a diverse range of books, genres, and authors encourages readers to step outside their comfort zones and embrace new reading experiences.

Additionally, collaborative recommendations can introduce followers to books from different cultures, historical periods, or with unique perspectives, further enriching their understanding of the world through literature.

Encouraging Thoughtful Discussions:

The process of collaborative book recommendations often leads to thoughtful and engaging discussions. As followers share their favorite books, they naturally express their reasons for loving those particular titles. This exchange of insights and reflections sparks conversations about literary themes, character development, writing styles, and the emotional impact of certain books.

Through these discussions, followers can explore different interpretations of books, discover shared reading experiences, and even respectfully debate their varying viewpoints. This interactive discourse not only enhances the reading experience but also deepens the bookstagram community's connection.

Empowering Diverse Voices:

Collaborative book recommendations offer an inclusive platform to amplify diverse voices and underrepresented authors. By suggesting books from diverse backgrounds and cultures, participants contribute to a more inclusive and equitable representation of literature. This creates an enriching reading experience for everyone involved and encourages followers to support a broader range of authors and stories.

The bookstagrammer's role in curating and featuring these recommendations is instrumental in promoting diversity and encouraging followers to explore books that offer unique perspectives and cultural insights.

IN CONCLUSION:

Collaborative book recommendations represent the collective power of a bookstagram community united by its passion for reading. By inviting followers to contribute their favorite books based on specific themes or topics, bookstagrammers create a collaborative and interactive reading experience. This concept not only strengthens the sense of community among followers but also expands their literary horizons, fosters thoughtful discussions, and empowers diverse voices within the bookstagram landscape. As this concept continues to evolve, it will undoubtedly remain a cherished tradition, inspiring readers to explore the vast world of literature together, one collaborative recommendation at a time.

FOUR
THEMED BOOKSHELF ORGANIZATION AND DISPLAY IDEAS:

SHOWCASING LITERATURE WITH ARTISTIC FLAIR

THE CONCEPT EXPLAINED:

Themed bookshelf organization and display ideas are an imaginative approach to arranging and presenting books in a visually cohesive and engaging manner. Instead of organizing books solely by author or title, this concept focuses on thematic elements that unite books under a common thread. This could range from genres like fantasy, mystery, or romance, to broader themes such as books set in specific time periods or featuring strong female protagonists.

Each themed bookshelf display becomes a curated collection, telling a story through its carefully chosen books and decorations. Bookstagrammers and book lovers take inspiration from literature, movies, seasons, historical events, or personal interests to craft these artful book arrangements.

Creative Themes and Concepts:

The beauty of themed bookshelf organization lies in its endless creative possibilities. The themes can be as diverse and imaginative as the human imagination itself. Some popular ideas include:

- ***Color-coordinated Bookshelves:*** Books are organized by the color of their spines, creating visually stunning rainbows or ombre effects.
- ***Seasonal Displays:*** Bookshelves are adorned with books that evoke the essence of a particular season, such as cozy reads for autumn or breezy beach reads for summer.
- ***Genre Showcase:*** Each shelf is dedicated to a specific genre, showcasing the best of fantasy, sci-fi, or historical fiction, allowing viewers to explore their preferred genres easily.
- ***Character-Centric Shelves:*** Books are arranged based on beloved characters or character archetypes, creating a tribute to literary icons.
- ***Book-to-Movie Displays:*** Books and their corresponding movie adaptations are paired together, highlighting the journey from the page to the screen.
- ***Historical Timeline:*** Books are organized chronologically, allowing readers to explore different eras in history through literature.
- ***Literary Quotes:*** Shelves feature books alongside framed quotes from the literature, adding an artistic touch and emphasizing the essence of the chosen theme.

Curating an Artistic Journey:

Themed bookshelf displays elevate the concept of book organization from a practical necessity to an artistic journey. As books are carefully selected and arranged, the bookshelf becomes a canvas where stories come alive through visual elements. The chosen theme guides the bookstagrammer's selection process, leading to thoughtful pairings and creative book arrangements that catch the eye and ignite curiosity.

Each themed bookshelf becomes a story in itself, inviting viewers to explore the world of books beyond individual titles and immerse themselves in a broader narrative that transcends the boundaries of single novels.

Inspiring Engagement and Discovery:

Themed bookshelf displays spark engagement and conversation within the bookstagram community and beyond. Followers are drawn to the creativity and effort put into crafting these displays, and they eagerly share their thoughts, book recommendations, and personal connections to the themes.

Additionally, themed displays inspire book lovers to discover new books that align with their interests and preferences. When books are organized by themes, it becomes easier for readers to find stories that resonate with their emotions or spark their curiosity.

Personal Expression and Connection:

Themed bookshelf displays offer bookstagrammers and bibliophiles an opportunity for personal expression. Each bookshelf is a reflection of its creator's interests, passions, and unique perspective on literature. As a result, the displays become a form of self-expression, allowing book lovers to share a piece of themselves through their favorite books and themes.

Viewers, too, find connections with these displays, recognizing shared interests or discovering new themes that resonate with them. The bookshelf becomes a space for like-minded individuals to bond over their love for literature and celebrate the beauty of storytelling.

IN CONCLUSION:

Themed bookshelf organization and display ideas breathe new life into bookshelves, transforming them into artistic showcases that celebrate literature and captivate the imagination. By curating books based on specific themes, colors, genres, or aesthetics, bookstagrammers and bibliophiles create visually stunning displays that spark engagement, inspire discovery, and offer a glimpse into their unique reading journeys. Through this concept, book lovers celebrate not only individual books but also the magic of storytelling as a whole. As the bookstagram community continues to thrive, themed bookshelf displays will remain a cherished tradition, inspiring readers to curate their literary worlds with passion and creativity.

FIVE
EXCLUSIVE BOOK GIVEAWAYS:
GRATITUDE IN THE LITERARY WORLD

THE CONCEPT EXPLAINED:

Exclusive book giveaways on bookstagram are a way for bookstagrammers, authors, and publishers to give back to their dedicated followers and express their gratitude for the continuous support they receive. The giveaways typically involve selecting a specific book or a set of books as prizes and announcing the giveaway through a post or story. Participants are required to follow certain entry rules, which might include liking the post, following the account, tagging friends, or sharing the giveaway in their stories.

The goal of these giveaways is not only to offer followers the chance to win a coveted book but also to create a sense of excitement and appreciation within the bookstagram community.

Fostering Community and Connection:

Exclusive book giveaways foster a strong sense of community and connection among bookstagrammers and their followers. As participants enter the giveaway, they share their enthusiasm for the books, the bookstagrammer, or the author, and often leave heartfelt comments expressing their gratitude for the impact the account has had on their reading journey.

The bookstagrammer, author, or publisher hosting the giveaway, in turn, has the opportunity to engage with followers through responses, messages, and appreciation posts. This interaction enhances the feeling of connection and camaraderie, turning the bookstagram account into a welcoming space where book lovers can share their love for literature.

Celebrating Reading and Literature:

Exclusive book giveaways are not just about the prizes; they also celebrate the joy of reading and the beauty of literature. The chosen books for the giveaway are often thoughtfully selected to align with the preferences and interests of the bookstagram community.

By featuring books that resonate with the community, the giveaways become a celebration of the stories, characters, and themes that have touched the hearts of readers. As participants enter the giveaway and express their excitement for these books, they are also celebrating the power of storytelling and the impact that literature can have on individuals' lives.

Building Anticipation and Excitement:

The announcement of an exclusive book giveaway generates anticipation and excitement within the bookstagram community. Followers eagerly wait for the reveal of the prize, and the act of entering the giveaway becomes an event in itself. This excitement extends to the selection of the winner, as participants keep an eye on the announcement to see who will be the lucky recipient of the exclusive book.

During this period, conversations and discussions about the featured book(s) flourish, fueling the sense of excitement and anticipation even further. As a result, the entire bookstagram community becomes involved in the celebration, even those who might not be participating in the giveaway directly.

Showing Gratitude and Appreciation:

Above all, exclusive book giveaways are a sincere expression of gratitude and appreciation towards followers. By offering coveted books as prizes, the bookstagrammer, author, or publisher is acknowledging the invaluable role that followers play in the success of the account or the book's promotion.

The giveaways serve as a way to say "thank you" to the community for their support, loyalty, and engagement. It is a gesture that resonates deeply with followers, as they feel recognized and valued by the account or author they admire.

IN CONCLUSION:

Exclusive book giveaways are a heartwarming tradition within the bookstagram community that celebrates the love for literature, fosters a strong sense of community, and expresses sincere gratitude towards followers. Through these giveaways, bookstagrammers, authors, and publishers give back to their loyal supporters and create moments of excitement and celebration within the literary world. As the bookstagram landscape continues to evolve, exclusive book giveaways will undoubtedly remain a cherished practice, epitomizing the joy of reading and the power of connection within the realm of books.

SIX
LIVE BOOK DISCUSSIONS:
UNITING READERS AND CREATORS IN REAL-TIME CONVERSATIONS

THE CONCEPT EXPLAINED:

Live book discussions on bookstagram are virtual events conducted in real-time using features like Instagram Live, Zoom, or other live streaming platforms. The concept revolves around bringing together authors, bookstagrammers, or even multiple bookstagrammers, to engage in live conversations about books, reading experiences, writing journeys, and various literary topics.

The discussions can take several formats, such as Q&A sessions with authors, book club discussions, author interviews, panel discussions on specific genres, or book reviews with multiple participants. The live nature of these conversations allows for instant interaction, audience participation, and spontaneous exchanges, making them an engaging and immersive experience for both participants and viewers.

Connecting Authors and Readers:

One of the primary aims of live book discussions is to bridge the gap between authors and their readers. By inviting authors to engage in real-time conversations, bookstagrammers provide their followers with an exclusive opportunity to interact directly with the creators of their favorite books. Participants can ask questions, share their thoughts, and gain deeper insights into the author's inspirations, writing process, and the stories behind their works.

These interactions humanize the author-reader relationship and create a personal connection that goes beyond the pages of the book. For authors, live book discussions offer a chance to connect with their audience, hear their feedback, and express their gratitude for the support they receive.

Fostering Book Discussions and Recommendations:

Live book discussions create a platform for in-depth book discussions and recommendations. During these conversations, participants share their thoughts and opinions on specific books, characters, themes, and literary techniques. They often engage in passionate debates about the merits of different books, encouraging diverse perspectives and enriching the reading experiences of viewers.

Bookstagrammers and authors also use these discussions to recommend books they have loved, drawing attention to hidden gems and new releases. Such recommendations inspire followers to explore new genres, discover fresh authors, and broaden their literary horizons.

Promoting Learning and Understanding:

The live format of book discussions allows for real-time learning opportunities. Bookstagrammers can invite authors or experts on specific subjects to share their knowledge, insights, and experiences related to literature, writing, or even historical contexts behind certain books. For example, a discussion on historical fiction might include a historian providing context and facts about the era the book is set in, enriching the readers' understanding of the narrative.

In addition to this, authors often share the challenges they faced while writing their books, the research they conducted, and the themes they intended to convey. These details give readers a deeper appreciation for the author's creative process and the messages embedded within the story.

Building a Bookish Community:

Live book discussions play a pivotal role in building a bookish community on bookstagram. They provide a space where like-minded individuals can come together to celebrate their shared love for literature. Participants often engage in lively conversations with one another during the live event, forming connections and discovering new bookish friends.

These discussions also serve as a focal point for book clubs or reading groups to gather virtually and exchange their thoughts on the selected books. This sense of community fosters a supportive and inclusive environment where everyone's voices are valued and heard.

IN CONCLUSION:

Live book discussions stand as a dynamic and immersive concept within the bookstagram community, uniting authors, bookstagrammers, and followers in real-time conversations about books and literature. Through these interactive events, readers gain valuable insights into the minds of authors, participate in passionate discussions, and discover new books to enrich their reading journeys. Moreover, the sense of community fostered by live book discussions enhances the overall bookstagram experience, turning it into a welcoming space for all who share the love for storytelling and the written word. As bookstagram continues to flourish, live book discussions will remain a cherished tradition, showcasing the power of literature to connect and inspire across virtual boundaries.

SEVEN
BOOK-INSPIRED RECIPES:
SAVORING LITERATURE ONE BITE AT A TIME

THE CONCEPT EXPLAINED:

Book-inspired recipes on bookstagram are culinary creations that draw inspiration from the meals, treats, and beverages featured in books. These recipes can be inspired by fictional feasts described in novels, the favorite foods of beloved characters, or even dishes that align with the setting and themes of the story. The bookstagrammer, acting as a culinary storyteller, brings these literary flavors to life by providing step-by-step recipes and inviting followers to recreate the dishes in their own kitchens.

The goal is to evoke the sensory experiences described in the books, enabling followers to savor the stories not just with their minds but also with their taste buds.

Culinary Journeys Through Literature:

Book-inspired recipes offer a delightful journey through literature, allowing followers to experience the world of books in a multisensory way. As followers try out the recipes, they step into the shoes of characters and immerse themselves in the fictional realms where the dishes originated. The taste of butterbeer from the Harry Potter series might transport them to the magical halls of Hogwarts, while a rich Turkish delight recipe from "The Chronicles of Narnia" could evoke the enchanting realm of Narnia itself.

These culinary journeys serve as a delicious and imaginative extension of the reading experience, deepening the emotional connection between readers and their favorite books.

Creating a Feast for the Senses:

Book-inspired recipes are more than just a collection of ingredients; they are a feast for the senses. As followers cook and bake the dishes, their kitchens are filled with the tantalizing aromas and flavors described in the books. The visual appeal of the dishes, captured in stunning food photography, further enhances the experience, inviting followers to appreciate the artistry of both literature and culinary craftsmanship.

These sensory elements add depth to the bookstagram experience, making it a truly immersive and delightful journey for followers.

Fostering Creativity and Experimentation:

Book-inspired recipes encourage creativity and experimentation in the kitchen. The act of translating literary descriptions into tangible dishes challenges both the bookstagrammer and followers to think outside the box and adapt recipes to suit real-life ingredients and tastes.

Moreover, bookstagrammers often add their own creative twists to the recipes, giving them a unique flair that reflects their culinary style. Followers, in turn, are inspired to do the same, experimenting with flavors and presentation to personalize the dishes and make them their own.

Uniting Literature and Food Enthusiasts:

Book-inspired recipes serve as a delightful meeting point for literature enthusiasts and food lovers alike. These culinary creations appeal to followers who have a passion for reading and storytelling, as well as those who enjoy exploring new recipes and cuisines.

The recipes spark conversations and connections among followers who share their experiences, modifications, and anecdotes while trying out the dishes. In this way, book-inspired recipes foster a supportive and enthusiastic community of bookstagrammers who bond over their love for literature and culinary delights.

Encouraging Engagement and Book Discoveries:

Book-inspired recipes also promote engagement and book discoveries within the bookstagram community. As bookstagrammers craft recipes inspired by their favorite books, they naturally introduce followers to new titles and authors. This exposure to diverse literature can lead followers to explore books they might not have encountered otherwise, enriching their reading experiences.

Conversely, followers might be inspired to pick up a book after trying out a recipe related to it, creating a delightful feedback loop between literature and culinary adventures.

IN CONCLUSION:

Book-inspired recipes offer a delectable and immersive concept within the bookstagram community, uniting the pleasures of reading with the joys of culinary exploration. By crafting recipes inspired by the food and drinks featured in books, bookstagrammers take their followers on a delightful culinary journey through literature. Through these recipes, followers savor the stories in a multisensory way, deepening their connection with beloved books. Moreover, book-inspired recipes foster creativity, encourage engagement, and create a vibrant community where literature and culinary passions intertwine harmoniously. As bookstagram continues to evolve, book-inspired recipes will remain a cherished tradition, inviting readers to savor literature one bite at a time.

EIGHT
MONTHLY BOOK CLUB:
EMPOWERING READERS' CHOICE AND SHARED READING EXPERIENCES

THE CONCEPT EXPLAINED:

The monthly book club on bookstagram operates as a recurring event where followers are invited to participate in choosing the book that the community will read and discuss for the upcoming month. At the beginning of each month, the bookstagrammer presents a curated list of book options, often with diverse genres, themes, and authors. The followers are then encouraged to vote for their preferred book through polls, direct messages, or comments.

The book with the highest number of votes becomes the chosen read for the month, and participants are invited to read the book at their own pace throughout the month. At the end of the month, a book discussion is hosted, providing an opportunity for followers to share their thoughts, reflections, and insights about the chosen book.

Empowering Readers' Choice:

The essence of the monthly book club lies in empowering readers to have a say in the book selection process. By involving followers in the voting process, the bookstagrammer allows them to take an active role in shaping the reading experience and exercising their literary preferences. This sense of agency not only fosters a feeling of ownership within the bookstagram community but also encourages followers to engage more deeply with the chosen book.

The freedom to vote for their favorite reads allows followers to explore diverse genres and discover books they might not have encountered through traditional reading avenues.

Creating a Sense of Community:

The monthly book club creates a cohesive and supportive community within the bookstagram space. As followers participate in the voting process and read the chosen book together, they form connections with others who share their reading interests. This shared reading experience becomes a catalyst for conversations, debates, and exchanges of recommendations.

The book discussion at the end of the month further solidifies this sense of community, as followers come together to engage in thoughtful conversations about the book's themes, characters, and impact. This collaborative spirit fosters a friendly and inclusive atmosphere, welcoming readers of all backgrounds and experiences to join the literary conversations.

Fostering Shared Reading Experiences:

The monthly book club nurtures shared reading experiences that transcend virtual boundaries. When followers read the same book, they embark on a collective literary journey, exploring the narrative world and delving into the emotions and ideas that the book evokes. As they share this experience, the book becomes a common thread that connects readers, regardless of their physical locations or backgrounds.

This shared reading experience enhances the enjoyment of the book, as readers feel a sense of camaraderie and understanding, knowing that others are also immersed in the same story.

Diverse Literary Exploration:

The book options presented for voting each month offer diverse literary exploration. By curating a range of genres, themes, and authors, the bookstagrammer ensures that followers encounter a variety of books that cater to different tastes and interests. Some months may feature classic literature, while others may focus on contemporary fiction, non-fiction, or even poetry.

This diverse literary exploration encourages followers to step outside their comfort zones, embrace new reading experiences, and discover hidden literary gems they might not have considered otherwise.

Nurturing Book Discussions and Analysis:

The monthly book club serves as a platform for in-depth book discussions and literary analysis. As followers read the chosen book together, they have the opportunity to analyze the plot, characters, writing style, and themes. The book discussion at the end of the month provides a space for participants to share their insights, ask questions, and engage in meaningful conversations.

These discussions deepen the readers' understanding of the book and enhance their overall reading experience. Participants gain fresh perspectives, learn from one another, and develop critical thinking skills through the exchange of ideas.

IN CONCLUSION:

The monthly book club, where followers can vote on the next read, offers a dynamic and interactive concept within the bookstagram community. By empowering readers to choose the books they read and discuss together, the bookstagrammer fosters a sense of community ownership, shared reading experiences, and engaging book discussions. This concept encourages diverse literary exploration, nurtures a welcoming community, and celebrates the joy of reading and literary connections. As bookstagram continues to flourish, the monthly book club will remain a cherished tradition, inspiring readers to embark on literary journeys together, one book at a time.

NINE
BEHIND-THE-SCENES SNEAK PEEKS:

UNVEILING THE MAGIC OF BOOKSTAGRAM

THE CONCEPT EXPLAINED:

Behind-the-scenes sneak peeks on bookstagram involve sharing candid and authentic glimpses into the bookstagrammer's reading and photography journey. This concept goes beyond the polished and final images posted on the bookstagram feed, offering followers a window into the creative process behind each captivating photo.

The behind-the-scenes content may include:

- ***Reading Nooks:*** The cozy corners where the bookstagrammer immerses themselves in the world of literature, complete with favorite blankets, mugs, and reading companions.
- ***Photography Setups:*** The carefully arranged props, lighting equipment, and camera angles that go into capturing the perfect bookstagram photo.
- ***Book Selection:*** The thought process behind selecting the books featured on the feed, along

with insights into the bookstagrammer's reading preferences and current TBR (To Be Read) pile.

- ***Editing Techniques:*** The post-processing steps and editing tools used to enhance the aesthetics and visual appeal of the bookstagram photos.
- ***Bloopers and Outtakes:*** Playful outtakes or bloopers that reveal the fun and lighthearted moments that occur during photoshoots.
- ***Book Hauls:*** Unveiling the latest book hauls and the excitement of adding new books to the collection.
- ***Bookish Discussions:*** Candid reflections, opinions, and discussions about the books being read or considered for future posts.

Creating Connection and Relatability:

Behind-the-scenes sneak peeks create a strong sense of connection and relatability between the bookstagrammer and their followers. By sharing the less polished, authentic moments, the bookstagrammer opens up to their community, allowing followers to see the human side behind the carefully curated feed.

This transparency fosters a feeling of familiarity and trust, as followers witness the passion and dedication that goes into creating the bookstagram content. As a result, the bookstagrammer becomes more than just a content creator; they become a relatable and approachable friend with shared interests in literature.

Inspiring Creativity and Learning:

Behind-the-scenes sneak peeks inspire creativity and learning among the bookstagram community. As followers observe the bookstagrammer's reading nooks, photography setups, and editing techniques, they gain insights into the artistic choices and technical skills that go into creating stunning bookish visuals.

These glimpses behind the curtain often prompt followers to experiment with their own photography, try out new editing techniques, or create their unique reading spaces. The bookstagrammer becomes a source of inspiration and learning, empowering followers to explore their own creativity and aesthetic expression.

Celebrating the Process:

Behind-the-scenes sneak peeks celebrate the process of content creation as much as the final results. Followers witness the joy, effort, and dedication that the bookstagrammer pours into each photo and post. This celebration of the journey, rather than just the destination, encourages followers to appreciate the artistry behind bookstagramming and the craft of storytelling.

Moreover, as followers witness the ups and downs, the challenges and breakthroughs, they gain a deeper understanding of the passion that drives the bookstagrammer's commitment to their craft.

Encouraging Interaction and Engagement:

Behind-the-scenes content invites interaction and engagement within the bookstagram community. As followers observe the bookstagrammer's reading selections and photography process, they are encouraged to share their thoughts, book recommendations, and personal experiences in the comments.

These interactions lead to vibrant discussions, where followers bond over shared reading interests, swap photography tips, and exchange book recommendations. The behind-the-scenes moments become a catalyst for meaningful conversations that go beyond the visual aspects of bookstagram.

IN CONCLUSION:

Behind-the-scenes sneak peeks unveil the magic of bookstagram, offering followers a glimpse into the bookstagrammer's reading and photography process. By sharing candid and authentic moments, bookstagrammers create a sense of connection, transparency, and inspiration within their community. The behind-the-scenes content fosters creativity, empowers learning, and celebrates the dedication that goes into crafting visually stunning and engaging bookish feeds. As bookstagram continues to thrive, behind-the-scenes sneak peeks will remain a cherished tradition, reminding us that bookstagram is not just about the pictures but also the passion, love, and artistry that breathe life into the world of literature.

TEN
BOOK-THEMED PHOTO CHALLENGES:

NLEASHING CREATIVITY THROUGH UNIQUE PROMPTS

THE CONCEPT EXPLAINED:

Book-themed photo challenges on bookstagram are recurring events that present participants with a curated list of unique prompts or themes. Each prompt corresponds to a specific book, genre, character, or literary element, inviting bookstagrammers to interpret and represent these themes through visually appealing and creative photos.

Participants are usually given a daily prompt throughout the challenge's duration, spanning from a week to a month. They then capture and post images that align with each day's prompt, infusing their unique style and perspective into the visual storytelling.

Unleashing Creativity and Imagination:

Book-themed photo challenges are an avenue for bookstagrammers to unleash their creativity and imagination. Each prompt serves as a creative springboard, inspiring participants to think outside the box and explore new visual concepts.

The challenge prompts often encourage bookstagrammers to experiment with different photography techniques, settings, props, and editing styles. Whether it's capturing a whimsical fairy tale-inspired scene or composing a minimalist photo that encapsulates a profound literary theme, the photo challenges challenge participants to push their creative boundaries.

Celebrating Literature in Visual Form:

The essence of book-themed photo challenges lies in celebrating literature through visual storytelling. By translating literary elements, characters, and themes into visually captivating images, participants pay homage to the power of storytelling.

The challenges become a tribute to beloved books, characters, and authors, inviting bookstagrammers to share their passion for literature with the broader community in an artful and expressive manner.

Fostering Community and Connection:

Book-themed photo challenges foster a strong sense of community and connection within the bookstagram world. As participants post their images for each prompt, they use common hashtags to label their posts, allowing others to discover and engage with their contributions easily.

The challenges encourage participants to explore and support one another's work, leaving encouraging comments and engaging in meaningful conversations about the books and prompts. Through these interactions, participants form connections, share recommendations, and celebrate their shared love for literature.

Interactive and Inclusive Participation:

The interactive nature of book-themed photo challenges makes them inclusive and accessible to bookstagrammers of all skill levels and interests. Participants are encouraged to interpret the prompts in their unique ways, ensuring a diverse range of responses to each theme.

As a result, the challenges become a celebration of individual perspectives, styles, and reading preferences. Whether someone is a seasoned bookstagrammer with professional photography skills or a newcomer eager to experiment with smartphone photography, they can all participate and contribute to the community-driven photo challenge.

Encouraging Daily Engagement:

Book-themed photo challenges encourage daily engagement within the bookstagram community. As participants are presented with a new prompt each day, they actively participate throughout the challenge's duration.

The challenges become a shared journey, as participants anticipate and look forward to each day's prompt, and the vibrant bookstagram community becomes a lively hub of activity and interaction.

IN CONCLUSION:

Book-themed photo challenges with unique prompts add an exciting and interactive dimension to the bookstagram experience. By inviting participants to visually interpret and celebrate literature through creative images, the challenges unleash the power of creativity and imagination within the bookstagram community. Participants embark on a delightful journey of self-expression, artistic exploration, and shared literary experiences, forming connections, and celebrating their passion for books. As bookstagram continues to thrive, book-themed photo challenges with unique prompts will remain a cherished tradition, inviting book lovers to express their love for literature in artful and visually captivating ways.

ELEVEN
BOOK-INSPIRED DIY CRAFTS:
TURNING IMAGINATION INTO TANGIBLE TREASURES

THE CONCEPT EXPLAINED:

Book-inspired DIY crafts on bookstagram revolve around sharing creative and crafty projects inspired by the enchanting world of literature. These projects may include handmade bookmarks, book covers, literary-themed decorations, character-inspired crafts, or even DIY journals for book reviews and reflections.

The bookstagrammer typically provides step-by-step tutorials, clear instructions, and creative ideas, encouraging followers to try out the crafts at their own pace. The goal is to offer bookish enthusiasts an opportunity to channel their love for literature into imaginative and hands-on creations.

Unleashing Artistic Expression:

Book-inspired DIY crafts unleash artistic expression within the bookstagram community. As followers engage in these craft projects, they have the creative freedom to put their unique spin on the designs, colors, and materials used.

Whether it's illustrating a favorite book quote on a handmade bookmark or crafting a magical wand inspired by a beloved character, these DIY projects become a canvas for artistic self-expression, allowing followers to infuse their personal touch into each creation.

Bridging Literature and Crafting:

The essence of book-inspired DIY crafts lies in bridging the worlds of literature and crafting. By drawing inspiration from books, characters, and themes, these projects become a celebration of the literary magic that has captured the hearts of readers.

Crafting becomes a tangible way to honor the stories and characters that have left a lasting impact, transforming them from beloved tales on the pages into cherished keepsakes and memorabilia.

Personalized Literary Treasures:

Book-inspired DIY crafts create personalized literary treasures for followers to cherish. As participants create these crafts, they develop a deeper connection with the stories and characters that inspire them. The crafts become tangible reminders of the emotions, adventures, and life lessons that literature has imparted.

Moreover, followers can gift these personalized literary crafts to fellow bookstagrammers, friends, or family members, creating meaningful and heartfelt presents that speak directly to the recipient's literary preferences.

Fostering a Sense of Accomplishment:

Book-inspired DIY crafts foster a sense of accomplishment and pride among followers. As participants complete these projects, they gain a tangible result for their efforts, boosting their confidence and providing a sense of fulfillment.

The act of crafting something with their own hands, inspired by their love for literature, is a rewarding experience that strengthens the connection between bookstagrammers and their passion for books.

Encouraging Community Engagement:

Book-inspired DIY crafts encourage community engagement and collaboration within the bookstagram world. As followers embark on these crafting projects, they often share their progress and completed works on their feeds or in stories.

This sharing of creativity sparks conversations, comments, and interactions with fellow bookstagrammers who appreciate and celebrate the crafts. Crafters exchange tips, offer encouragement, and inspire one another to try new projects, fostering a supportive and inspiring community.

Creating Interactive Challenges and Events:

Bookstagrammers often host interactive challenges and events centered around book-inspired DIY crafts. These challenges may involve a themed crafting contest, where participants compete for creative excellence, or a collaborative crafting project where followers work together to create a larger craft installation.

These interactive events create a buzz of excitement, encouraging more participants to join in the crafting fun and fostering a sense of camaraderie among bookstagrammers.

IN CONCLUSION:

Book-inspired DIY crafts offer an imaginative and interactive concept within the bookstagram community. By sharing craft projects and tutorials inspired by books, characters, and literary themes, bookstagrammers invite followers to transform their love for literature into tangible and personalized creations. These DIY crafts unleash artistic expression, bridge the worlds of literature and crafting, and create personalized literary treasures that deepen the connection between bookstagrammers and their favorite stories. As bookstagram continues to flourish, book-inspired DIY crafts will remain a cherished tradition, sparking creativity and turning the enchantment of books into tangible treasures crafted with love.

TWELVE
INTERACTIVE POLLS:
EMPOWERING FOLLOWERS' VOICES IN BOOKSTAGRAM

THE CONCEPT EXPLAINED:

Interactive polls on bookstagram are engaging features that allow followers to cast their votes on various topics related to books, reading, and literary preferences. Bookstagrammers use the poll feature on platforms like Instagram to present followers with two or more options, and followers can choose their preferred option by simply tapping on their choice.

The topics for polls can vary widely, such as voting for favorite books in a specific genre, selecting the next book for a book club, deciding the theme for the next photo challenge, or even choosing a character for a fictional face-off.

Empowering Followers' Voices:

The essence of interactive polls lies in empowering followers' voices within the bookstagram community. By participating in polls, followers feel seen, heard, and valued for their opinions and preferences.

The act of voting allows followers to actively contribute to decision-making processes, making them feel like they have a stake in the content and events on the bookstagram account. This empowerment fosters a sense of ownership and belonging, creating a more engaged and invested bookstagram community.

Encouraging Active Participation:

Interactive polls encourage active participation and engagement within the bookstagram community. The simplicity of tapping on a choice in a poll makes it easy and accessible for followers to participate without any barriers.

Bookstagrammers can leverage this feature to spark discussions, gain insights into their followers' interests, and encourage participation in bookish activities like book clubs, photo challenges, or read-alongs. Polls become an avenue for bookstagrammers to connect with their audience in a fun and interactive way.

Facilitating Reader Recommendations:

Interactive polls serve as a valuable tool for gathering reader recommendations and insights. For example, a bookstagrammer might create a poll asking followers for recommendations on the best books they've read in a particular genre.

The responses from followers provide a wealth of book recommendations that can be shared with the entire community, allowing readers to discover new titles and authors they might not have encountered otherwise. This sharing of recommendations fosters a supportive and collaborative bookstagram environment.

Fostering Community Engagement:

Interactive polls foster community engagement and interactions within the bookstagram space. As followers participate in polls, they see the choices and preferences of others, sparking conversations and debates about books, characters, and literary themes.

The poll results often lead to lively discussions in the comments, where followers share their reasons for voting a certain way or express their excitement about the winning choice. This engagement enhances the sense of community and camaraderie within the bookstagram space.

Creating Interactive Book Clubs and Read-Alongs:

Interactive polls are particularly effective in shaping book clubs and read-alongs within the bookstagram community. By asking followers to vote on the next book to read together, bookstagrammers ensure that the chosen book aligns with the interests of the majority.

This democratic process creates a sense of inclusivity, where followers have a say in the collective reading experience. Book club discussions become more vibrant and meaningful when everyone has had the chance to participate in choosing the book.

Driving Content Tailored to Followers:

Interactive polls enable bookstagrammers to create content tailored to their followers' preferences and interests. By seeking input through polls, bookstagrammers gain insights into the topics and themes that resonate most with their audience.

This data-driven approach allows bookstagrammers to fine-tune their content strategy, ensuring that they are providing valuable and engaging content that aligns with their followers' tastes and preferences.

IN CONCLUSION:

Interactive polls represent a powerful and engaging concept within the bookstagram community. By using polls to invite followers to vote on their favorite books, characters, genres, and even to shape content decisions, bookstagrammers empower their followers' voices and encourage active participation. Polls foster community engagement, facilitate reader recommendations, and create a collaborative and inclusive environment within the bookish space. As bookstagram continues to thrive, interactive polls will remain a cherished tradition, ensuring that the bookstagram community remains vibrant, connected, and driven by the collective passions of its avid readers.

THIRTEEN
"CAPTION THIS" CONTESTS:

UNLEASHING CREATIVITY WITH BOOK-RELATED PHOTOS

THE CONCEPT EXPLAINED:

"Caption This" contests on bookstagram are light-hearted and fun challenges that present followers with book-related photos or images. These photos often feature book covers, literary quotes, bookish props, or scenes inspired by specific books or themes.

Followers are then invited to participate in the contest by providing captions for the photos. The captions can be humorous, witty, punny, or even reflective, capturing the essence of the image in a few words.

Unleashing Creativity and Humor:

The essence of "Caption This" contests lies in unleashing creativity and humor within the bookstagram community. Participants have the opportunity to put their wit and wordplay to the test as they craft captions that complement the book-related images.

These contests provide a fun and lighthearted platform for followers to showcase their cleverness and literary humor, creating an atmosphere of laughter and amusement within the bookish community.

Fostering Connection and Engagement:

"Caption This" contests foster connection and engagement among followers. As participants submit their captions, they interact with the bookstagrammer and one another in the comments section, sharing laughter and appreciation for the clever and entertaining entries.

The contests become a shared experience, where followers bond over their love for books, wordplay, and humorous creativity. This sense of camaraderie strengthens the bookstagram community and encourages followers to return for more interactive challenges.

Exploring Literary Themes and Quotes:

"Caption This" contests provide an opportunity to explore literary themes and quotes in a playful and imaginative manner. The book-related photos often feature elements that reference specific books, characters, or iconic quotes, prompting participants to draw inspiration from their favorite literature.

This exploration of literary themes allows followers to celebrate the magic of books, characters, and stories while engaging in a playful and interactive way.

Encouraging Unique Perspectives:

"Caption This" contests encourage participants to bring their unique perspectives and interpretations to the photos. Each caption becomes a personal expression of the participant's literary preferences, sense of humor, and creativity.

By embracing diverse perspectives, these contests celebrate the richness and variety within the bookstagram community, showcasing the myriad ways that books touch the hearts and minds of readers.

Creating Friendly Competitions:

"Caption This" contests add an element of friendly competition to the bookstagram space. As followers vie for the most clever or amusing caption, they engage in a good-natured race of humor and creativity.

While the contests may have winners or feature highlighted captions, the focus remains on the enjoyment of participating and appreciating the witty contributions of fellow bookstagrammers.

Showcasing Bookstagrammer's Photography:

For bookstagrammers with photography skills, "Caption This" contests provide an opportunity to showcase their creativity and visual storytelling. The book-related photos become a canvas for their artistic expression, setting the stage for the humorous captions that follow.

Incorporating captivating and eye-catching bookish images enhances the overall experience of the contests and elevates the visual appeal of the bookstagrammer's feed.

IN CONCLUSION:

"Caption This" contests with book-related photos offer an interactive and imaginative concept within the bookstagram community. By inviting followers to provide clever and witty captions, bookstagrammers unleash creativity, foster engagement, and create a sense of literary camaraderie. These contests celebrate the magic of books, explore literary themes, and showcase the diverse perspectives of the bookstagram community. As bookstagram continues to flourish, "Caption This" contests will remain a cherished tradition, inviting followers to engage in playful wordplay and celebrate the joy of literature with laughter and creativity.

FOURTEEN
COLLABORATIVE FAN ART SHOWCASES:
CELEBRATING THE ARTISTRY OF BOOKSTAGRAM FOLLOWERS

THE CONCEPT EXPLAINED:

Collaborative fan art showcases on bookstagram involve inviting followers to submit their original artwork inspired by books, characters, scenes, or quotes. The artwork can take various forms, including illustrations, digital art, paintings, sketches, or even crafts.

The bookstagrammer then curates and shares the submitted artwork in a dedicated post, story highlight, or series of posts, showcasing the talent and creativity of the bookstagram community.

Celebrating Artistry and Creativity:

The essence of collaborative fan art showcases lies in celebrating the artistry and creativity of bookstagram followers. By inviting them to contribute their original artwork, bookstagram accounts highlight the talent that thrives within the community.

These showcases become a platform for bookstagrammers to express their love for literature through visual storytelling, offering a fresh and artistic perspective on beloved books and characters.

Fostering a Sense of Belonging:

Collaborative fan art showcases foster a strong sense of belonging and community within the bookstagram world. As participants see their artwork featured and appreciated, they feel acknowledged and valued for their contributions.

This sense of belonging encourages further engagement and participation, as followers are inspired by one another's work and celebrate the diversity of artistic styles and interpretations within the community.

Encouraging Interaction and Support:

The interactive nature of collaborative fan art showcases encourages followers to engage with one another's artwork. As followers view and appreciate the submitted art, they often leave encouraging comments, expressing admiration for the creativity and talent displayed.

This support and interaction create a positive and encouraging environment where bookstagrammers lift each other up, fostering a spirit of collaboration and artistic growth.

Building a Creative Archive:

Collaborative fan art showcases build a creative archive of artwork inspired by literature. As bookstagram accounts curate and save the submitted artwork in story highlights or dedicated posts, they create a treasure trove of book-inspired creativity that can be revisited by followers and the broader bookstagram community.

This creative archive becomes a source of inspiration for future artwork and encourages continuous engagement with beloved books and characters.

Enhancing the Visual Appeal of the Feed:

For bookstagram accounts that prioritize visual aesthetics, collaborative fan art showcases add depth and visual appeal to their feeds. The inclusion of stunning artwork complements the bookish photography and creates a diverse and engaging feed for followers.

The art showcases add a touch of uniqueness and creativity to the bookstagrammer's content, distinguishing their feed as a hub that celebrates both literature and visual art.

Connecting with Authors and Publishers:

Collaborative fan art showcases can also lead to connections with authors and publishers. As bookstagram accounts feature fan art inspired by specific books, authors may take notice and appreciate the visual tributes to their work.

These connections may lead to interactions, shoutouts, or even collaborations with authors and publishers, further enhancing the bookstagrammer's engagement and reach within the literary community.

IN CONCLUSION:

Collaborative fan art showcases featuring artwork created by followers offer an inclusive and celebratory concept within the bookstagram community. By inviting followers to contribute their original artwork inspired by literature, bookstagram accounts celebrate the artistry and creativity of their community members. These showcases foster a sense of belonging, encourage interaction and support among followers, and create a vibrant archive of book-inspired art. As bookstagram continues to thrive, collaborative fan art showcases will remain a cherished tradition, uniting the love for literature and visual storytelling within the enchanting world of bookstagram.

FIFTEEN
"BOOK OF THE MONTH" HIGHLIGHT:
A LITERARY JOURNEY THROUGH IN-DEPTH REVIEWS AND DISCUSSIONS

THE CONCEPT EXPLAINED:

"Book of the Month" highlights on bookstagram are recurring features where a bookstagrammer selects and showcases a single book each month. The chosen book may belong to any genre, ranging from fiction, non-fiction, fantasy, classic literature, and more.

Throughout the month, the bookstagrammer devotes dedicated posts, stories, and discussions to the selected book, offering in-depth reviews, reflections, and thought-provoking insights. Followers are encouraged to read the book alongside the bookstagrammer, creating a collective reading experience.

Embracing the Joy of Reading:

The essence of "Book of the Month" highlights lies in embracing the joy of reading and exploring literature together as a community. By featuring a different book each month, bookstagrammers celebrate the vast world of literature and encourage followers to engage with a diverse range of books and authors.

This concept promotes a culture of reading and learning, where followers can discover new literary gems, revisit beloved classics, or explore genres outside their comfort zones.

Creating a Sense of Community and Connection:

"Book of the Month" highlights foster a strong sense of community and connection within the bookstagram space. As followers read the selected book alongside the bookstagrammer, they become part of a shared reading experience.

The discussions and reflections in the comments section, direct messages, or even virtual book clubs create meaningful interactions, encouraging followers to connect with one another over their shared love for literature.

In-Depth Reviews and Discussions:

The heart of "Book of the Month" highlights lies in providing in-depth reviews and discussions about the selected book. The bookstagrammer may analyze the plot, characters, writing style, and themes, offering thoughtful insights and reflections.

These in-depth reviews go beyond surface-level summaries, encouraging followers to engage deeply with the book's content and sparking meaningful discussions about literary elements and interpretations.

Encouraging Meaningful Conversations:

"Book of the Month" highlights encourage meaningful conversations among followers. As bookstagrammers share their thoughts and reviews, followers are inspired to contribute their own opinions, perspectives, and interpretations.

These conversations often reveal diverse viewpoints, allowing followers to gain fresh insights and deepen their understanding of the book. The exchange of ideas fosters critical thinking and broadens literary horizons.

Creating Excitement and Anticipation:

"Book of the Month" highlights create excitement and anticipation within the bookstagram community. At the beginning of each month, followers eagerly await the announcement of the chosen book, looking forward to embarking on a literary journey together.

The anticipation builds as the month progresses, with followers eagerly reading and participating in the discussions, creating a dynamic and engaging reading experience.

Exploring a Variety of Literary Genres:

The concept of "Book of the Month" highlights allows bookstagrammers to explore a variety of literary genres and themes. Each month's selection may vary, ranging from contemporary fiction to historical novels, fantasy epics, thought-provoking non-fiction, or even poetry collections.

This diversity in literary choices ensures that followers are exposed to a rich tapestry of books, broadening their reading interests and introducing them to new genres and authors.

Fostering Lifelong Reading Habits:

"Book of the Month" highlights foster lifelong reading habits among followers. By consistently featuring and discussing books, bookstagrammers inspire followers to maintain a regular reading practice.

The shared reading experiences and discussions provide encouragement and motivation, nurturing a love for reading that extends beyond the virtual bookstagram world.

IN CONCLUSION:

"Book of the Month" highlights featuring in-depth reviews and discussions offer an immersive and enriching concept within the bookstagram community. By selecting and showcasing a single book each month, bookstagrammers celebrate the joy of reading, create a sense of community, and foster meaningful discussions among followers. These highlights encourage a diverse exploration of literary genres, spark excitement and anticipation, and cultivate lifelong reading habits. As bookstagram continues to thrive, "Book of the Month" highlights will remain a cherished tradition, uniting book lovers in a shared literary journey through the enchanting world of books.

SIXTEEN
FUN AND CREATIVE BOOK-RELATED HASHTAGS:
IGNITING BOOKSTAGRAM'S DIGITAL TAPESTRY

THE CONCEPT EXPLAINED:

Fun and creative book-related hashtags on bookstagram are hashtags designed specifically to capture the essence of books, characters, themes, or reading experiences. These hashtags often incorporate wordplay, puns, alliterations, or references to famous literary quotes.

When bookstagrammers use these hashtags in their posts, stories, or captions, they join a broader conversation with fellow book lovers who share similar interests or are exploring similar literary themes.

Fostering Community and Connection:

The essence of fun and creative book-related hashtags lies in fostering community and connection within the bookstagram world. By encouraging followers to use these hashtags, bookstagrammers create a digital gathering space where readers can find one another, interact, and share their love for literature.

These hashtags become virtual meeting points, connecting bookstagrammers from different corners of the world through their shared passion for books.

Sparking Conversations and Discoveries:

Fun and creative book-related hashtags spark conversations and discoveries among followers. As bookstagrammers use these hashtags, they open themselves to engaging with others who share similar reading preferences or have recommendations for books within specific genres.

These hashtags become a catalyst for book discussions, where followers swap book recommendations, share their thoughts on beloved characters, and explore new literary worlds.

Encouraging Book Challenges and Photo Prompts:

Book-related hashtags often play a central role in book challenges and photo prompts. Bookstagrammers use these hashtags to curate themed challenges, encouraging followers to post bookish photos that align with specific prompts.

These challenges create a dynamic and interactive space where followers can participate, showcasing their creativity and love for books through visual storytelling.

Embracing Wordplay and Creativity:

Fun and creative book-related hashtags celebrate the power of wordplay and creativity. By incorporating puns, alliterations, or references to literary quotes, these hashtags add a touch of playfulness and artistic expression to the bookstagram captions and content.

Followers are encouraged to come up with their unique interpretations and join in the fun of crafting clever hashtags that capture the spirit of their bookish posts.

Creating a Themed Digital Tapestry:

Through the use of fun and creative book-related hashtags, bookstagrammers curate a themed digital tapestry of bookish content. When followers use these hashtags, their posts become part of the broader bookstagram conversation, forming a cohesive and vibrant collage of book-related content.

The themed digital tapestry showcases a diverse array of bookish perspectives, celebrating the richness and diversity of literature and reading experiences.

Building a Sense of Bookish Identity:

The regular use of fun and creative book-related hashtags can contribute to building a bookish identity for followers. As users consistently use these hashtags in their bookstagram content, they align themselves with a specific bookish community, genre, or theme.

These hashtags become a way for followers to express their unique reading interests and to signal to others what type of bookish content they can expect from their feed.

IN CONCLUSION:

Fun and creative book-related hashtags offer a vibrant and engaging concept within the bookstagram community. By crafting unique and catchy hashtags, bookstagrammers foster community, spark conversations, and celebrate the magic of storytelling. These hashtags become digital meeting points, encouraging bookish interactions, book challenges, and creative expressions. As bookstagram continues to thrive, fun and creative book-related hashtags will remain a cherished tradition, uniting book lovers in a joyful and imaginative celebration of literature within the enchanting world of bookstagram.

SEVENTEEN

"MEET THE READER" FEATURES:

CELEBRATING THE DIVERSE VOICES OF BOOKSTAGRAM FOLLOWERS

THE CONCEPT EXPLAINED:

"Meet the Reader" features on bookstagram are recurring posts, stories, or series dedicated to showcasing the stories and experiences of followers. Bookstagrammers invite their followers to participate by sharing their own bookish stories, which can include personal reading journeys, favorite book memories, book-related travel experiences, book hauls, and more.

The bookstagrammer may create a questionnaire or prompts to guide the submissions and ensure that each "Meet the Reader" feature provides a unique and authentic glimpse into the bookish lives of followers.

Celebrating Diverse Bookish Experiences:

The essence of "Meet the Reader" features lies in celebrating the diverse bookish experiences and perspectives of followers. By inviting them to share their stories, bookstagrammers recognize that each reader's journey is unique and worthy of celebration.

These features become a space for followers to feel seen, heard, and appreciated for their individual connections with books and literature.

Fostering a Sense of Belonging:

"Meet the Reader" features foster a strong sense of belonging within the bookstagram community. As followers share their bookish stories, they contribute to the collective tapestry of experiences and create a supportive environment where readers can relate to one another.

These features create a virtual gathering place where bookstagrammers connect over shared reading habits, cherished book memories, and the emotional impact of literature.

Encouraging Empathy and Understanding:

Through the sharing of bookish stories, "Meet the Reader" features encourage empathy and understanding among followers. As bookstagrammers read about the experiences and perspectives of others, they gain insights into different literary journeys and the ways books have influenced and shaped each reader's life.

This understanding fosters a deeper appreciation for the diverse ways that literature resonates with individuals, fostering a compassionate and inclusive bookstagram community.

Inspiring Book Recommendations and Discovery:

"Meet the Reader" features become a source of inspiration for book recommendations and literary discovery. As followers share their favorite books, genres, and authors, others in the community are introduced to new reading possibilities and potential book treasures.

These features become a valuable resource for followers seeking their next literary adventure, showcasing a wide range of bookish interests and recommendations.

Building Personal Connections:

The concept of "Meet the Reader" features creates an opportunity for bookstagrammers to build personal connections with their followers. As bookstagrammers read and engage with the submissions, they learn more about the individuals behind the accounts, forging meaningful connections beyond the virtual world.

These personal connections add authenticity and depth to the bookstagram experience, creating a sense of friendship and camaraderie among readers.

Sharing Bookish Enthusiasm and Moments:

"Meet the Reader" features provide a space for followers to share their bookish enthusiasm and moments of joy. From sharing the excitement of a long-awaited book release to reliving favorite book quotes, these features become a celebration of the moments that make reading such a cherished and joyful experience.

These shared moments of enthusiasm create a positive and uplifting atmosphere within the bookstagram community.

IN CONCLUSION:

"Meet the Reader" features that showcase the bookish stories and experiences of followers offer an inclusive and inspiring concept within the bookstagram community. By celebrating the diverse voices and perspectives of readers, bookstagrammers create a sense of connection, understanding, and shared love for literature. These features become a virtual gathering place, fostering empathy, personal connections, and bookish inspiration. As bookstagram continues to thrive, "Meet the Reader" features will remain a cherished tradition, uniting book lovers in a heartfelt and meaningful celebration of literature within the enchanting world of bookstagram.

EIGHTEEN
VIRTUAL AUTHOR INTERVIEWS OR Q&A SESSIONS:
BRIDGING THE LITERARY WORLD AND BOOKSTAGRAM

THE CONCEPT EXPLAINED:

Virtual author interviews or Q&A sessions on bookstagram are online events where bookstagrammers invite authors to participate in live or pre-recorded interviews or Q&A sessions. These sessions can take place on platforms like Instagram Live, YouTube, or through Instagram stories.

During the sessions, bookstagrammers may ask authors questions about their writing process, inspiration behind their books, characters, themes, and literary journey. Followers are often encouraged to submit their own questions in advance or during the live session.

Bridging the Gap between Authors and Readers:

The essence of virtual author interviews or Q&A sessions lies in bridging the gap between authors and their readers. By facilitating direct interactions between bookstagrammers and authors, these sessions create a sense of connection and intimacy.

Readers have the opportunity to gain insights into the minds of their favorite authors, learning about the creative process and the stories that have captured their imaginations.

Fostering Deeper Appreciation for Literature:

Through virtual author interviews or Q&A sessions, followers gain a deeper appreciation for literature and the craft of writing. Hearing authors discuss their work, characters, and themes adds depth and context to the reading experience, allowing readers to engage with the books on a more profound level.

The sessions create a richer understanding of the stories, characters, and worlds created by the authors, enhancing the overall literary experience for bookstagrammers.

Offering Behind-the-Scenes Insights:

Virtual author interviews or Q&A sessions offer behind-the-scenes insights into the literary world. Authors often share anecdotes, challenges, and triumphs related to their writing journey, giving followers a glimpse into the life of a writer.

These intimate details create a more personal connection between authors and readers, fostering a sense of camaraderie and shared passion for literature.

Empowering Followers to Ask Questions:

Through virtual author interviews or Q&A sessions, followers are empowered to ask questions directly to the authors. This direct interaction breaks down barriers and makes the literary world more accessible to readers.

Followers can seek clarification, delve deeper into the themes of the books, or even ask about the authors' favorite reads and literary inspirations, fostering a meaningful and interactive dialogue.

Creating a Sense of Community:

Virtual author interviews or Q&A sessions create a sense of community within the bookstagram space. As followers come together to engage with authors, they share a collective love for literature and a curiosity about the stories that have touched their hearts.

The sessions become a shared experience where bookstagrammers celebrate the magic of books and storytelling together.

Promoting New Book Releases:

Virtual author interviews or Q&A sessions often coincide with new book releases. Authors use these sessions as an opportunity to promote their latest works, offering followers exclusive insights and previews.

The sessions generate excitement and anticipation for upcoming books, encouraging followers to support and engage with the authors' new releases.

Expanding Literary Horizons:

Virtual author interviews or Q&A sessions also expand literary horizons for bookstagrammers. By featuring a diverse range of authors and genres, these sessions introduce followers to new writers and stories they might not have encountered otherwise.

This exposure broadens readers' reading interests and encourages them to explore a wider range of books and literary themes.

IN CONCLUSION:

Virtual author interviews or Q&A sessions on bookstagram offer an engaging and enriching concept within the bookstagram community. By connecting readers with authors, these sessions bridge the gap between the literary world and bookstagram, fostering a deeper appreciation for literature and the creative process. These sessions empower followers to ask questions and gain behind-the-scenes insights, creating a sense of community and expanding literary horizons. As bookstagram continues to thrive, virtual author interviews or Q&A sessions will remain a cherished tradition, uniting book lovers in a shared celebration of literature within the enchanting world of bookstagram.

NINETEEN
FLASH SALES OR DISCOUNTS ON BOOKISH MERCHANDISE:

UNLEASHING BOOKSTAGRAM'S SHOPPING FRENZY

THE CONCEPT EXPLAINED:

Flash sales or discounts on bookish merchandise on bookstagram are time-sensitive promotions during which bookstagrammers offer special deals, price reductions, or exclusive discounts on a curated selection of book-themed products. These promotions may last for a few hours, a day, or a weekend, creating a sense of urgency and excitement among followers.

Bookstagrammers may partner with bookish brands, small businesses, or independent artists to feature their merchandise during the flash sales, showcasing a diverse range of products inspired by literature.

Creating a Sense of Excitement and Urgency:

The essence of flash sales or discounts on bookish merchandise lies in creating a sense of excitement and urgency among followers. The limited-time nature of the promotions generates a feeling of exclusivity, encouraging followers to act quickly to secure their favorite bookish items at discounted prices.

This excitement motivates followers to engage with the flash sale posts, stories, and updates, heightening the overall bookstagram experience.

Fostering a Passionate Bookish Community:

Flash sales or discounts on bookish merchandise foster a passionate and engaged bookish community on bookstagram. As followers eagerly browse through the showcased products, they bond over their shared love for literature and the creative ways it is brought to life through merchandise.

The flash sales become a vibrant space where followers interact, share their favorite finds, and celebrate their unique bookish style.

Supporting Bookish Brands and Artists:

By featuring bookish merchandise from various brands and independent artists, flash sales encourage followers to support small businesses and creators within the bookish community.

The promotions provide exposure to lesser-known brands and artists, giving them a platform to showcase their talent and connect with a broader audience of bookstagrammers.

Celebrating Literary Style and Identity:

Flash sales or discounts on bookish merchandise celebrate the unique literary style and identity of each bookstagrammer. Followers have the opportunity to find merchandise that aligns with their favorite books, characters, or literary themes, allowing them to express their love for literature in a personal and stylish way.

The merchandise becomes an extension of the followers' bookish identity, adding a touch of literary flair to their everyday lives.

Sparking Creativity and Inspiration:

Flash sales on bookish merchandise spark creativity and inspiration among followers. The wide variety of products, including book-themed apparel, accessories, home decor, and artwork, inspire followers to curate their own bookish collections and create personalized bookish spaces.

The merchandise becomes a source of inspiration for bookstagrammers to curate aesthetically pleasing and unique book-related content.

Offering Affordable Bookish Delights:

Flash sales or discounts on bookish merchandise make book-inspired products more accessible and affordable to followers. The special deals and price reductions allow bookstagrammers to acquire their favorite bookish items at a more budget-friendly cost.

This affordability enhances the overall bookstagram experience, making it easier for followers to incorporate bookish delights into their everyday lives.

Enhancing Bookstagram's Shopping Experience:

The concept of flash sales or discounts on bookish merchandise enhances the shopping experience on bookstagram. As followers browse through the curated selection of products, they enjoy a seamless shopping experience directly within the bookstagram platform.

The flash sales add an interactive and engaging element to bookstagram, transforming it into a delightful shopping destination for book lovers.

IN CONCLUSION:

Flash sales or discounts on bookish merchandise offer an exciting and enticing concept within the bookstagram community. By offering limited-time promotions on a curated selection of book-related products, bookstagrammers create a thrilling and engaging space that fosters excitement and urgency among followers. These promotions support bookish brands and independent artists, celebrate literary style and identity, and enhance the overall shopping experience on bookstagram. As bookstagram continues to thrive, flash sales or discounts on bookish merchandise will remain a cherished tradition, unleashing bookstagram's shopping frenzy and uniting book lovers in the enchanting world of bookish delights.

TWENTY
"RATE THE COVER" POSTS:
UNLEASHING AESTHETIC CRITIQUES AND BOOKISH OPINIONS

THE CONCEPT EXPLAINED:

"Rate the Cover" posts on bookstagram are dedicated posts or stories where bookstagrammers showcase the covers of specific books and invite followers to share their opinions. Followers are encouraged to rate the covers on a scale, provide comments on the visual appeal, design elements, color choices, typography, and overall aesthetics.

The bookstagrammer may use polls, question stickers, or open ended questions in the captions to encourage participation and facilitate meaningful discussions.

Celebrating the Artistry of Book Covers:

The essence of "Rate the Cover" posts lies in celebrating the artistry of book covers. Bookstagrammers curate a collection of visually striking and diverse book covers, showcasing the creativity and thoughtfulness that goes into designing book jackets.

These posts become a platform for followers to express their admiration for the captivating artwork that enhances the reading experience.

Encouraging Aesthetic Critiques:

"Rate the Cover" posts encourage aesthetic critiques and thoughtful analyses of book covers. Followers have the opportunity to share their perspectives on the use of colors, symbolism, imagery, and how well the cover represents the book's content or genre.

This process of aesthetic critique fosters a deeper engagement with the visual aspects of literature, elevating the bookstagram experience beyond the written word.

Unleashing Bookish Discussions:

Through "Rate the Cover" posts, bookstagrammers unleash bookish discussions and encourage followers to interact with one another. As followers rate and comment on the covers, they engage in conversations about their preferences, favorite design elements, and memorable covers.

These discussions often lead to book recommendations and shared excitement about books with eye-catching covers.

Exploring Diverse Cover Designs:

"Rate the Cover" posts provide an opportunity to explore diverse cover designs and artistic styles. Bookstagrammers can feature books from different genres, time periods, and regions, showcasing the vast range of visual artistry that graces bookshelves.

Followers are exposed to covers they might not have encountered otherwise, broadening their appreciation for the art that accompanies literature.

Gaining Insight into Visual Preferences:

For bookstagrammers, "Rate the Cover" posts offer insights into their followers' visual preferences. As followers share their opinions on various covers, bookstagrammers can gain a better understanding of what appeals to their audience.

This insight can inform future content, allowing bookstagrammers to curate posts and recommendations that align with their followers' tastes.

Creating Engagement and Interaction:

"Rate the Cover" posts create engagement and interaction within the bookstagram community. Followers enjoy participating in the polls and discussions, expressing their opinions, and comparing their ratings with others.

These interactive posts foster a sense of community and camaraderie among bookstagrammers, encouraging them to return for more discussions and visual analyses.

Adding a Visual Element to Bookstagram:

The concept of "Rate the Cover" posts adds a visual element to bookstagram. While bookstagram is primarily focused on the written word, these posts celebrate the visual beauty that accompanies literature. The inclusion of aesthetically pleasing book covers enhances the overall aesthetic appeal of bookstagram feeds.

IN CONCLUSION:

"Rate the Cover" posts featuring aesthetic critiques and bookish opinions offer an engaging and interactive concept within the bookstagram community. By showcasing the artistry of book covers and encouraging followers to share their perspectives, bookstagrammers create a dynamic space that celebrates visual artistry and fosters bookish discussions. These posts explore diverse cover designs, gain insights into followers' visual preferences, and add a delightful visual element to bookstagram. As bookstagram continues to thrive, "Rate the Cover" posts will remain a cherished tradition, uniting book lovers in a shared celebration of the visual allure that accompanies the enchanting world of books.

TWENTY-ONE
BOOK-INSPIRED FASHION LOOKBOOKS OR OUTFIT OF THE DAY (OOTD) POSTS:
WHERE LITERATURE MEETS STYLE

THE CONCEPT EXPLAINED:

Book-inspired fashion lookbooks or OOTD posts on bookstagram are dedicated posts or stories where bookstagrammers share photographs or visual collages of outfits that draw inspiration from books. These outfits may reflect the style of beloved book characters, the color palette of a book cover, the ambiance of a literary setting, or the overall theme of a particular book.

The bookstagrammer may provide captions that explain the inspiration behind each outfit, detailing how specific elements relate to the chosen book or literary reference.

Celebrating the Fusion of Literature and Fashion:

The essence of book-inspired fashion lookbooks or OOTD posts lies in celebrating the fusion of literature and fashion. Bookstagrammers combine their love for books with their personal style, creating outfits that pay homage to the worlds and characters they adore.

These posts become a visual celebration of the interconnectedness between literature and style, highlighting the influence of books on fashion choices.

Curating Outfits with Literary References:

Bookstagrammers curate outfits with thoughtful literary references. Each outfit may embody the essence of a specific book or character, drawing from the book's themes, atmosphere, or time period.

The choice of clothing items, accessories, and colors is carefully curated to evoke the spirit of the book and immerse followers in its literary universe.

Inviting Followers into Imaginative Fashion Realms:

Through book-inspired fashion lookbooks or OOTD posts, bookstagrammers invite followers into imaginative fashion realms. These posts transport followers beyond the written word, allowing them to visualize the sartorial aspects of literature.

By showcasing how literature can inspire personal style, bookstagrammers ignite creativity and curiosity among their followers.

Encouraging Bookish Style Exploration:

Book-inspired fashion lookbooks and OOTD posts encourage followers to explore bookish style choices of their own. Followers may be inspired to recreate the showcased outfits or experiment with their interpretations of book-inspired fashion.

These posts expand the notion of book appreciation beyond reading, encouraging followers to integrate literature into their everyday lives through fashion expression.

Infusing Bookstagram with Aesthetic Appeal:

The concept of book-inspired fashion lookbooks or OOTD posts adds aesthetic appeal to bookstagram. These visually captivating posts showcase bookstagrammers' fashion sense and creativity, enhancing the overall visual experience for followers.

The inclusion of stylish outfits and artful presentations elevates the bookstagram feed, creating a delightful blend of literature and aesthetics.

Celebrating Book Characters and Themes:

Book-inspired fashion lookbooks or OOTD posts celebrate beloved book characters and themes. Followers have the opportunity to see how bookstagrammers envision the style of iconic protagonists or immerse themselves in the world of a favorite book through clothing choices.

These posts deepen the appreciation for characters and stories by incorporating visual representations of their personalities and journeys.

Fostering Bookish Discussions:

Through book-inspired fashion lookbooks or OOTD posts, bookstagrammers foster bookish discussions among followers. As followers interact with the posts, they may share their own interpretations, favorite book characters, or personal style choices inspired by literature.

These discussions create a vibrant and engaging bookstagram community, where fashion and literature enthusiasts unite in shared admiration for the written word and artistic style.

IN CONCLUSION:

Book-inspired fashion lookbooks or OOTD posts that blend literature with style offer a stylish and creative concept within the bookstagram community. By curating outfits with thoughtful literary references, bookstagrammers celebrate the fusion of literature and fashion, inviting followers into imaginative fashion realms. These posts encourage bookish style exploration, infuse bookstagram with aesthetic appeal, and deepen the appreciation for book characters and themes. As bookstagram continues to thrive, book-inspired fashion lookbooks or OOTD posts will remain a cherished tradition, uniting book lovers in a stylish celebration of literature and fashion within the enchanting world of bookstagram.

TWENTY-TWO
THEMED READING SPRINTS:
AN ENCHANTING JOURNEY OF COLLECTIVE READING AND CONNECTION

THE CONCEPT EXPLAINED:

Themed reading sprints on bookstagram are organized reading sessions where bookstagrammers set a specific time duration for reading and invite their followers to join in. The reading sprints are centered around a particular theme, genre, or book, adding an element of excitement and focus to the reading experience.

During the reading sprints, bookstagrammers may share updates, quotes, or thoughts about their current reads on their stories or posts, fostering real-time engagement and discussion among followers.

Creating a Sense of Collective Reading:

The essence of themed reading sprints lies in creating a sense of collective reading among bookstagrammers. By participating in the sprints, followers engage in simultaneous reading experiences, sharing the joy and discoveries that books bring.

This collective reading experience fosters a feeling of togetherness and shared passion for literature within the bookstagram community.

Setting a Focused Reading Goal:

Themed reading sprints provide a focused reading goal for followers. With a specific theme or genre guiding the reading choices, followers can curate their reading list accordingly, immersing themselves in books that align with the chosen theme.

This focus adds intentionality to the reading experience and encourages followers to explore new books or revisit beloved ones that fit the theme.

Fostering Camaraderie and Connection:

Through themed reading sprints, bookstagrammers foster camaraderie and connection among followers. As readers share updates and reactions during the sprints, they engage in discussions and bond over their shared experiences.

These interactions create a supportive and encouraging environment where bookstagrammers connect with like-minded readers and form meaningful connections.

Inspiring Reading Enthusiasm:

Themed reading sprints inspire reading enthusiasm among followers. The anticipation of participating in the collective reading event motivates readers to set aside dedicated time for reading and engage with the chosen theme.

The sprints infuse the bookstagram community with a renewed sense of excitement and passion for books.

Encouraging Diverse Reading Choices:

The concept of themed reading sprints encourages diverse reading choices within the bookstagram community. As bookstagrammers explore different themes or genres through the sprints, they broaden their reading horizons and discover books they might not have otherwise encountered.

This exposure to diverse reading experiences enriches the overall literary journey of followers.

Adding an Interactive Element to Reading:

Themed reading sprints add an interactive element to the act of reading. The real-time updates, quotes, and discussions shared by bookstagrammers during the sprints transform reading into a social and interactive experience.

The sprints turn the solitary act of reading into a communal event, where followers feel connected and engaged with other readers.

Creating a Sense of Accomplishment:

Themed reading sprints create a sense of accomplishment among followers. Completing the set reading duration and participating actively in the discussions instills a feeling of achievement and satisfaction.

This sense of accomplishment motivates readers to continue their literary explorations beyond the sprints.

IN CONCLUSION:

Themed reading sprints offer an enchanting and immersive concept within the bookstagram community. By organizing collective reading sessions around specific themes or genres, bookstagrammers create a sense of camaraderie and connection among followers. These sprints set focused reading goals, inspire reading enthusiasm, and encourage diverse reading choices. The interactive nature of the sprints adds an exciting dimension to reading, turning it into a shared and enriching experience. As bookstagram continues to thrive, themed reading sprints will remain a cherished tradition, uniting book lovers in an enchanting journey of collective reading and connection within the enchanting world of bookstagram.

TWENTY-THREE
VIRTUAL BOOK TOURS:
EXPLORING LITERARY LANDMARKS AND BOOKSTORES AROUND THE WORLD

THE CONCEPT EXPLAINED:

Virtual book tours on bookstagram are interactive and visually captivating tours where bookstagrammers share their experiences exploring literary landmarks, author's homes, or unique bookstores. These tours are conducted through a combination of visual content, such as photos and videos, along with engaging captions and stories that provide historical context and interesting facts about each location.

The bookstagrammer may also invite followers to join in the virtual journey by sharing their own literary travel memories or dream destinations.

Transporting Followers to Literary Places:

The essence of virtual book tours lies in transporting followers to literary places they may not have had the opportunity to visit in person. Through captivating visuals and informative captions, bookstagrammers recreate the magic of famous literary landmarks, such as Shakespeare's birthplace in Stratford-upon-Avon, England, or the Louisa May Alcott Orchard House in Massachusetts, USA.

Followers are immersed in the rich history and literary heritage of these iconic places, forging a deeper connection with the stories and authors that have shaped literature.

Celebrating Literary Heritage:

Virtual book tours celebrate the literary heritage of various regions and countries. As bookstagrammers explore the homes of beloved authors or significant locations from classic literature, they pay homage to the literary legacy that continues to captivate readers around the world.

These tours become a tribute to the timeless power of books and the authors who have left an indelible mark on literary history.

Inspiring Literary Wanderlust:

Through virtual book tours, bookstagrammers inspire literary wanderlust among their followers. The breath-taking visuals and captivating stories ignite a desire to explore the world and experience the literary wonders that await in different corners of the globe.

Followers are encouraged to dream of their own literary travel adventures and add new destinations to their reading and travel bucket lists.

Promoting Cultural Exchange:

Virtual book tours promote cultural exchange and global appreciation for literature. As bookstagrammers share the beauty of literary landmarks and bookstores from diverse countries, they foster a deeper understanding of different cultures and literary traditions.

These tours become a window into the literary worlds of various nations, promoting cross-cultural connections within the bookstagram community.

Discovering Unique Bookstores:

In addition to exploring literary landmarks, virtual book tours also take followers on a journey to discover unique and charming bookstores from around the world. From quaint independent bookshops with rich histories to modern literary havens, bookstagrammers showcase a variety of bookstores that celebrate the love for books and reading.

Followers are introduced to hidden gems and delightful literary sanctuaries they might wish to visit in the future.

Fostering Bookish Discussions:

Virtual book tours foster bookish discussions among followers. As followers engage with the captivating content, they may share their favorite literary landmarks, bookstores they have visited, or dream destinations they hope to explore.

These discussions create a lively and interactive bookstagram community, where readers bond over their shared love for literature and literary travel.

Promoting Lifelong Learning:

The concept of virtual book tours promotes lifelong learning among followers. As bookstagrammers share historical and cultural insights about each location, followers gain knowledge about literary history, authors' lives, and the impact of specific settings on literature.

The tours become an educational and inspiring experience that enriches the literary journey of bookstagrammers.

IN CONCLUSION:

Virtual book tours offering captivating journeys to explore literary landmarks and bookstores around the world offer an exciting and immersive concept within the bookstagram community. By transporting followers to iconic literary places and spaces, bookstagrammers celebrate the literary heritage, inspire literary wanderlust, and promote cultural exchange. These tours also introduce followers to unique bookstores and foster bookish discussions, creating an engaging and interactive bookstagram community. As bookstagram continues to thrive, virtual book tours will remain a cherished tradition, uniting book lovers in an enchanting journey of exploration and appreciation for the written word within the captivating world of bookstagram.

TWENTY-FOUR
BOOKISH WOULD YOU RATHER GAMES:

A FUN AND ENGAGING JOURNEY OF LITERARY DILEMMAS

THE CONCEPT EXPLAINED:

"Bookish Would You Rather" games on bookstagram are interactive posts or stories where bookstagrammers present their followers with a series of engaging book-related dilemmas. Each dilemma comprises two options, and followers are asked to choose the one they prefer.

The dilemmas may revolve around literary scenarios, such as choosing between living in a library forever or being able to visit any book world, or between having the ability to read minds or being able to speak any language in the world.

Sparking Curiosity and Imagination:

The essence of "Bookish Would You Rather" games lies in sparking curiosity and igniting the imagination of followers. As followers encounter the intriguing dilemmas, they are prompted to reflect on their reading preferences, bookish desires, and the imaginative possibilities that books offer.

These games encourage followers to delve deeper into their relationship with literature and explore the whimsical aspects of literary scenarios.

Fostering Bookish Discussions:

"Bookish Would You Rather" games foster bookish discussions among followers. As followers engage with the dilemmas, they may share their chosen options in the comments or respond with explanations for their decisions.

These discussions create a lively and interactive bookstagram community, where readers bond over their shared love for literature and engage in friendly debates over the various choices.

Adding Playfulness to Bookstagram:

The concept of "Bookish Would You Rather" games adds a sense of playfulness to bookstagram. Amidst the serious book reviews and discussions, these games inject a dose of fun and amusement into the bookstagram feed.

Followers enjoy the lightheartedness of the dilemmas and the opportunity to playfully ponder bookish scenarios.

Engaging Bookstagram Followers:

"Bookish Would You Rather" games engage bookstagram followers on a deeper level. As followers participate in the games, they become active participants in the bookstagram content, rather than passive observers.

The interactive nature of the games creates a sense of involvement and investment among followers, encouraging them to return for more engaging content.

Celebrating Bookish Preferences:

Through "Bookish Would You Rather" games, bookstagrammers celebrate the diverse bookish preferences of their followers. The dilemmas touch upon various aspects of the reading experience, such as favorite genres, bookish abilities, or dream bookish scenarios.

These games acknowledge and embrace the unique tastes and perspectives of each follower, creating an inclusive and welcoming bookstagram environment.

Encouraging Personal Reflection:

"Bookish Would You Rather" games encourage personal reflection among followers. As followers contemplate their choices, they gain insights into their own reading preferences, literary aspirations, and bookish dreams.

The games become a journey of self-discovery, where followers explore their relationship with books and the imaginative possibilities they envision.

Promoting Creativity and Bookish Imagination:

The concept of "Bookish Would You Rather" games promotes creativity and bookish imagination among followers. The dilemmas challenge followers to think outside the box, envisioning fantastical scenarios and contemplating the unlimited potential that books offer.

These games inspire followers to tap into their creative minds and explore the boundless worlds of literature.

IN CONCLUSION:

"Bookish Would You Rather" games offering a series of intriguing literary dilemmas offer a fun and engaging concept within the bookstagram community. By sparking curiosity, fostering bookish discussions, and promoting creativity, these games celebrate the joy of books and ignite the imaginations of followers. These games add playfulness to bookstagram, engage followers on a deeper level, and encourage personal reflection. As bookstagram continues to thrive, "Bookish Would You Rather" games will remain a cherished tradition, uniting book lovers in a delightful journey of literary dilemmas and shared appreciation for the enchanting world of books within the captivating world of bookstagram.

TWENTY-FIVE
BOOK UNBOXING VIDEOS:
UNVEILING LITERARY TREASURES IN SPECIAL EDITIONS AND SUBSCRIPTION BOXES

THE CONCEPT EXPLAINED:

Book unboxing videos on bookstagram are visual experiences where bookstagrammers record themselves unboxing special edition books or book subscription boxes. These videos are often posted as stories or highlights and offer a step-by-step journey of unwrapping and revealing the contents of the box.

The bookstagrammer shares their genuine reactions and emotions as they explore the carefully curated literary delights, from the cover design to exclusive bookish merchandise or bonus items.

Capturing the Excitement of Unveiling Literary Treasures:

The essence of book unboxing videos lies in capturing the excitement and joy of unveiling literary treasures. As bookstagrammers unwrap the packaging and reveal the carefully curated contents, they share their genuine enthusiasm and delight with their followers.

These videos become a visual celebration of the magic of books and the thrill of discovering hidden bookish gems.

Sharing the Beauty of Special Editions:

Book unboxing videos offer followers a glimpse into the beauty of special edition books. From intricate cover designs and embossed details to exclusive illustrations or signed copies, the videos showcase the unique features that make these editions true collector's items.

Followers can appreciate the craftsmanship and artistic elements that elevate these editions beyond the ordinary.

Creating a Sense of Anticipation and Surprise:

Through book unboxing videos, bookstagrammers create a sense of anticipation and surprise among their followers. As they gradually reveal each item in the box, followers are kept on the edge of their seats, eagerly awaiting the next literary treasure.

The element of surprise adds to the excitement of the unboxing experience, making it a thrilling journey for both the bookstagrammer and the followers.

Highlighting the Magic of Book Subscription Boxes:

Book unboxing videos also highlight the magic of book subscription boxes. These boxes often include not only a carefully selected book but also bookish merchandise, themed goodies, or exclusive items related to the book.

The videos showcase the thoughtfulness and creativity that go into curating these boxes, making them a delightful surprise for bookstagrammers and a unique reading experience.

Fostering Engagement and Discussion:

Book unboxing videos foster engagement and discussion among followers. As followers watch the videos, they may comment on their favorite items, express their excitement, or share their own unboxing experiences.

These discussions create a sense of community and camaraderie among bookstagrammers, who bond over their shared love for books and bookish delights.

Inspiring Bookish Recommendations:

The concept of book unboxing videos inspires bookish recommendations among followers. As bookstagrammers showcase the books and items they receive, they introduce their followers to new and intriguing reads and bookish merchandise.

These videos become a source of inspiration for followers to explore new authors, genres, or book subscription boxes.

Celebrating the Joy of Book Collecting:

Through book unboxing videos, bookstagrammers celebrate the joy of book collecting. Special edition books and curated book subscription boxes often hold sentimental value for readers, becoming cherished additions to their bookshelves.

The videos honor the passion of book collectors and elevate the bookstagram experience beyond reading to include the thrill of discovering bookish treasures.

IN CONCLUSION:

Book unboxing videos that unveil literary treasures in special editions or book subscription boxes offer a captivating and immersive concept within the bookstagram community. By capturing the excitement of unboxing, sharing the beauty of special editions, and celebrating the magic of book subscription boxes, bookstagrammers create a sense of wonder and shared delight among their followers. These videos foster engagement and discussion, inspire bookish recommendations, and honor the joy of book collecting. As bookstagram continues to thrive, book unboxing videos will remain a cherished tradition, uniting book lovers in an enchanting journey of literary surprises and shared appreciation for the enchanting world of books within the captivating world of bookstagram.

TWENTY-SIX
"BOOKSHELFIE" CONTESTS:
SHOWCASING THE BEAUTY AND PERSONALITIES OF BOOKSHELVES

THE CONCEPT EXPLAINED:

"Bookshelfie" contests on bookstagram are interactive posts or stories where bookstagrammers encourage their followers to share photographs of their bookshelves. Participants, or "bookshelfie enthusiasts," submit images of their bookshelves, displaying their book collections, organizational methods, and decorative touches.

The bookstagrammer hosting the contest may set specific themes, such as color-coded bookshelves, themed book displays, or cozy reading nooks, to add an element of creativity to the contest.

Celebrating the Beauty and Diversity of Bookshelves:

The essence of "Bookshelfie" contests lies in celebrating the beauty and diversity of bookshelves. Each participant's bookshelf reflects their reading preferences, book collections, and personal style.

Through these contests, bookstagrammers create a visual feast of bookshelves, celebrating the creativity and uniqueness of each bookshelfie.

Fostering Bookstagram Community:

"Bookshelfie" contests foster a sense of community and camaraderie among bookstagram followers. As participants proudly share their bookshelves, they connect with fellow book lovers who appreciate and admire their book collections.

These contests become a platform for bookstagrammers to interact, exchange ideas, and bond over their shared passion for books and bookish spaces.

Inspiring Creative Bookshelf Displays:

The concept of "Bookshelfie" contests inspires participants to get creative with their bookshelf displays. Whether it's organizing books by color, showcasing favorite series, or incorporating bookish merchandise and decorations, participants take pride in curating their bookshelves to reflect their individual tastes.

The contests encourage bookshelf enthusiasts to reimagine their book displays and discover new ways to make their shelves visually appealing and unique.

Promoting Organizational Ideas:

"Bookshelfie" contests promote organizational ideas and tips within the bookstagram community. As participants share their well-organized bookshelves, they may also offer insights into their organizing methods or share strategies for keeping books tidy and accessible.

These contests become an opportunity for bookstagrammers to learn from one another and improve their own bookshelf organization.

Creating a Sense of Pride and Accomplishment:

Through "Bookshelfie" contests, participants experience a sense of pride and accomplishment. Sharing their bookshelves with others and receiving positive feedback from fellow bookstagrammers boosts their confidence and reaffirms their love for books and reading.

These contests become a celebration of the effort and care participants put into curating their bookish spaces.

Inspiring Bookish Wishlist Ideas:

The concept of "Bookshelfie" contests also inspires bookish wishlist ideas among participants and followers. As bookstagrammers spot intriguing books or bookshelves featuring unique bookish merchandise, they may add new titles or items to their reading and bookish collections.

These contests serve as a source of inspiration for bookish discoveries and encourage followers to explore new reads and book-related products.

Promoting Aesthetic and Cozy Reading Spaces:

"Bookshelfie" contests promote aesthetic and cozy reading spaces within the bookstagram community. Participants often share images of their bookshelves in cozy corners, adorned with cushions, blankets, or cozy reading nooks.

These contests encourage followers to create inviting and inspiring reading spaces where they can immerse themselves in the world of books.

IN CONCLUSION:

"Bookshelfie" contests offering a platform for bookstagram followers to proudly showcase their own bookshelves offer an engaging and visually captivating concept within the bookstagram community. By celebrating the beauty, diversity, and creativity of bookshelves, these contests foster a sense of community, inspiration, and admiration for the shared love of books and the spaces that hold them. The contests inspire creative bookshelf displays, promote organizational ideas, and create a sense of pride and accomplishment among participants. As bookstagram continues to thrive, "Bookshelfie" contests will remain a cherished tradition, uniting book lovers in a delightful journey of bookish spaces and shared appreciation for the enchanting world of books within the captivating world of bookstagram.

TWENTY-SEVEN
CURATED LIST OF UNDERRATED BOOKS:
UNEARTHING HIDDEN GEMS IN THE LITERARY WORLD

THE CONCEPT EXPLAINED:

Curated lists of underrated books on bookstagram are meticulously crafted posts or stories where bookstagrammers share a selection of books that they believe deserve more attention and recognition. These lists may revolve around various themes, genres, or authors, depending on the bookstagrammer's focus and expertise.

The books featured in these lists are often lesser-known works that may not have received extensive media coverage or popular acclaim but are cherished by readers who have discovered their literary brilliance.

Unearthing Hidden Gems:

The essence of curated lists of underrated books lies in unearthing hidden gems within the literary world. Bookstagrammers delve beyond the well-known bestsellers and acclaimed titles to explore the lesser-known works that hold profound stories, unique perspectives, and exceptional writing.

These lists become a treasure trove of literary discoveries, inviting followers to explore new and uncharted territories within the vast landscape of books.

Promoting Diverse Voices and Perspectives:

Curated lists of underrated books promote diverse voices and perspectives in literature. As bookstagrammers curate their lists, they may include books written by authors from marginalized backgrounds, authors representing various cultures, or books exploring less mainstream themes.

These lists become a celebration of literary diversity, encouraging followers to embrace a wide range of experiences and stories through reading.

Fostering a Sense of Community and Inclusivity:

Through curated lists of underrated books, bookstagrammers foster a sense of community and inclusivity within the bookstagram community. By highlighting lesser-known works, they create an environment where readers from different backgrounds and tastes can find books that resonate with them.

These lists encourage followers to engage in bookish discussions, share their thoughts on the featured works, and bond over their shared appreciation for literary gems.

Providing a Platform for Discovery:

Curated lists of underrated books provide a platform for book discovery among followers. As bookstagrammers share their carefully selected titles, followers can explore new authors, genres, or themes they might not have otherwise encountered.

These lists become a gateway to new reading experiences, enriching the literary journey of bookstagrammers.

Nurturing a Deeper Appreciation for Literature:

The concept of curated lists of underrated books nurtures a deeper appreciation for literature among followers. By shining a spotlight on lesser-known works, bookstagrammers highlight the vast diversity and richness of the literary landscape.

Followers are encouraged to broaden their reading horizons and recognize the value of each book, regardless of its popularity or commercial success.

Celebrating Unsung Authors and Hidden Talents:

Through curated lists of underrated books, bookstagrammers celebrate unsung authors and hidden talents. Lesser-known authors often possess immense talent and storytelling prowess, deserving recognition for their contributions to the literary world.

These lists become a tribute to the dedication and creativity of writers who may not have received widespread acclaim but have left a lasting impact on readers.

Promoting a Balanced Reading Diet:

The concept of curated lists of underrated books promotes a balanced reading diet among followers. By adding lesser-known works to their reading lists, bookstagrammers can complement their reading of popular bestsellers and well-known titles.

These lists encourage followers to seek a diverse range of reading experiences, enriching their literary journey with hidden gems and unexpected delights.

IN CONCLUSION:

Curated lists of underrated books offering thoughtfully selected literary treasures within the bookstagram community offer a valuable and insightful concept. By unearthing hidden gems, promoting diverse voices, and fostering a sense of community, bookstagrammers celebrate the depth and diversity of literature. These lists provide a platform for discovery, nurture a deeper appreciation for lesser-known works, and celebrate unsung authors. As bookstagram continues to thrive, curated lists of underrated books will remain a cherished tradition, uniting book lovers in an enchanting journey of literary exploration and shared appreciation for the enchanting world of books within the captivating world of bookstagram.

TWENTY-EIGHT
WEEKLY BOOK-RELATED MEMES OR HUMOR POSTS:
SPREADING LAUGHTER AND LITERARY FUN

THE CONCEPT EXPLAINED:

Weekly book-related memes or humor posts on bookstagram are regular content updates where bookstagrammers share funny and witty images, gifs, or captions related to books and reading. These posts may take the form of memes, which are humorous images or text that convey relatable bookish situations, or humorous captions that accompany bookish photos or illustrations.

The bookstagrammer may choose a specific day of the week to share these posts regularly, such as "Meme Monday" or "Funny Friday," to create a sense of anticipation and regularity among followers.

Spreading Laughter and Literary Fun:

The essence of weekly book-related memes or humor posts lies in spreading laughter and literary fun within the bookstagram community. As followers encounter these humorous posts, they are met with relatable and amusing bookish scenarios that bring smiles to their faces.

These posts become a source of light-hearted amusement, fostering a positive and joyful atmosphere on bookstagram.

Creating a Sense of Connection and Relatability:

Weekly book-related memes or humor posts create a sense of connection and relatability among bookstagram followers. The humor in these posts often stems from shared experiences, such as the joy of book hauls, the struggle of unread books piling up, or the dedication to finishing an enticing book in one sitting.

These posts become a way for bookstagrammers to bond over their shared love for books and the funny moments that come with being an avid reader.

Adding Playfulness to Bookstagram:

The concept of weekly book-related memes or humor posts adds a touch of playfulness to bookstagram. Amidst the serious book reviews and discussions, these posts inject a dose of humor and light-heartedness into the bookstagram feed.

Followers enjoy the moments of amusement and laughter, which serve as a refreshing break from the regular bookish content.

Fostering Bookish Discussions and Engagement:

Weekly book-related memes or humor posts foster bookish discussions and engagement among followers. As followers encounter the humorous content, they may comment on the posts, sharing their thoughts, experiences, or their own book-related funny stories.

These discussions create a lively and interactive booksta-gram community, where readers engage with one another and find camaraderie in their bookish adventures.

Encouraging Creativity and Wit:

The concept of weekly book-related memes or humor posts encourages creativity and wit among bookstagrammers. Creating humorous content that resonates with followers requires ingenuity and an understanding of bookish culture.

Bookstagrammers have the opportunity to showcase their creative talents and wit, making these posts an extension of their unique personalities.

Promoting Positive Bookish Vibes:

Through weekly book-related memes or humor posts, bookstagrammers promote positive bookish vibes within the community. The humor and laughter shared through these posts create an environment where followers feel uplifted and entertained.

These posts become a source of positivity and joy, enhancing the overall bookstagram experience for followers.

Relieving Bookish Stress and Tensions:

The concept of weekly book-related memes or humor posts provides a way to relieve bookish stress and tensions. Reading can be a deeply emotional and immer-sive experience, and sometimes, humor offers a welcome escape from intense plotlines or emotional narratives.

These posts become a breath of fresh air, offering a moment of lightheartedness in the midst of literary adventures.

IN CONCLUSION:

Weekly book-related memes or humor posts offering laughter and literary fun within the bookstagram community offer a delightful and entertaining concept. By spreading laughter, creating a sense of connection, and adding playfulness to bookstagram, these posts foster bookish discussions and promote positive bookish vibes. The humor and wit showcased in these posts reflect the creativity and personalities of bookstagrammers, making them a cherished tradition that unites book lovers in the enchanting world of books within the captivating world of bookstagram.

TWENTY-NINE
COLLABORATIVE BOOK PLAYLISTS:

FUSING LITERATURE AND MUSIC IN AN ENCHANTING SYMPHONY

THE CONCEPT EXPLAINED:

Collaborative book playlists on bookstagram are interactive experiences where bookstagrammers invite their followers to contribute songs to playlists based on different genres or moods related to books. The bookstagrammer may set a specific theme for each playlist, such as "Fantasy Adventure Vibes," "Heartfelt Romance," or "Spooky Mysteries."

Followers participate by suggesting songs that evoke the essence and emotions of the chosen book genres or moods. The bookstagrammer then curates the playlist, combining the suggestions into a harmonious and atmospheric collection of songs.

Fusing Literature and Music:

The essence of collaborative book playlists lies in fusing the worlds of literature and music. By selecting songs that resonate with the themes, characters, or settings of books, these playlists enhance the reading experience with an added layer of emotional depth and connection The playlists become an enchanting symphony that elevates the power of storytelling and evokes a wide range of emotions among readers.

Creating Immersive Reading Experiences:

Collaborative book playlists create immersive reading experiences for followers. As readers dive into the world of a book, they can also immerse themselves in the curated playlist, which serves as a companion soundtrack to their literary journey. The music amplifies the mood, atmosphere, and emotions of the story, enriching the reader's connection with the narrative.

Celebrating Book-Induced Emotions:

Through collaborative book playlists, bookstagrammers celebrate the emotions evoked by books. Followers contribute songs that remind them of the exhilaration of epic adventures, the tenderness of love stories, or the suspense of thrilling mysteries. These playlists become a collective expression of the impact books have on readers' hearts and souls.

Fostering Community Participation:

The concept of collaborative book playlists fosters community participation within the bookstagram community. As followers contribute their song suggestions, they actively engage with the bookstagrammer and fellow readers, forming a sense of community and connection. The collaborative nature of these playlists creates a shared experience that unites bookstagrammers and their followers in their love for both books and music.

Adding Personal Touches to Reading Recommendations:

Collaborative book playlists add personal touches to reading recommendations. As bookstagrammers curate playlists based on their followers' song suggestions, they tailor the playlists to match their readers' tastes and preferences.

The playlists become personalized reading companions that reflect the unique perspectives and emotions of the bookstagram community.

Enhancing Mood and Atmosphere:

The concept of collaborative book playlists enhances the mood and atmosphere of the reading experience. Whether it's a playlist that transports readers to the magical realms of fantasy or one that immerses them in the nostalgia of classic literature, the music complements the literary ambiance.

The playlists set the tone and create an emotional backdrop for the reader's journey through the pages of a book.

Promoting Interdisciplinary Appreciation:

Collaborative book playlists promote interdisciplinary appreciation between literature and music. By exploring how the two art forms complement and enhance each other, bookstagrammers and their followers develop a deeper understanding and appreciation for the intricacies of storytelling and musical expression.

These playlists become an avenue for exploring the intersections of creativity and emotion across different art forms.

IN CONCLUSION:

Collaborative book playlists, fusing literature and music into an enchanting symphony within the bookstagram community, offer a unique and immersive concept. By celebrating emotions inspired by books, fostering community participation, and enhancing mood and atmosphere, these playlists elevate the reading experience to new heights. The playlists become personal and evocative reading companions that amplify the power of storytelling and unite book lovers in a shared appreciation for the enchanting world of books and the captivating melodies of music within the captivating world of bookstagram.

THIRTY
BOOKSHELF SCAVENGER HUNT:
UNLEASHING THE ADVENTURER WITHIN BOOKSTAGRAMMERS

THE CONCEPT EXPLAINED:

"Bookshelf Scavenger Hunt" challenges on bookstagram are interactive posts or stories where bookstagrammers invite their followers to participate in a virtual scavenger hunt within their own bookshelves. The bookstagrammer creates a list of specific items, prompts, or clues related to books or bookish objects.

Participants, or "bookshelf adventurers," set out to find the items within their bookshelves and share photos or stories of their discoveries in the comments or through direct messages.

Unleashing the Adventurer Within:

The essence of "Bookshelf Scavenger Hunt" challenges lies in unleashing the adventurer within bookstagrammers. As participants search for specific items on their bookshelves, they embark on a virtual journey, exploring their bookish treasures and delving into the depths of their literary collections.

These challenges awaken the spirit of adventure and curiosity, turning bookshelves into treasure troves waiting to be discovered.

Adding Fun and Playfulness to Bookstagram:

The concept of "Bookshelf Scavenger Hunt" challenges adds a sense of fun and playfulness to bookstagram. Amidst serious book reviews and discussions, these challenges inject an element of excitement and lightheartedness into the bookstagram feed.

Followers enjoy the interactive nature of the challenges and the opportunity to explore their bookshelves in a creative and engaging way.

Fostering a Sense of Community and Participation:

"Bookshelf Scavenger Hunt" challenges foster a sense of community and participation within the bookstagram community. As participants share their discoveries and engage with the bookstagrammer's prompts, they form connections with fellow book lovers who are on the same adventurous quest.

These challenges become a shared experience that unites bookstagrammers and their followers in their love for exploration and books.

Promoting Bookshelf Organization and Rediscovery:

The concept of "Bookshelf Scavenger Hunt" challenges promotes bookshelf organization and rediscovery among participants. As bookstagrammers search for specific items, they may rearrange their bookshelves, rediscovering hidden gems and long-forgotten titles.

These challenges encourage participants to reimagine their book displays and appreciate the treasures hidden within their bookshelves.

Enhancing Creativity and Imagination:

"Bookshelf Scavenger Hunt" challenges enhance creativity and imagination among participants. The bookstagrammer's prompts may require participants to find books with specific colors, themes, or genres, prompting them to think outside the box and explore their literary collections from new perspectives. These challenges inspire participants to tap into their creative minds and reimagine the possibilities within their bookshelves.

Creating a Sense of Accomplishment:

The concept of "Bookshelf Scavenger Hunt" challenges creates a sense of accomplishment among participants. As they complete the scavenger hunt and find the specific items on their bookshelves, they experience a feeling of success and fulfillment. These challenges become a rewarding journey that celebrates the joy of bookish exploration.

Encouraging Friendly Competition and Encouragement:

"Bookshelf Scavenger Hunt" challenges encourage friendly competition and encouragement within the bookstagram community. Participants may compete to find items quickly or creatively interpret the prompts. At the same time, these challenges foster a supportive environment where participants cheer each other on and celebrate each other's discoveries.

IN CONCLUSION:

"Bookshelf Scavenger Hunt" challenges, unleashing the adventurer within bookstagrammers, offer a thrilling and interactive concept within the bookstagram community. By adding fun and playfulness, fostering a sense of community and participation, and promoting bookshelf organization and rediscovery, these challenges turn bookshelves into treasure troves waiting to be explored. The challenges inspire creativity and imagination, create a sense of accomplishment, and encourage friendly competition and encouragement. As bookstagram continues to thrive, "Bookshelf Scavenger Hunt" challenges will remain a cherished tradition, uniting book lovers in a thrilling literary journey and shared appreciation for the enchanting world of books within the captivating world of bookstagram.

THIRTY-ONE
READ-A-THON EVENTS:
A LITERARY MARATHON OF READING CHALLENGES AND PROGRESS UPDATES

THE CONCEPT EXPLAINED:

Read-a-thon events on bookstagram are time-limited reading challenges where bookstagrammers and their followers set aside specific periods, often ranging from a few hours to several days, for concentrated reading. The event may have a set start and end date, during which participants dedicate their time to reading as many books or pages as possible.

Bookstagrammers announce the Read-a-thon, set reading challenges or goals, and invite followers to participate by sharing their own reading aspirations for the event.

Throughout the Read-a-thon, participants provide progress updates, sharing the books they've read, their page counts, and their thoughts on the reading experience.

Fostering Camaraderie and Motivation:

The essence of Read-a-thon events lies in fostering camaraderie and motivation within the bookstagram community. As participants embark on their reading journey together, they feel connected to fellow book lovers who share the same dedication to reading. The support and encouragement from others inspire participants to persevere and achieve their reading goals during the event.

Creating a Shared Literary Experience:

Read-a-thon events create a shared literary experience among bookstagrammers and their followers. As participants read books during the event, they can discuss their progress, favorite moments, and book recommendations with others taking part. This shared experience enhances the joy of reading and deepens the sense of community within the bookstagram community.

Challenging Reading Aspirations:

The concept of Read-a-thon events challenges participants' reading aspirations. Bookstagrammers may set specific challenges, such as reading a certain number of books, completing a particular series, or delving into a new genre. These challenges push participants to explore new literary horizons and read outside their comfort zones, enriching their reading experiences.

Encouraging Time for Reading:

Read-a-thon events encourage participants to dedicate specific time for reading. In a world filled with busy schedules and distractions, Read-a-thons provide an opportunity for bookstagrammers to set aside uninterrupted moments for the love of reading. The events promote the joy of immersing oneself in the pages of a book and savoring the written word.

Celebrating Reading Progress:

The concept of Read-a-thon events celebrates reading progress and achievements. As participants share their updates and accomplishments, they receive support, praise, and encouragement from fellow bookstagrammers. These celebrations of progress motivate participants to continue reading and revel in the sense of accomplishment as they reach their goals.

Promoting Reading Accountability:

Read-a-thon events promote reading accountability among participants. As followers share their reading goals and progress, they commit to their aspirations, knowing that others are cheering them on. The sense of accountability helps participants stay focused and dedicated to their reading during the event.

Creating a Sense of Excitement and Anticipation:

The concept of Read-a-thon events creates a sense of excitement and anticipation within the bookstagram community. As the event approaches, participants eagerly prepare their reading lists, set goals, and anticipate the joy of diving into books during the event. The energy and enthusiasm surrounding the Read-a-thon add a vibrant atmosphere to the bookstagram community.

IN CONCLUSION:

Read-a-thon events, infusing bookstagram with a literary marathon of reading challenges and progress updates, offer an exhilarating and immersive concept within the bookstagram community. By fostering camaraderie, creating a shared literary experience, and challenging reading aspirations, these events celebrate the joy of reading and deepen the sense of community among bookstagrammers. The events encourage dedicated time for reading, promote reading accountability, and create a sense of excitement and anticipation. As bookstagram continues to thrive, Read-a-thon events will remain a cherished tradition, uniting book lovers in an enchanting journey of literary exploration and shared appreciation for the captivating world of books within the captivating world of bookstagram.

THIRTY-TWO
"PICK YOUR NEXT READ" STORIES:

EMPOWERING FOLLOWERS IN THE BOOKSTAGRAMMER'S READING JOURNEY

THE CONCEPT EXPLAINED:

"Pick Your Next Read" stories on bookstagram are interactive and time-limited posts where bookstagrammers present a selection of books they are considering reading next. The bookstagrammer may choose to include book covers, titles, or brief summaries of each book to provide context for the followers' voting choices.

In the story, the bookstagrammer invites followers to participate by voting on their preferred book choice using interactive polls or other voting features. Followers can then cast their votes, indicating which book they would like the bookstagrammer to read next.

After the voting period ends, the bookstagrammer tallies the votes and announces the winning book, which they will subsequently read and share their thoughts about with their followers.

Empowering Followers in the Reading Journey:

The essence of "Pick Your Next Read" stories lies in empowering bookstagram followers in the bookstagrammer's reading journey. By inviting followers to vote on the book, the bookstagrammer shows appreciation for their opinions and values their input in choosing the next literary adventure.

These stories create a sense of inclusivity, as followers actively participate in shaping the bookstagrammer's reading list.

Creating a Virtual Book Club Experience:

"Pick Your Next Read" stories create a virtual book club-style experience within the bookstagram community. The voting process, where followers collectively decide on the book, mirrors the democratic approach of a book club where members suggest and vote on books to read together.

The bookstagrammer's reading experience becomes a shared endeavor, akin to reading with friends in a virtual book club.

Fostering Community Engagement and Interaction:

The concept of "Pick Your Next Read" stories fosters community engagement and interaction among bookstagram followers. As participants cast their votes and share their preferences, they engage in bookish discussions and connect with fellow readers who share similar literary tastes.

These stories create opportunities for bookstagrammers to interact with their followers, building a strong sense of community within the bookstagram platform.

Instilling Anticipation and Excitement:

"Pick Your Next Read" stories instill anticipation and excitement among bookstagram followers. As they await the results of the voting, followers eagerly anticipate the bookstagrammer's final decision and look forward to embarking on the reading journey together.

The element of suspense adds an extra layer of enjoyment to the reading experience.

Promoting Diverse Book Selections:

The concept of "Pick Your Next Read" stories promotes diverse book selections within the bookstagram community. By presenting a curated list of books for followers to choose from, the bookstagrammer introduces their audience to a wide range of genres, authors, and literary themes.

The voting process becomes an opportunity to discover new and diverse reads, enriching the reading horizons of bookstagram followers.

Encouraging Honest and Authentic Reading Recommendations:

"Pick Your Next Read" stories encourage honest and authentic reading recommendations from bookstagram followers. As they vote for their preferred books, followers express their genuine interest and excitement for the titles they believe the bookstagrammer would enjoy. The voting process ensures that the bookstagrammer receives well-curated book suggestions from their engaged and enthusiastic audience.

Sharing the Reading Journey with Followers:

The concept of "Pick Your Next Read" stories creates a sense of togetherness in the reading journey between bookstagrammers and their followers. As the bookstagrammer reads the winning book, they share their thoughts, reviews, and reactions with their followers. These shared experiences deepen the connection between the bookstagrammer and their audience, fostering a strong and supportive bookstagram community.

IN CONCLUSION:

"Pick Your Next Read" stories, empowering followers in the bookstagrammer's reading journey, offer an engaging and interactive concept within the bookstagram community. By creating a virtual book club experience, fostering community engagement, and instilling anticipation and excitement, these stories unite bookstagrammers and their followers in the joy of discovering and reading books together. The voting process promotes diverse book selections, encourages honest reading recommendations, and allows the bookstagrammer to share their reading journey authentically with their audience. As bookstagram continues to thrive, "Pick Your Next Read" stories will remain a cherished tradition, reflecting the inclusive and communal spirit of the captivating world of books within the captivating world of bookstagram.

THIRTY-THREE
BOOK-INSPIRED MAKEUP OR NAIL ART TUTORIALS:
WHERE LITERATURE MEETS ARTISTIC EXPRESSION

THE CONCEPT EXPLAINED:

Book-inspired makeup or nail art tutorials on bookstagram are captivating posts or stories where bookstagrammers delve into the world of literature to find inspiration for their creative makeup looks or nail art designs. Each tutorial centers around a specific book, character, or theme, with the bookstagrammer using makeup products or nail art tools to bring the chosen literary inspiration to life on their face or nails.

The bookstagrammer begins the tutorial by introducing the book or character that served as their muse, sharing the reasons why they found it inspiring. They then demonstrate the step-by-step process of creating the makeup look or nail art design, providing tips, techniques, and product recommendations for their followers to follow along.

Throughout the tutorial, the bookstagrammer may incorporate quotes, symbols, or elements from the book to further emphasize the connection between the literary inspiration and the makeup or nail art.

The Fusion of Literature and Artistic Expression:

The essence of book-inspired makeup or nail art tutorials lies in the fusion of literature and artistic expression. As bookstagrammers translate the themes, aesthetics, and emotions of books into makeup looks or nail art, they create a visually stunning homage to their favorite literature.

The tutorials become a celebration of the symbiotic relationship between literature and art, showcasing the power of storytelling through visual representation.

Bringing Books to Life:

Book-inspired makeup or nail art tutorials bring books to life in a vivid and enchanting manner. By reimagining characters, scenes, or book covers on their faces or nails, bookstagrammers give physical form to the magic and allure of literature.

The tutorials become a visual journey through the pages of beloved books, allowing followers to witness the beauty and depth of their favorite stories in a new and captivating way.

Encouraging Creativity and Self-Expression:

The concept of book-inspired makeup or nail art tutorials encourages creativity and self-expression among bookstagrammers. As they experiment with different makeup techniques or nail art designs, they explore their artistic talents and develop their unique style.

The tutorials become a canvas for bookstagrammers to express their love for literature and their passion for art.

Connecting with Literary Characters and Themes:

Book-inspired makeup or nail art tutorials allow bookstagrammers to form a deeper connection with their favorite literary characters and themes. As they recreate iconic looks or symbols associated with the book, they embody the essence and personality of the characters, immersing themselves in the world of the story.

The tutorials become a bridge that connects bookstagrammers to the fictional worlds and beloved characters that have left a lasting impact on their hearts.

Inspiring Bookish Discussions and Interactions:

The concept of book-inspired makeup or nail art tutorials inspires bookish discussions and interactions within the bookstagram community. Followers may comment on the tutorials, sharing their thoughts on the chosen book, their admiration for the makeup or nail art, or their own creative interpretations of literary inspirations.

These discussions create a lively and interactive bookstagram community, where readers engage with one another through the lens of literature and art.

Promoting Diverse Literary Influences:

Book-inspired makeup or nail art tutorials promote diverse literary influences within the bookstagram community. As bookstagrammers draw inspiration from various genres, authors, and literary works, they introduce their audience to a wide range of books and stories they may not have encountered before.

The tutorials become a source of discovery, encouraging followers to explore new literary horizons.

IN CONCLUSION:

Book-inspired makeup or nail art tutorials, where literature meets artistic expression within the bookstagram community, offer a unique and imaginative concept. By fusing literature and art, these tutorials bring books to life, celebrating the power of storytelling through visual representation. The tutorials encourage creativity and self-expression, connecting bookstagrammers with their favorite literary characters and themes. They also inspire bookish discussions and promote diverse literary influences, creating a vibrant and captivating world of books within the captivating world of bookstagram. As bookstagram continues to thrive, book-inspired makeup or nail art tutorials will remain a cherished tradition, uniting book lovers in a visual celebration of the enchanting world of books.

THIRTY-FOUR
BOOKSTAGRAMMER-HOSTED READ-ALOUD SESSIONS:
UNLEASHING THE POWER OF VOICE IN LITERATURE

THE CONCEPT EXPLAINED:

Bookstagrammer-hosted read-aloud sessions on bookstagram are engaging posts, stories, or live sessions where bookstagrammers showcase their love for literature through the spoken word. The bookstagrammer selects specific short stories or poetry that hold special meaning to them or align with a chosen theme or event.

During the session, the bookstagrammer reads the selected literary pieces aloud, providing an enchanting and immersive auditory experience for their followers. They may add dramatic intonations, pauses, and expressive delivery to bring the words to life and evoke the emotions and nuances of the written text.

After the session, the bookstagrammer may engage with their followers by discussing the chosen pieces, inviting reflections, or answering questions related to the literature shared.

Unleashing the Power of Voice in Literature:

The essence of bookstagrammer-hosted read-aloud sessions lies in unleashing the power of voice in literature. As the bookstagrammer breathes life into the written words through their expressive delivery, they transform the static pages of a book into a dynamic and emotive experience for their audience.

The sessions highlight the beauty of storytelling through oral tradition and remind us of the timeless connection between the spoken word and the human heart.

Creating an Enchanting Auditory Experience:

Bookstagrammer-hosted read-aloud sessions create an enchanting auditory experience for listeners. As the bookstagrammer reads with passion and fervor, their followers are captivated by the melodious flow of words and the magic of storytelling.

These sessions become a treat for the ears, offering a sensory journey into the world of literature.

Fostering a Sense of Connection and Intimacy:

The concept of bookstagrammer-hosted read-aloud sessions fosters a sense of connection and intimacy within the bookstagram community. As followers listen to the bookstagrammer's voice, they feel a personal connection with the reader, akin to sitting beside a friend sharing stories.

The sessions create a warm and inviting atmosphere that draws listeners closer to the heart of literature.

Promoting Appreciation for Short Stories and Poetry:

Bookstagrammer-hosted read-aloud sessions promote appreciation for short stories and poetry within the bookstagram community. By featuring these often overlooked literary forms, the bookstagrammer introduces their audience to the beauty and power of concise and evocative storytelling.

The sessions become a platform for celebrating the artistry of short fiction and poetry.

Enhancing the Emotional Impact of Literature:

The concept of bookstagrammer-hosted read-aloud sessions enhances the emotional impact of literature on listeners. As the bookstagrammer reads with emotion and depth, they evoke feelings of joy, sorrow, laughter, or contemplation in their audience.

The sessions become an immersive experience that touches the hearts and minds of listeners, making literature come alive in a profound way.

Creating a Shared Literary Experience:

Bookstagrammer-hosted read-aloud sessions create a shared literary experience within the bookstagram community. As followers listen to the same literary pieces, they form a collective appreciation for the chosen works and engage in discussions or reflections related to the literature shared.

The sessions become a virtual book club-style experience that unites bookstagrammers and their followers through the love of literature.

Encouraging Oral Tradition in the Digital Age:

The concept of bookstagrammer-hosted read-aloud sessions encourages oral tradition in the digital age. In a world dominated by text and screens, these sessions honor the time-honored tradition of storytelling through spoken words.

The sessions become a modern-day celebration of the timeless art of oral storytelling.

IN CONCLUSION:

Bookstagrammer-hosted read-aloud sessions, unleashing the power of voice in literature within the bookstagram community, offer a captivating and immersive concept. By creating an enchanting auditory experience, fostering a sense of connection and intimacy, and promoting appreciation for short stories and poetry, these sessions celebrate the magic of storytelling through the spoken word. They enhance the emotional impact of literature, create a shared literary experience, and encourage oral tradition in the digital age. As bookstagram continues to thrive, bookstagrammer-hosted read-aloud sessions will remain a cherished tradition, weaving the threads of voice and literature into the captivating world of books within the captivating world of bookstagram.

THIRTY-FIVE
INTERACTIVE "CREATE YOUR OWN ADVENTURE" STORIES:

UNRAVELING LITERARY JOURNEYS IN THE HANDS OF READERS

THE CONCEPT EXPLAINED:

Interactive "Create Your Own Adventure" stories on bookstagram are captivating and interactive posts or stories where bookstagrammers reimagine the worlds of their favorite books and invite their followers to shape the narrative through choices.

The bookstagrammer starts the story by setting the scene, introducing the characters, and outlining the initial dilemma or situation. At a crucial turning point in the narrative, the bookstagrammer presents followers with a series of choices, each representing a different direction the story can take.

Followers are encouraged to vote or provide input on which choice they want the characters to make. Based on the majority's decision, the bookstagrammer continues the story, building upon the chosen path.

The interactive story unfolds through multiple decision points, with followers continuously influencing the plot and the outcome with each choice they make.

Unraveling Literary Journeys in the Hands of Readers:

The essence of interactive "Create Your Own Adventure" stories lies in unraveling literary journeys in the hands of readers. By allowing followers to be active participants and decision-makers in the story, these narratives turn the bookstagram platform into a collaborative storytelling experience.

The bookstagrammer becomes the guide, leading their audience on a unique and personalized journey through the world of the chosen book.

Engaging Followers in Immersive Storytelling:

Interactive "Create Your Own Adventure" stories engage followers in immersive storytelling within the bookstagram community. As followers vote on the choices presented, they become emotionally invested in the characters and the outcome, eagerly awaiting the next installment of the narrative.

These stories blur the line between reader and writer, making storytelling a collective and interactive endeavor.

Unlocking Endless Possibilities:

The concept of interactive "Create Your Own Adventure" stories unlocks endless possibilities for the narrative. With each choice, the trajectory of the story changes, offering multiple plotlines and potential endings.

Followers can explore different paths and witness the consequences of their decisions, creating a sense of exploration and discovery within the story.

Fostering Connection with Literary Characters:

Interactive "Create Your Own Adventure" stories foster a deeper connection with literary characters within the bookstagram community. As followers influence the choices the characters make, they form emotional bonds and empathy with the fictional personas, experiencing the story through their eyes.

These stories bring characters to life in a dynamic and interactive way, making them feel like close companions on the literary journey.

Promoting Book Discussions and Conversations:

The concept of interactive "Create Your Own Adventure" stories promotes book discussions and conversations within the bookstagram community. As followers engage with the choices and outcomes, they share their thoughts, predictions, and reactions in the comments, fostering lively discussions and interactions.

These stories become a catalyst for meaningful bookish exchanges, where readers analyze the characters' decisions and motivations.

Creating a Sense of Ownership in the Storytelling Process:

Interactive "Create Your Own Adventure" stories create a sense of ownership in the storytelling process among followers. As they influence the plot and direction of the narrative, they feel a sense of authorship and agency in the unfolding story.

The stories become a testament to the collaborative power of storytelling in the digital age.

Inspiring Creativity and Storytelling Skills:

The concept of interactive "Create Your Own Adventure" stories inspires creativity and storytelling skills within the bookstagram community. As followers engage with the narrative and make choices, they may also be encouraged to craft their own interactive stories or participate in writing challenges.

These stories become a wellspring of creativity and literary exploration.

IN CONCLUSION:

Interactive "Create Your Own Adventure" stories, unraveling literary journeys in the hands of readers within the bookstagram community, offer an engaging and immersive concept. By engaging followers in immersive storytelling, unlocking endless possibilities, and fostering a connection with literary characters, these stories celebrate the magic of books in a collaborative and interactive way. They promote book discussions and conversations, create a sense of ownership in the storytelling process, and inspire creativity and storytelling skills among followers. As bookstagram continues to thrive, interactive "Create Your Own Adventure" stories will remain a cherished tradition, bridging the gap between readers and writers in the captivating world of books within the captivating world of bookstagram.

THIRTY-SIX
BOOKISH PUZZLES OR RIDDLES:

UNLOCKING LITERARY ENIGMAS IN THE WORLD OF BOOKS

THE CONCEPT EXPLAINED:

Bookish puzzles or riddles on bookstagram are captivating posts, stories, or interactive challenges where bookstagrammers present followers with a range of puzzling questions, conundrums, or riddles related to literature.

The bookstagrammer may craft puzzles based on plot twists, character identities, famous quotes, or obscure book references. They may also create word games, anagrams, or literary quizzes to challenge their followers' knowledge and literary acumen.

Followers are invited to participate in solving the puzzles by leaving their answers in the comments, direct messages, or through interactive poll features.

After a designated period, the bookstagrammer reveals the correct answers and acknowledges participants who cracked the literary codes.

Unlocking Literary Enigmas:

The essence of bookish puzzles or riddles lies in unlocking literary enigmas in the world of books. As followers engage with the mind-boggling challenges, they embark on a quest to decipher the hidden clues and unravel the literary mysteries.

These puzzles add a sense of adventure and exploration to the bookstagram experience, inviting readers to delve deeper into the books they love.

Sparkling Intellectual Curiosity:

Bookish puzzles or riddles spark intellectual curiosity within the bookstagram community. As followers ponder over the challenging questions and search for clues in their favorite books, they exercise their minds and engage in critical thinking.

These puzzles become an opportunity to enhance literary knowledge while having fun with brain-teasing challenges.

Adding Playful Mystery to Bookstagram:

The concept of bookish puzzles or riddles adds a playful sense of mystery to the bookstagram community. Followers eagerly anticipate the arrival of new puzzles, wondering what clever enigmas the bookstagrammer will present next.

These puzzles create an interactive and playful atmosphere that keeps the bookstagram audience entertained and engaged.

Encouraging Bookish Engagement:

Bookish puzzles or riddles encourage bookish engagement among followers. As they try to solve the challenges, readers revisit their favorite books, search for clues, and engage in book-related discussions to find the answers.

The puzzles become a catalyst for active participation and interaction within the bookstagram community.

Building a Sense of Community:

The concept of bookish puzzles or riddles fosters a sense of community within the bookstagram platform. As followers collaborate, share their thoughts, and celebrate their collective successes in solving the puzzles, they bond over their shared love for literature.

The puzzles create a space for camaraderie and friendly competition among bookstagrammers.

Promoting Literary Exploration and Discovery:

Bookish puzzles or riddles promote literary exploration and discovery among followers. As they encounter new challenges inspired by different books and authors, readers may be inspired to explore new genres, authors, or literary works.

The puzzles become a gateway to expanding one's reading horizons and discovering hidden literary gems.

Inspiring Creativity in Puzzlemaking:

The concept of bookish puzzles or riddles inspires creativity in puzzlemaking within the bookstagram community. As followers encounter intriguing challenges, they may also be encouraged to craft their own book-themed puzzles or contribute to bookish games on the platform.

The puzzles become a catalyst for creativity and innovation within the bookstagram space.

IN CONCLUSION:

Bookish puzzles or riddles, unlocking literary enigmas in the world of books within the bookstagram community, offer a delightful and engaging concept. By sparking intellectual curiosity, adding playful mystery, and encouraging bookish engagement, these puzzles celebrate the magic of literature in an interactive and interactive way. They build a sense of community, promote literary exploration and discovery, and inspire creativity in puzzlemaking among followers. As bookstagram continues to thrive, bookish puzzles or riddles will remain a cherished tradition, challenging minds and hearts in the captivating world of books within the captivating world of bookstagram.

THIRTY-SEVEN
THEMED BOOK AESTHETICS:
ILLUMINATING LITERARY WORLDS WITH QUOTES AND IMAGES

THE CONCEPT EXPLAINED:

Themed book aesthetics on bookstagram are captivating posts or stories where bookstagrammers design visual collages that capture the essence of specific themes, genres, or beloved books.

The bookstagrammer begins by selecting a particular theme, such as "mystery," "fantasy," "classics," or a specific book like "Pride and Prejudice" or "Harry Potter."

They then curate a collection of high-quality images that align with the chosen theme or book. These images may depict relevant landscapes, scenes, objects, or symbols that are significant to the literary world being represented.

To complete the aesthetic, the bookstagrammer incorporates carefully chosen quotes from the featured book or other relevant literary works. These quotes add depth and emotion to the visual collage, providing context and insight into the theme or book being celebrated.

Illuminating Literary Worlds:

The essence of themed book aesthetics lies in illuminating literary worlds through a visual medium. By carefully selecting images and quotes that resonate with the theme or book, the bookstagrammer recreates the atmosphere and emotions found within the pages of beloved literature.

The aesthetics offer followers a visual journey into the heart of the story, evoking nostalgia or introducing them to new literary wonders.

Eliciting Emotions and Imaginations:

Themed book aesthetics elicit emotions and spark imaginations within the bookstagram community. As followers immerse themselves in the visual collages and read the carefully chosen quotes, they experience a range of feelings and thoughts related to the themes or books presented.

The aesthetics become a gateway to experiencing the magic of literature through images and words.

Showcasing Creativity and Design:

The concept of themed book aesthetics showcases creativity and design skills among bookstagrammers. As they curate and arrange images, colors, and quotes, they exercise their artistic talents to create visually stunning and cohesive collages.

The aesthetics become a testament to the bookstagrammer's ability to merge art and literature seamlessly.

Fostering Bookish Connections:

Themed book aesthetics foster bookish connections among followers within the bookstagram community. As followers resonate with the themes or books showcased, they may share their thoughts, memories, or personal experiences related to the literature.

The aesthetics become a catalyst for meaningful bookish discussions and interactions.

Celebrating Diverse Themes and Genres:

The concept of themed book aesthetics celebrates diverse themes and genres within the bookstagram platform. From romance to dystopia, historical fiction to science fiction, bookstagrammers curate aesthetics that cater to a wide range of literary interests.

The aesthetics become a treasure trove of literary wonders that cater to diverse reading preferences.

Inspiring Reading Recommendations:

Themed book aesthetics inspire reading recommendations among followers. As they encounter captivating visuals and compelling quotes, they may feel compelled to explore the featured books or similar works, expanding their reading horizons.

The aesthetics become a source of literary inspiration and discovery.

Adding Aesthetic Appeal to Bookstagram:

The concept of themed book aesthetics adds aesthetic appeal to the bookstagram platform. As followers scroll through visually stunning collages, their bookstagram experience is enriched by the beauty and artistry that these aesthetics bring to the literary world.

The aesthetics become a visual treat that elevates the bookstagram experience.

IN CONCLUSION:

Themed book aesthetics, illuminating literary worlds with quotes and images within the bookstagram community, offer a visually captivating and expressive concept. By eliciting emotions and sparking imaginations, showcasing creativity and design skills, and fostering bookish connections, these aesthetics celebrate the magic of literature through an artistic and visual lens. They celebrate diverse themes and genres, inspire reading recommendations, and add aesthetic appeal to the bookstagram platform. As bookstagram continues to thrive, themed book aesthetics will remain a cherished tradition, enchanting readers with glimpses into the enchanting worlds of literature within the captivating world of bookstagram.

THIRTY-EIGHT
"CHARACTER COSPLAY" CHALLENGES:
BRINGING BOOK CHARACTERS TO LIFE IN THE BOOKSTAGRAM COMMUNITY

THE CONCEPT EXPLAINED:

"Character Cosplay" challenges on bookstagram are captivating posts or stories where bookstagrammers invite their followers to dress up as characters from their favorite books.

The bookstagrammer selects a specific book, series, or theme for the challenge. It could be centered around a popular novel like "Harry Potter," a classic like "Pride and Prejudice," or a genre like "fantasy" or "dystopia."

They encourage their followers to use their creativity and imagination to interpret and embody the chosen characters through costumes, makeup, and props.

Followers participate by sharing photos of their character cosplays, either in their main feeds, stories, or by using a designated hashtag. The bookstagrammer may also feature some of the best cosplays on their own account or stories to showcase the community's talent and dedication.

Bringing Book Characters to Life:

The essence of "Character Cosplay" challenges lies in bringing book characters to life within the bookstagram community. As followers don the personas of their favorite fictional personalities, they step into the shoes of the characters they've grown to love, immersing themselves in the magical worlds of literature.

The challenges create a visual spectacle that celebrates the influence of literature on readers' lives.

Celebrating Creativity and Imagination:

"Character Cosplay" challenges celebrate creativity and imagination among bookstagrammers. As followers brainstorm and assemble their costumes, they exercise their artistic talents to recreate the iconic appearances and distinctive traits of the characters.

The challenges become a canvas for showcasing individuality and originality within the bookstagram community.

Fostering a Sense of Community and Belonging:

The concept of "Character Cosplay" challenges fosters a sense of community and belonging among bookstagrammers. As followers participate and share their cosplays, they create a space where book lovers come together to celebrate their shared love for specific books or genres.

The challenges become a unifying force that bridges readers across diverse backgrounds and locations.

Promoting Bookish Engagement and Interaction:

"Character Cosplay" challenges promote bookish engagement and interaction within the bookstagram community. As followers post their cosplays and interact with one another through comments or messages, they share their admiration for the characters and exchange thoughts on the featured books.

The challenges become a catalyst for meaningful bookish discussions and connections.

Encouraging a Deeper Connection with Literature:

The concept of "Character Cosplay" challenges encourages a deeper connection with literature among followers. As they embody the characters they've grown to love, readers develop a profound understanding of the fictional personas, empathizing with their struggles and triumphs.

The challenges enhance the emotional impact of the books, making the reading experience more immersive and unforgettable.

Inspiring Book Recommendations and Discoveries:

"Character Cosplay" challenges inspire book recommendations and discoveries within the bookstagram community. As followers encounter diverse character cosplays, they may feel inspired to explore the featured books or discover new literary works with captivating characters.

The challenges become a wellspring of literary inspiration and exploration.

Adding Playful Fun to Bookstagram:

The concept of "Character Cosplay" challenges adds playful fun to the bookstagram platform. As followers dress up as their favorite characters and engage in friendly competitions, they inject a sense of joy and excitement into the bookstagram experience.

The challenges create an atmosphere of celebration and amusement.

IN CONCLUSION:

"Character Cosplay" challenges, bringing book characters to life in the bookstagram community, offer an exciting and creative concept. By celebrating creativity and imagination, fostering a sense of community and belonging, and promoting bookish engagement and interaction, these challenges honor the magic of literature and its profound impact on readers' lives. They encourage a deeper connection with literature, inspire book recommendations and discoveries, and add playful fun to the bookstagram platform. As bookstagram continues to thrive, "Character Cosplay" challenges will remain a cherished tradition, celebrating the beloved characters and worlds that have captured the hearts of readers within the captivating world of bookstagram.

THIRTY-NINE
BOOKISH TAROT OR FORTUNE-TELLING SESSIONS:
UNRAVELING LITERARY DESTINIES THROUGH BOOK COVERS

THE CONCEPT EXPLAINED:

Bookish tarot or fortune-telling sessions on bookstagram are captivating posts, stories, or interactive challenges where bookstagrammers use book covers to conduct tarot readings or fortune-telling sessions for their followers.

The bookstagrammer begins by selecting a specific book or a set of books that represent the tarot cards or symbols they wish to use in the reading. For instance, they might choose books with distinct themes or motifs, such as love, adventure, mystery, or self-discovery, to correspond with specific tarot cards.

They then assign book covers to different tarot cards or symbols, using the visual elements and symbolism of the covers to align with the traditional meanings of the cards.

Followers participate by asking questions or seeking guidance on specific aspects of their lives, just like in a traditional tarot reading or fortune-telling session.

The bookstagrammer responds by interpreting the selected book covers in the context of the follower's questions, offering insights and advice based on the visual cues and symbolism found on the covers.

Unraveling Literary Destinies:

The essence of bookish tarot or fortune-telling sessions lies in unraveling literary destinies through book covers. As bookstagrammers conduct the readings and interpret the symbolism of the chosen book covers, they offer followers a glimpse into the paths and possibilities that lie ahead within the captivating worlds of literature.

The sessions become a fusion of mystical divination and the magic of storytelling.

Tapping into the Mystical Allure of Literature:

Bookish tarot or fortune-telling sessions tap into the mystical allure of literature within the bookstagram community. As followers seek guidance and insights through the visual symbolism of book covers, they embrace the enigmatic and magical nature of the reading experience.

The sessions become an invitation to explore the unknown and embrace the mysteries of literature.

Offering Unique Insights and Interpretations:

The concept of bookish tarot or fortune-telling sessions offers unique insights and interpretations among followers. As the bookstagrammer draws connections between the visual elements on the book covers and the traditional meanings of tarot cards or symbols, they provide followers with personalized and creative readings.

The sessions become a testament to the bookstagrammer's ability to weave literary magic into divination.

Fostering a Sense of Connection with Books:

Bookish tarot or fortune-telling sessions foster a sense of connection with books within the bookstagram community. As followers seek guidance through the book covers, they develop a deeper appreciation for the visual artistry and symbolism found in literature.

The sessions become a celebration of the captivating power of book covers and their ability to evoke emotions and imagination.

Creating a Playful and Interactive Experience:

The concept of bookish tarot or fortune-telling sessions creates a playful and interactive experience on the bookstagram platform. As followers engage with the readings, ask questions, and receive insights, they become active participants in the mystical journey, adding an element of excitement and wonder to the bookstagram experience.

The sessions become an enchanting blend of storytelling and divination.

Inspiring Literary Explorations:

Bookish tarot or fortune-telling sessions inspire literary explorations among followers. As they encounter unique book covers in the readings, they may feel inspired to explore the featured books and discover new literary gems that align with their questions or interests.

The sessions become a source of literary inspiration and discovery.

IN CONCLUSION:

Bookish tarot or fortune-telling sessions, unraveling literary destinies through book covers within the bookstagram community, offer a unique and fascinating concept. By tapping into the mystical allure of literature, offering unique insights and interpretations, and fostering a sense of connection with books, these sessions celebrate the magic of storytelling and divination. They create a playful and interactive experience, inspiring literary explorations, and inviting followers to explore the mystical realms hidden within the captivating world of books within the captivating world of bookstagram. As bookstagram continues to thrive, bookish tarot or fortune-telling sessions will remain a cherished tradition, unlocking the secrets and destinies concealed within the visual artistry of book covers.

FORTY

BOOKSHELF BINGO:

A LITERARY ADVENTURE WITH BOOK-RELATED CHALLENGES IN A BINGO FORMAT

THE CONCEPT EXPLAINED:

"Bookshelf Bingo" on bookstagram is a captivating and interactive game where bookstagrammers create a bingo card with book-related challenges or prompts.

The bingo card consists of a grid with different squares, each containing a unique challenge. These challenges can range from reading tasks like "Read a classic novel" or "Finish a book in one day" to bookshelf organization challenges like "Rearrange your bookshelf by color" or "Create a themed book display."

Participants can mark off the squares on the bingo card as they complete the corresponding challenges. They can either print out physical cards or use digital templates to track their progress.

The bookstagrammer may host the "Bookshelf Bingo" as a stand-alone event or as part of a larger reading challenge or bookish event.

A Literary Adventure:

The essence of "Bookshelf Bingo" lies in embarking on a literary adventure within the bookstagram community. As participants complete various book-related challenges, they traverse through diverse literary landscapes and genres, expanding their reading horizons.

The game becomes a thrilling journey of exploration and discovery.

Exploring Diverse Genres and Authors:

"Bookshelf Bingo" challenges participants to explore diverse genres and authors they might not have encountered otherwise. As they complete tasks like "Read a book by an author from a different culture" or "Try a genre you rarely read," readers are encouraged to step outside their comfort zones and embrace the diversity of literature.

The game becomes a gateway to literary exploration and new reading experiences.

Adding an Element of Excitement and Camaraderie:

The concept of "Bookshelf Bingo" adds an element of excitement and camaraderie to the bookstagram community. As participants share their progress and experiences through posts or stories, they create a sense of shared enthusiasm and support.

The game becomes a collaborative endeavor that fosters connection and friendly competition among bookstagrammers.

Promoting Bookish Engagement and Interaction:

"Bookshelf Bingo" challenges promote bookish engagement and interaction within the bookstagram community.

As participants complete challenges and share their achievements, they engage in lively discussions about the books they've read, authors they've discovered, and bookshelf organization ideas.

The game becomes a catalyst for meaningful bookish conversations.

Encouraging Reading Goals and Accomplishments:

The concept of "Bookshelf Bingo" encourages participants to set and achieve reading goals. As they mark off squares on the bingo card, they experience a sense of accomplishment and progress in their reading journey.

The game becomes a source of motivation and inspiration to read more and explore further.

Inspiring Book Recommendations:

"Bookshelf Bingo" inspires book recommendations among participants. As they complete challenges like "Read a book recommended by a friend" or "Read a book with a beautiful cover," they share their discoveries with others, leading to a cascade of bookish recommendations. The game becomes a treasure trove of book suggestions and literary gems.

Fostering Creativity and Bookshelf Organization:

The concept of "Bookshelf Bingo" fosters creativity and bookshelf organization among bookstagrammers. As participants complete challenges related to book displays and organization, they get creative with arranging their bookshelves, incorporating aesthetics and themes that reflect their personalities and reading preferences.

The game becomes an opportunity for self-expression and artistic flair.

IN CONCLUSION:

"Bookshelf Bingo," a literary adventure with book-related challenges in a bingo format within the bookstagram community, offers a creative and engaging concept. By exploring diverse genres and authors, adding excitement and camaraderie, and promoting bookish engagement and interaction, this interactive game celebrates the magic of literature and its power to bring readers together. It encourages reading goals and accomplishments, inspires book recommendations, and fosters creativity in bookshelf organization. As bookstagram continues to thrive, "Bookshelf Bingo" will remain a cherished tradition, leading readers on a delightful journey through the captivating world of books within the captivating world of bookstagram.

FORTY-ONE
AUTHOR SPOTLIGHT:
ILLUMINATING NEW WRITERS AND CELEBRATING LITERARY TALENT

THE CONCEPT EXPLAINED:

"Author Spotlight" features on bookstagram are captivating posts or stories where bookstagrammers introduce their followers to new and emerging writers.

The bookstagrammer selects a specific author or a group of authors to feature. These authors may be debut writers, self-published authors, or writers who have recently released a book that deserves more attention.

The feature typically includes an introduction to the author, highlighting their background, writing journey, and literary achievements. Bookstagrammers may also include personal anecdotes or thoughts about the author's work to add a personal touch to the spotlight.

To enhance the feature, bookstagrammers may share captivating images of the author's book covers, reading spaces, or events where they have participated.

Followers are encouraged to interact with the "Author Spotlight" feature by asking questions, sharing their thoughts on the author's works, or expressing their appreciation for the introduction.

Illuminating New Writers:

The essence of "Author Spotlight" features lies in illuminating new writers within the bookstagram community. By introducing followers to talented authors and their literary works, bookstagrammers provide a platform for these writers to reach a wider audience and gain recognition.

The features become a celebration of literary talent and creativity.

Fostering a Sense of Community:

The concept of "Author Spotlight" features fosters a sense of community between writers and readers. As bookstagrammers introduce followers to new authors and their works, they create a space where readers can connect with writers on a more personal level.

The features become a bridge that brings writers and readers closer together.

Creating a Platform for Discovery:

"Author Spotlight" features create a platform for discovery among followers. As they encounter new writers and learn about their books, readers may feel inspired to explore the featured works and discover hidden literary gems.

The features become a gateway to literary exploration and new reading experiences.

Celebrating Literary Diversity:

The concept of "Author Spotlight" features celebrates literary diversity within the bookstagram community. As bookstagrammers feature writers from different backgrounds, genres, and writing styles, they embrace the richness and versatility of literature.

The features become a tribute to the power of storytelling and its ability to connect people from various walks of life.

Supporting Emerging Authors:

"Author Spotlight" features provide vital support to emerging authors within the bookstagram community. By introducing their works to a larger audience, bookstagrammers contribute to the visibility and success of these writers, fostering a positive impact on their careers.

The features become a stepping stone for authors to flourish in their literary journeys.

Inspiring Meaningful Conversations:

The concept of "Author Spotlight" features inspires meaningful conversations among followers. As readers share their thoughts on the featured works, engage in discussions about the author's writing process, or express their appreciation for the introduction, they enrich the bookstagram experience with insightful dialogues.

The features become a catalyst for engaging and thought-provoking conversations about literature.

Promoting a Love for Reading:

"Author Spotlight" features promote a love for reading among followers. As readers discover new writers and immerse themselves in the world of the featured books, they nurture their passion for literature and reading.

The features become a source of inspiration and encouragement to explore more books.

IN CONCLUSION:

"Author Spotlight" features, illuminating new writers and celebrating literary talent within the bookstagram community, offer a powerful and engaging concept. By fostering a sense of community, creating a platform for discovery, and supporting emerging authors, these features enhance the bookstagram experience and contribute to the growth of literary appreciation. They celebrate diversity, inspire meaningful conversations, and promote a love for reading among followers. As bookstagram continues to thrive, "Author Spotlight" features will remain a cherished tradition, shining a spotlight on talented writers and igniting the magic of literature within the captivating world of bookstagram.

FORTY-TWO
BOOK-TO-MOVIE OR BOOK-TO-TV SHOW COMPARISONS AND DISCUSSIONS:

UNRAVELING THE MAGIC OF LITERARY ADAPTATIONS

THE CONCEPT EXPLAINED:

"Book-to-Movie" or "Book-to-TV Show" comparisons and discussions on bookstagram are captivating posts, stories, or interactive challenges where bookstagrammers and their followers explore and analyze the process of adapting a literary work into a film or television show.

The bookstagrammer selects a specific book that has been adapted into a movie or TV show. They may choose popular adaptations, classics, or recent releases that have sparked interest among readers and viewers.

They begin the discussion by providing an overview of the literary work, highlighting its plot, themes, and central characters. They may also share their personal thoughts and experiences with the book.

The comparison and discussion extend to the adaptation process, where the bookstagrammer explores how the story was transformed into a visual medium. They may analyze changes made to the plot, character portrayals, and key events.

Followers are encouraged to participate in the discussion by sharing their thoughts on the adaptation, comparing it to the original book, and expressing their appreciation for the storytelling choices.

Unraveling the Magic of Literary Adaptations:

The essence of "Book-to-Movie" or "Book-to-TV Show" comparisons and discussions lies in unraveling the magic of literary adaptations within the bookstagram community. As bookstagrammers and their followers delve into the journey of a book from page to screen, they gain insights into the complexities and creative decisions involved in bringing a beloved story to life in a different medium.

The discussions become an exploration of the interplay between literature and visual storytelling.

Fostering Appreciation for Both Mediums:

The concept of "Book-to-Movie" or "Book-to-TV Show" comparisons and discussions fosters appreciation for both literature and visual media within the bookstagram community. As participants explore the strengths and limitations of each medium in storytelling, they develop a greater understanding of the unique qualities that make books and adaptations compelling in their own ways.

The discussions become a celebration of storytelling diversity.

Engaging in Meaningful Analysis:

"Book-to-Movie" or "Book-to-TV Show" comparisons and discussions inspire meaningful analysis among followers.

As they compare the book and its adaptation, they examine narrative choices, character developments, and thematic changes, leading to thought-provoking discussions about storytelling techniques.

The discussions become a platform for critical thinking and literary exploration.

Sparking Book and Movie Recommendations:

The concept of "Book-to-Movie" or "Book-to-TV Show" comparisons and discussions sparks book and movie recommendations among participants. As they encounter adaptations or books they may not have previously considered, they may feel inspired to explore the featured works, leading to a cascade of recommendations.

The discussions become a treasure trove of literary and cinematic gems.

Encouraging Discussions About Adaptation Choices:

"Book-to-Movie" or "Book-to-TV Show" comparisons and discussions encourage discussions about adaptation choices within the bookstagram community. As participants analyze changes made to the original story, they share their perspectives on how these choices affected the overall impact of the adaptation.

The discussions become a platform for constructive conversations about artistic interpretation.

Building a Sense of Community:

The concept of "Book-to-Movie" or "Book-to-TV Show" comparisons and discussions builds a sense of community among followers. As participants engage in conversations about shared interests and experiences with books and adaptations, they strengthen their connections with one another.

The discussions become a catalyst for camaraderie and mutual appreciation for literature and visual storytelling.

IN CONCLUSION:

"Book-to-Movie" or "Book-to-TV Show" comparisons and discussions, unraveling the magic of literary adaptations within the bookstagram community, offer a fascinating and engaging concept. By fostering appreciation for both mediums, engaging in meaningful analysis, and sparking book and movie recommendations, these discussions celebrate the synergy between literature and visual storytelling. They encourage discussions about adaptation choices, building a sense of community among followers. As bookstagram continues to thrive, "Book-to-Movie" or "Book-to-TV Show" comparisons and discussions will remain a cherished tradition, inviting readers and viewers to explore the enchanting world of storytelling in all its diverse forms within the captivating world of bookstagram.

FORTY-THREE
"THIS OR THAT" POSTS:
EXPLORING BOOK-RELATED CHOICES AND FOSTERING ENGAGING DISCUSSIONS

THE CONCEPT EXPLAINED:

"This or That" posts on bookstagram are captivating images or graphics where bookstagrammers present their followers with book-related choices in a fun and interactive manner.

The bookstagrammer selects a specific theme or topic for the "This or That" post. This could include genres like "Fantasy or Contemporary," book formats like "Physical Books or E books," or reading preferences like "Morning Reading or Night Reading."

The post features two contrasting options side by side, each representing a different choice for the selected theme. For example, it could display two book covers, one from a fantasy novel and the other from a contemporary book, and ask followers to choose their favorite genre.

Followers participate by engaging with the post and making their choices known through comments or direct messages. They may also elaborate on their decisions, sharing reasons for their preferences or personal anecdotes related to the choices.

The bookstagrammer may encourage followers to tag friends or fellow book lovers, inviting them to join the discussion and express their own opinions.

Exploring Book-Related Choices:

The essence of "This or That" posts lies in exploring book-related choices within the bookstagram community. By presenting followers with different options and asking them to make decisions, bookstagrammers create a platform for readers to express their preferences and showcase their unique tastes in literature.

The posts become a celebration of individuality and diversity in reading.

Fostering Engaging Discussions:

The concept of "This or That" posts fosters engaging discussions among followers. As readers share their choices and reasons for their decisions, they initiate lively conversations about the featured themes and preferences, creating an interactive and dynamic exchange of ideas.

The posts become a catalyst for meaningful bookish conversations.

Celebrating the Diversity of Literary Tastes:

"This or That" posts celebrate the diversity of literary tastes within the bookstagram community. As followers express their preferences for different genres, book formats, and reading habits, they showcase the vast array of books and reading experiences that appeal to various readers.

The posts become a tribute to the rich tapestry of literature and its ability to resonate with different individuals.

Building a Sense of Camaraderie:

The concept of "This or That" posts builds a sense of camaraderie among followers. As participants engage with the post and discuss their choices, they discover common interests with fellow book lovers, forming connections based on shared reading preferences.

The posts become a source of connection and unity within the bookstagram community.

Encouraging Book Recommendations:

"This or That" posts encourage book recommendations among followers. As readers express their choices and share their favorite books within the featured themes, they inspire others to explore the suggested works, leading to a chain of bookish discoveries.

The posts become a treasure trove of reading suggestions and literary gems.

Adding a Fun and Interactive Element:

The concept of "This or That" posts adds a fun and interactive element to the bookstagram experience. As followers participate in the decision-making process and engage with the post, they enjoy a lighthearted and enjoyable activity centered around their passion for books.

The posts become an entertaining and immersive way to interact with bookstagram content.

IN CONCLUSION:

"This or That" posts, exploring book-related choices and fostering engaging discussions within the bookstagram community, offer an interactive and captivating concept. By celebrating the diversity of literary tastes, building a sense of camaraderie, and encouraging book recommendations, these posts celebrate the magic of literature and its power to connect readers from all walks of life. They add a fun and interactive element to the bookstagram experience, creating an atmosphere of enjoyment and camaraderie. As bookstagram continues to thrive, "This or That" posts will remain a cherished tradition, inviting readers to express their preferences, showcase their unique tastes, and embrace the endless possibilities of the captivating world of books within the captivating world of bookstagram.

FORTY-FOUR
VIRTUAL BOOK EXCHANGES AND PEN PAL PROGRAMS:
FOSTERING BOOKISH CONNECTIONS AND LITERARY BONDS

THE CONCEPT EXPLAINED:

Virtual Book Exchanges:

Virtual book exchanges on bookstagram are engaging events where bookstagrammers organize and facilitate the exchange of books among followers.

The bookstagrammer sets the theme and guidelines for the exchange. For example, they may organize a genre-specific exchange like "Fantasy Book Exchange" or a book recommendation exchange where participants send their favorite reads to each other.

Interested followers sign up to participate in the virtual book exchange. The bookstagrammer matches participants, ensuring that each person is paired with someone to exchange books with.

Participants receive their assigned partner's details, including reading preferences and mailing addresses.

They then select and send a book that aligns with their partner's interests, adding a personal touch such as a handwritten note or a bookish trinket.

Once the books are received, participants share their excitement and gratitude by posting about the exchanged books on their bookstagram profiles.

Pen Pal Programs:

Pen pal programs on bookstagram are delightful initiatives where bookstagrammers connect followers as pen pals to exchange letters and share their love for books and reading.

The bookstagrammer announces the pen pal program and invites interested followers to sign up.

Participants are paired with pen pals based on shared reading interests, literary preferences, or geographic locations.

Pen pals begin exchanging letters, sharing book recommendations, and discussing their reading experiences through heartfelt and personalized correspondence.

As pen pals continue to correspond, they develop a strong bond centered around their mutual passion for literature and reading.

Fostering Bookish Connections:

The essence of virtual book exchanges and pen pal programs lies in fostering bookish connections within the bookstagram community. By facilitating the exchange of books or letters among followers, these initiatives create opportunities for readers to connect with like-minded individuals who share their enthusiasm for literature.

The exchanges become a celebration of shared bookish passions and experiences.

Celebrating the Joy of Sharing Stories:

Virtual book exchanges and pen pal programs celebrate the joy of sharing stories and experiences with fellow book lovers. As participants send books or letters to their partners, they not only share literary treasures but also open a window into their reading journeys and bookish insights.

The exchanges become an embodiment of the joy of storytelling and the power of shared narratives.

Building a Sense of Community:

The concept of virtual book exchanges and pen pal programs builds a sense of community and friendship within the bookstagram community. As participants interact with their exchange partners or pen pals, they form meaningful connections based on a shared love for books, creating a supportive and inclusive bookish community.

The exchanges become a catalyst for building literary bonds and enduring friendships.

Encouraging Book Discovery and Recommendations:

Virtual book exchanges and pen pal programs encourage book discovery and recommendations among participants. As readers select books or discuss their favorite reads in their letters, they inspire each other to explore new literary worlds and broaden their reading horizons.

The exchanges become a wellspring of literary inspiration and discovery.

Embracing Personal Touch and Thoughtfulness:

The concept of virtual book exchanges and pen pal programs embraces personal touch and thoughtfulness. Participants go beyond the simple act of exchanging books or letters by adding handwritten notes, bookish trinkets, or personalized touches to their packages.

The exchanges become heartfelt expressions of appreciation and care.

IN CONCLUSION:

Virtual book exchanges and pen pal programs, fostering bookish connections and literary bonds within the bookstagram community, offer heartwarming and enriching concepts. By celebrating the joy of sharing stories, building a sense of community, and encouraging book discovery and recommendations, these initiatives enrich the bookstagram experience and create a supportive and inclusive bookish community. They embrace personal touch and thoughtfulness, turning simple exchanges into heartfelt gestures of appreciation and friendship. As bookstagram continues to thrive, virtual book exchanges and pen pal programs will remain cherished traditions, uniting readers through the captivating world of books within the captivating world of bookstagram.

FORTY-FIVE
BOOKISH CONFESSIONS:
CELEBRATING GUILTY PLEASURES IN THE WORLD OF BOOKS

THE CONCEPT EXPLAINED:

"Bookish Confessions" on bookstagram are captivating posts, stories, or interactive challenges where bookstagrammers invite their followers to share their book-related guilty pleasures.

The bookstagrammer introduces the concept of "Bookish Confessions," explaining that it is a celebration of the guilty pleasures readers indulge in within the world of books.

Followers are encouraged to share their confessions openly and authentically, with the assurance that they will be embraced and accepted for their unique reading preferences.

Participants comment on the post or respond through direct messages, sharing their bookish confessions with fellow book lovers.

Embracing Guilty Pleasures:

The essence of "Bookish Confessions" lies in embracing guilty pleasures in the world of books. Readers are encouraged to admit and celebrate the books, genres, or reading habits that might be considered unconventional or outside their usual literary tastes.

The confessions become a celebration of personal preferences and individual reading journeys.

Creating a Safe and Accepting Space:

The concept of "Bookish Confessions" creates a safe and accepting space within the bookstagram community. As readers share their guilty pleasures, they are met with understanding and encouragement from fellow bookstagrammers, fostering a sense of camaraderie and inclusivity.

The confessions become an opportunity for vulnerability and connection.

Fostering Authenticity in Reading:

"Bookish Confessions" foster authenticity in reading experiences. By encouraging readers to be honest about their guilty pleasures, bookstagrammers promote a culture where readers feel free to express their true selves, free from judgment or criticism.

The confessions become a tribute to the diverse ways books touch readers' hearts.

Celebrating Reading Diversity:

The concept of "Bookish Confessions" celebrates reading diversity within the bookstagram community. As participants share their confessions, they highlight the vast array of literary experiences that bring joy and fulfillment to different readers.

The confessions become a celebration of the multiplicity of literary tastes.

Encouraging Shared Experiences:

"Bookish Confessions" encourage shared experiences among participants. As readers find resonance with each other's confessions, they realize that their guilty pleasures are not solitary pursuits but shared joys experienced by many.

The confessions become a catalyst for shared understanding and connection.

Inspiring Guilt-Free Enjoyment:

The concept of "Bookish Confessions" inspires guilt-free enjoyment in reading. By celebrating guilty pleasures, bookstagrammers encourage readers to embrace the books they love wholeheartedly, regardless of whether they align with popular opinions or critical acclaim.

The confessions become an invitation to revel in unapologetic bookish pleasure.

Creating Positive Discussions:

"Bookish Confessions" create positive and uplifting discussions among followers. As readers engage with the confessions, they might express their agreement, share similar experiences, or recommend books that align with the confessed guilty pleasures.

The confessions become a source of lively and constructive bookish conversations.

IN CONCLUSION:

"Bookish Confessions," celebrating guilty pleasures in the world of books within the bookstagram community, offer a delightful and liberating concept. By embracing guilty pleasures, creating a safe and accepting space, and fostering authenticity in reading experiences, these confessions celebrate the diverse ways books touch readers' hearts. They encourage shared experiences and inspire guilt-free enjoyment, promoting a culture of positivity and inclusivity within the bookstagram community. As bookstagram continues to thrive, "Bookish Confessions" will remain a cherished tradition, inviting readers to share and celebrate the joyful and diverse ways books bring happiness and fulfillment within the captivating world of bookstagram.

FORTY-SIX
STORYTIME SESSIONS:
CONNECTING THROUGH PERSONAL ANECDOTES AND THE MAGIC OF BOOKS

THE CONCEPT EXPLAINED:

"Storytime Sessions" on bookstagram are captivating posts, stories, or live sessions where bookstagrammers share personal anecdotes related to books and their reading journeys.

The bookstagrammer introduces the concept of "Storytime Sessions," explaining that they will be sharing personal stories and experiences that have been shaped by the books they have read.

The anecdotes could range from heartwarming tales of discovering a favorite childhood book to more profound reflections on how a specific book influenced their perspective on life.

Celebrating the Impact of Literature:

The essence of "Storytime Sessions" lies in celebrating the impact of literature on our lives. By sharing personal anecdotes, bookstagrammers illustrate how books can evoke emotions, spark memories, and shape our understanding of the world.

The sessions become a tribute to the transformative power of storytelling.

Creating an Intimate Connection:

The concept of "Storytime Sessions" creates an intimate connection between the bookstagrammer and their followers. As readers listen to personal stories, they glimpse a deeper and more personal side of the bookstagrammer, forging a stronger bond based on shared experiences with literature.

The sessions become a window into the lives of bookstagrammers and readers alike.

Fostering Empathy and Understanding:

"Storytime Sessions" foster empathy and understanding within the bookstagram community. As readers hear about the bookstagrammer's experiences, they may relate to the emotions and situations described, creating a shared sense of connection and camaraderie.

The sessions become a catalyst for empathy and compassion among followers.

Inspiring Reflection and Self-Discovery:

The concept of "Storytime Sessions" inspires reflection and self-discovery among followers. As readers listen to personal anecdotes, they may find themselves revisiting their own memories and experiences with books, leading to moments of introspection and self-awareness.

The sessions become a source of personal growth and discovery.

Highlighting Diverse Reading Journeys:

"Storytime Sessions" highlight the diverse reading journeys within the bookstagram community. As bookstagrammers share their experiences with different books, genres, and authors, they showcase the richness and variety of literary exploration.

The sessions become a celebration of reading diversity and individuality.

Creating a Safe Space for Sharing:

The concept of "Storytime Sessions" creates a safe and accepting space for sharing among followers. As bookstagrammers open up about their personal experiences, they set an example that encourages others to share their own stories and feelings related to books.

The sessions become an invitation to share and connect.

Celebrating the Joy of Storytelling:

"Storytime Sessions" celebrate the joy of storytelling within the bookstagram community. As bookstagrammers share their personal tales, they reaffirm the profound impact that stories can have on our lives, whether through laughter, tears, or moments of enlightenment.

The sessions become a reminder of the magic of books and the joy of storytelling.

IN CONCLUSION:

"Storytime Sessions," connecting through personal anecdotes and the magic of books within the bookstagram community, offer a captivating and authentic concept. By celebrating the impact of literature, creating an intimate connection, and fostering empathy and understanding, these sessions remind readers of the transformative power of storytelling. They inspire reflection and self-discovery, highlighting diverse reading journeys, and creating a safe space for sharing and connecting. As bookstagram continues to thrive, "Storytime Sessions" will remain a cherished tradition, weaving the threads of personal stories and the enchanting world of books within the captivating world of bookstagram.

FORTY-SEVEN
COLLABORATIVE STORYTELLING:

WEAVING A COLLECTIVE NARRATIVE WITH BOOKSTAGRAM FOLLOWERS

THE CONCEPT EXPLAINED:

Initiating the Collaborative Narrative:

Collaborative storytelling on bookstagram is an interactive and participatory experience where the bookstagrammer initiates a collective narrative, providing the opening lines or the beginning of a story.

The bookstagrammer introduces the concept of collaborative storytelling, inviting followers to join in the creative journey and contribute to the development of the narrative.

Engaging Followers as Co-creators:

The essence of collaborative storytelling lies in engaging followers as co-creators of the narrative. As bookstagrammers present the opening lines, they encourage followers to continue the story by adding their own contributions in the comments or through direct messages.

Participants' contributions can take the form of a few sentences, paragraphs, or even entire chapters, each building on the ideas of the previous contributor and shaping the direction of the story.

Fostering a Sense of Community:

The concept of collaborative storytelling fosters a sense of community and togetherness within the bookstagram community. As followers join in the narrative, they become part of a creative collective, working together to craft a unique and interconnected story.

The collaborative storytelling becomes a celebration of shared creativity and collective imagination.

Unleashing Limitless Possibilities:

Collaborative storytelling on bookstagram unleashes limitless possibilities for the narrative. As participants from diverse backgrounds and perspectives contribute to the story, the plot can take unexpected twists and turns, incorporating a wide range of genres and themes.

The storytelling becomes an exploration of boundless creativity and imagination.

Encouraging Diverse Voices:

The concept of collaborative storytelling encourages diverse voices to be heard and valued. As participants contribute to the narrative, they bring their unique storytelling styles, ideas, and perspectives to the table, enriching the story with their individual creativity.

The storytelling becomes an inclusive and encompassing tapestry of voices.

Promoting Interactive Engagement:

Collaborative storytelling promotes interactive engagement among followers. As participants read the previous contributions and build upon them, they actively engage with the narrative, immersing themselves in the unfolding story.

The storytelling becomes an immersive and interactive experience.

Creating a Sense of Ownership:

The concept of collaborative storytelling creates a sense of ownership among participants. As followers contribute to the narrative, they become emotionally invested in the story's development and eagerly await subsequent updates and additions.

The storytelling becomes a shared creation to which all participants feel connected.

Weaving a Tapestry of Creativity:

Collaborative storytelling weaves a tapestry of creativity within the bookstagram community. As followers from different backgrounds come together to contribute, they create a collective work of art that reflects the collaborative spirit of the community.

The storytelling becomes a masterpiece of collective creativity and ingenuity.

IN CONCLUSION:

Collaborative storytelling, weaving a collective narrative with bookstagram followers, offers a captivating and imaginative concept. By engaging followers as co-creators, fostering a sense of community, and unleashing limitless possibilities for the narrative, collaborative storytelling celebrates the power of collective imagination and the joy of shared creativity. It encourages diverse voices to be heard and valued, promoting interactive engagement and creating a sense of ownership among participants. As bookstagram continues to thrive, collaborative storytelling will remain a cherished tradition, uniting readers and creators in the enchanting world of books and the captivating world of bookstagram.

FORTY-EIGHT
BOOKISH TOUR VIDEOS:
IMMERSING IN THE WORLD OF BOOKS THROUGH VIRTUAL VISITS TO BOOK EVENTS, SIGNINGS, AND CONVENTIONS

THE CONCEPT EXPLAINED:

Virtual Visits to Book Events, Signings, and Conventions:

"Bookish Tour" videos on bookstagram are captivating and informative visual journeys that take followers on virtual visits to various book events, signings, and conventions.

The bookstagrammer introduces the concept of "Bookish Tour" videos, explaining that they will be sharing firsthand experiences and insights from literary gatherings they have attended.

Transporting Viewers into the Literary World:

The essence of "Bookish Tour" videos lies in transporting viewers into the literary world. Through a combination of video footage, photos, and engaging narration, bookstagrammers recreate the atmosphere and excitement of book events, signings, and conventions.

Viewers feel as if they are part of the experience, even from afar.

Fostering Excitement and Camaraderie:

The concept of "Bookish Tour" videos fosters excitement and camaraderie within the bookstagram community. As viewers watch their favorite bookstagrammers immerse themselves in literary gatherings, they share in the enthusiasm and passion for books and authors.

The videos become a celebration of shared excitement and connection.

Showcasing the Vibrant Literary Community:

"Bookish Tour" videos showcase the vibrant and dynamic nature of the literary community. As bookstagrammers explore various events, signings, and conventions, they capture the diversity of readers, authors, and bookish activities that thrive within these gatherings.

The videos become a tribute to the rich tapestry of the bookish world.

Sharing Personal Experiences and Insights:

The concept of "Bookish Tour" videos involves bookstagrammers sharing their personal experiences and insights from the events they attend. They may talk about meeting favorite authors, discovering new books, or participating in engaging discussions and workshops.

The videos become a glimpse into the bookstagrammer's literary journey.

Highlighting Author Interactions:

"Bookish Tour" videos highlight the bookstagrammer's interactions with authors at book events and signings. Viewers witness heartwarming moments of connection between readers and writers, witnessing the magic of meeting the creators behind their beloved books.

The videos become a celebration of author-reader relationships.

Celebrating Bookish Swag and Goodies:

The concept of "Bookish Tour" videos celebrates bookish swag and goodies that attendees often receive at conventions and signings. Bookstagrammers may showcase book-related merchandise, signed copies, or exclusive items that make these events even more memorable.

The videos become a treasure trove of bookish delights.

Promoting Literary Discoveries:

"Bookish Tour" videos promote literary discoveries among viewers. As bookstagrammers share their experiences and the books they encountered at events, signings, and conventions, they inspire viewers to explore new authors and genres.

The videos become a source of literary inspiration and recommendations.

IN CONCLUSION:

"Bookish Tour" videos, featuring virtual visits to book events, signings, and conventions within the bookstagram community, offer an enthralling and immersive concept. By transporting viewers into the literary world, fostering excitement and camaraderie, and showcasing the vibrant literary community, these videos celebrate the joys of being part of a book-loving community. They offer a glimpse into the bookstagrammer's personal experiences and insights, highlighting author interactions and bookish swag. As bookstagram continues to thrive, "Bookish Tour" videos will remain a cherished tradition, transporting viewers into the enchanting world of books and the captivating world of bookstagram.

FORTY-NINE
CURATED LIST OF BOOKS:
EMBRACING DIVERSITY AND AMPLIFYING VOICES

THE CONCEPT EXPLAINED:

Thoughtfully Curated Lists:

"A Curated List of Books Featuring Diverse Representation and Perspectives" on bookstagram are carefully selected and thoughtfully compiled lists of books that represent a wide range of identities, cultures, and experiences. The bookstagrammer introduces the concept, explaining that the goal is to promote diversity and inclusivity in literature by showcasing books that reflect a multitude of perspectives.

Representation and Empowerment:

The essence of the curated list lies in representation and empowerment. By featuring books that portray diverse characters and stories, the bookstagrammer aims to amplify voices that are often underrepresented in mainstream literature. The list becomes a powerful platform for marginalized voices to be heard and celebrated.

Showcasing Cultural Richness:

"A Curated List of Books Featuring Diverse Representation and Perspectives" showcases the cultural richness and diversity of human experiences. The books chosen may explore different ethnicities, religions, genders, sexual orientations, abilities, and socio-economic backgrounds. The list becomes a celebration of the tapestry of human existence.

Promoting Empathy and Understanding:

The concept of the curated list promotes empathy and understanding within the bookstagram community. As readers engage with books that offer diverse perspectives, they gain insights into the challenges, joys, and complexities of lived experiences different from their own. The list becomes a pathway to building bridges of understanding and compassion.

Encouraging Inclusivity in Reading:

The curated list encourages inclusivity in reading choices. By offering a diverse array of books, the bookstagrammer invites readers to broaden their literary horizons and explore stories beyond their comfort zones. The list becomes an invitation to embrace a wide range of narratives.

Supporting Underrepresented Authors:

"A Curated List of Books Featuring Diverse Representation and Perspectives" supports underrepresented authors and creators. Many of the books on the list may be written by authors from marginalized backgrounds, whose voices deserve recognition and appreciation. The list becomes a platform for elevating diverse literary talent.

Fostering Conversations on Diversity:

The concept of the curated list fosters conversations on diversity and representation in literature. As bookstagrammers and followers discuss the books on the list, they reflect on the importance of diverse stories in shaping our understanding of the world. The list becomes a catalyst for meaningful discussions on representation and inclusivity.

Celebrating Intersectionality:

"A Curated List of Books Featuring Diverse Representation and Perspectives" celebrates intersectionality, recognizing that individuals have multiple identities that shape their experiences. The list becomes a celebration of the multifaceted nature of humanity.

Sparking Social Awareness:

The curated list sparks social awareness and consciousness. By recommending books that shed light on social issues, the bookstagrammer encourages readers to engage with literature that inspires change and reflection. The list becomes a call to action for a more equitable and inclusive world.

IN CONCLUSION:

"A Curated List of Books Featuring Diverse Representation and Perspectives" on bookstagram offers a powerful and meaningful concept. By thoughtfully compiling books that amplify diverse voices and cultures, this curated list promotes inclusivity, empathy, and understanding within the bookstagram community. It showcases the cultural richness of human experiences and encourages readers to explore a wide range of narratives. The list becomes a platform for marginalized voices to be heard and celebrated, supporting underrepresented authors and creators. It fosters conversations on diversity, intersectionality, and social awareness, inspiring readers to engage with literature that sparks change. As bookstagram continues to thrive, "A Curated List of Books Featuring Diverse Representation and Perspectives" will remain a cherished tradition, reminding us of the transformative power of stories and the beauty of diversity within the captivating world of bookstagram.

FIFTY
BOOKISH DEBATE CLUB:
A PLATFORM FOR LIVELY BOOK DISCUSSIONS AND INTELLECTUAL EXPLORATION

THE CONCEPT EXPLAINED:

Virtual Space for Lively Discussions:

The "Bookish Debate Club" on bookstagram is a designated platform or series of posts/stories where followers can engage in lively discussions and debates related to books. The bookstagrammer introduces the concept, explaining that the club aims to create a stimulating and respectful environment for intellectual exploration.

Topics Covering Various Aspects of Books:

The essence of the "Bookish Debate Club" lies in its diverse array of book-related topics. The bookstagrammer may pose questions or statements related to character analysis, plot development, controversial themes, authorial intent, or the impact of literature on society. The topics become a gateway to deeper understanding and exploration of literature.

Fostering Critical Thinking:

The concept of the "Bookish Debate Club" fosters critical thinking among followers. As participants engage in debates, they are encouraged to examine different angles and aspects of a literary work, considering multiple perspectives before forming opinions. The debates become an exercise in intellectual growth and reflection.

Respectful Exchange of Ideas:

The "Bookish Debate Club" encourages a culture of respectful exchange of ideas and opinions. Participants are reminded to engage with civility and empathy, creating an environment where diverse perspectives are welcomed and valued. The debates become an opportunity for open-minded discussions.

Promoting Engagement and Participation:

The concept of the "Bookish Debate Club" promotes engagement and active participation among followers. As readers respond to the questions or statements, they become an integral part of the bookstagrammer's virtual book club. The debates become a shared intellectual endeavor.

Nurturing a Sense of Community:

The "Bookish Debate Club" nurtures a sense of community within the bookstagram community. As followers engage with each other's responses, they realize that they are part of a like-minded group of individuals passionate about books and reading. The debates become a source of camaraderie and belonging.

Encouraging Exploration of Diverse Literature:

The concept of the "Bookish Debate Club" encourages participants to explore diverse literature to contribute to the discussions effectively. As the club covers various topics and themes, readers may discover new books and authors that broaden their reading horizons. The debates become a catalyst for literary exploration.

Celebrating the Beauty of Literary Complexity:

"A Bookish Debate Club" celebrates the beauty of literary complexity. As participants delve into the intricacies of different works, they come to appreciate the depth and richness of literature, recognizing that there are no simple answers or singular interpretations. The debates become a tribute to the artistry of storytelling.

Deepening Reader-Writer Connections:

The concept of the "Bookish Debate Club" deepens the connections between readers and writers. As readers discuss their interpretations and engage in debates, they gain a deeper understanding of an author's craft and intentions. The debates become a bridge between readers and the creative minds behind the books they love.

IN CONCLUSION:

The "Bookish Debate Club" on bookstagram offers an engaging and intellectually stimulating concept. By providing a virtual space for lively book discussions and debates, this club fosters critical thinking, encourages respectful exchange of ideas, and promotes engagement and participation among followers. It nurtures a sense of community and belonging within the bookstagram community while celebrating the beauty of literary complexity. As readers explore diverse literature and deepen their connections with writers, "A Bookish Debate Club" remains a cherished tradition, inviting readers to embark on an intellectual journey within the captivating world of bookstagram.

FIFTY-ONE
BOOK-INSPIRED TRAVEL GUIDES:

EMBARKING ON LITERARY JOURNEYS TO ENCHANTING LITERARY LOCATIONS AND SETTINGS

THE CONCEPT EXPLAINED:

Bringing Books to Life Through Travel:

"Book-Inspired Travel Guides" on bookstagram are enchanting and informative posts or stories that transport readers to real-life locations and settings featured in books.

The bookstagrammer introduces the concept, explaining that these guides offer a unique opportunity to explore the world of literature through travel.

Unveiling Literary Landscapes:

The essence of "Book-Inspired Travel Guides" lies in unveiling the literary landscapes that exist in reality. These guides highlight destinations and places that authors have immortalized in their works, offering followers a chance to step into the pages of their favorite books. The guides become a portal to a magical fusion of fiction and reality.

Connecting Stories to Tangible Places:

The concept of "Book-Inspired Travel Guides" connects the stories that readers love to tangible places that hold literary significance. The guides may include destinations like the countryside of Jane Austen's England, the streets of Victorian London featured in Charles Dickens' novels, or the mystical landscapes of J.R.R. Tolkien's Middle-earth. The guides become a bridge between the imaginary and the real.

Inspiring Literary Pilgrimages:

"Book-Inspired Travel Guides" inspire literary pilgrimages among followers. As readers discover the real-life locations that inspired their favorite authors, they may feel compelled to embark on their own literary journeys to walk in the footsteps of literary greats. The guides become an invitation to embark on enchanted adventures.

Offering Background and Historical Context:

The concept of "Book-Inspired Travel Guides" offers background and historical context to enrich readers' understanding of the locations. The bookstagrammer may share insights into the author's connection to the place or the historical significance of the setting in the book. The guides become a treasure trove of literary knowledge and history.

Encouraging Cultural Exploration:

"Book-Inspired Travel Guides" encourage cultural exploration as readers delve into the rich tapestry of places depicted in books. The guides may include recommendations for local cuisine, museums, and cultural experiences that enhance the travel experience. The guides become a celebration of diverse cultures and traditions.

Promoting Literary Wanderlust:

The concept of "Book-Inspired Travel Guides" promotes literary wanderlust among followers. As readers discover new destinations linked to their favorite books, they may feel inspired to create their own reading-inspired travel bucket lists. The guides become a source of inspiration for future literary adventures.

Celebrating the Magic of Reading and Travel:

"Book-Inspired Travel Guides" celebrate the magic of reading and travel as intertwined experiences. The guides highlight the transformative power of books, igniting a desire to explore the world and discover the stories that exist beyond the page. The guides become a tribute to the enchantment of literature and the allure of travel.

IN CONCLUSION:

"Book-Inspired Travel Guides" on bookstagram offer an enchanting and immersive concept. By connecting readers to real-life locations and settings featured in books, these guides bring literature to life through travel. They inspire literary pilgrimages, cultural exploration, and literary wanderlust while celebrating the magic of reading and the allure of travel. As followers embark on their own literary journeys and explore literary landscapes, "Book-Inspired Travel Guides" remain a cherished tradition within the captivating world of bookstagram, inviting readers to journey through the pages of their favorite stories and discover the magic that exists beyond the book's covers.

FIFTY-TWO
"GUESS THE FIRST LINE" CHALLENGES:
UNRAVELING THE MAGIC OF BOOK OPENINGS

THE CONCEPT EXPLAINED:

Unveiling the Magic of Book Beginnings:

"Guess the First Line" challenges on bookstagram are engaging and interactive posts or stories where bookstagrammers present the opening lines of different books to their followers. The bookstagrammer introduces the concept, explaining that the challenge celebrates the captivating art of book beginnings.

Testing Readers' Literary Knowledge:

The essence of "Guess the First Line" challenges lies in testing readers' literary knowledge and recognition of famous book openings. Followers are invited to identify the books from which the presented lines originate. The challenges become a playful test of readers' literary memory.

Celebrating Authors' Craftsmanship:

The concept of "Guess the First Line" challenges celebrates the craftsmanship of authors who skillfully craft captivating opening lines. As followers try to identify the books, they may be reminded of the beauty and significance of an author's words in drawing readers into a story. The challenges become a tribute to the artistry of literary beginnings.

Inspiring Curiosity and Intrigue:

"Guess the First Line" challenges inspire curiosity and intrigue among followers. As readers encounter intriguing and evocative openings, they may be enticed to explore the books in their entirety, uncovering the stories that lie beyond the first lines. The challenges become an invitation to embark on literary explorations.

Promoting Interaction and Engagement:

The concept of "Guess the First Line" challenges promotes interaction and engagement within the bookstagram community. As followers participate in the guessing game, they connect with fellow book lovers and share their thoughts and insights. The challenges become a shared literary experience.

Introducing Readers to New Books:

"Guess the First Line" challenges introduce readers to new books and authors they might not be familiar with. As participants encounter lines from diverse genres and styles, they may discover fresh literary gems. The challenges become a source of literary recommendations.

Fostering Appreciation for Book Openings:

The concept of "Guess the First Line" challenges fosters appreciation for the power of book openings. As readers immerse themselves in the opening lines, they realize the significance of a strong beginning in setting the tone and capturing their imagination. The challenges become an exploration of literary craftsmanship.

Creating a Playful Literary Atmosphere:

"Guess the First Line" challenges create a playful literary atmosphere on bookstagram. Followers may eagerly anticipate new challenges, delighting in their ability to recognize beloved book beginnings.The challenges become a source of enjoyment and entertainment.

Incorporating Quotes and Artistic Presentations:

The concept of "Guess the First Line" challenges may incorporate artistic presentations and visually appealing layouts. Bookstagrammers may pair the lines with thematic images or use creative typography to enhance the guessing experience. The challenges become a fusion of visual art and literary magic.

IN CONCLUSION:

"Guess the First Line" challenges on bookstagram offer an intriguing and interactive concept. By presenting the opening lines of various books, these challenges test readers' literary knowledge and celebrate the captivating artistry of authors. They inspire curiosity, engagement, and appreciation for book beginnings, introducing readers to new literary treasures. As followers immerse themselves in the world of "Guess the First Line" challenges, they celebrate the magic of book openings and embark on a delightful journey through the captivating world of bookstagram.

FIFTY-THREE
BOOKSTAGRAMMER-CREATED BOOK TAGS:

FOSTERING CREATIVITY AND COMMUNITY IN THE WORLD OF BOOKS

THE CONCEPT EXPLAINED:

Creative Sets of Bookish Questions or Prompts:

"Bookstagrammer-Created Book Tags" on bookstagram are imaginative and interactive posts or stories where bookstagrammers design sets of bookish questions or prompts related to various themes or aspects of books. The bookstagrammer introduces the concept, explaining that the tags are meant to inspire fun and engaging discussions.

Inviting Followers to Participate:

The essence of "Bookstagrammer-Created Book Tags" lies in inviting followers to participate in the bookish fun. Bookstagrammers may tag specific followers or encourage anyone interested to join in. The tags become an invitation to be part of a literary conversation.

Connecting Book Lovers and Creating Community:

The concept of "Bookstagrammer-Created Book Tags" creates a sense of community among book lovers. As followers participate in the tags, they connect with fellow readers, forming bonds over shared interests and bookish enthusiasm. The tags become a platform for building bookish connections.

Fostering Creativity and Personal Expression:

"Bookstagrammer-Created Book Tags" foster creativity and personal expression among participants. Readers can interpret and respond to the questions or prompts in unique ways, showcasing their individual tastes and preferences. The tags become a canvas for bookish self-expression.

Exploring Diverse Book Themes and Genres:

The concept of "Bookstagrammer-Created Book Tags" encourages exploration of diverse book themes and genres. Bookstagrammers may design tags that revolve around specific genres, diverse authors, favorite book-to-movie adaptations, or even seasonal reads. The tags become an opportunity to discover new books and genres.

Generating Engaging Bookish Discussions:

"Bookstagrammer-Created Book Tags" generate engaging bookish discussions among followers. As participants respond to the questions or prompts, they share their thoughts on beloved books, memorable characters, and literary experiences. The tags become a platform for thought-provoking conversations.

Discovering Hidden Gems and Recommendations:

The concept of "Bookstagrammer-Created Book Tags" leads to the discovery of hidden literary gems and recommendations. As participants share their responses, they may recommend lesser-known books that captivated them. The tags become a treasure trove of book recommendations.

Promoting Reading Diversity and Inclusivity:

"Bookstagrammer-Created Book Tags" promote reading diversity and inclusivity. Bookstagrammers may design tags that highlight books by diverse authors or stories that shed light on important social issues. The tags become a celebration of diverse voices in literature.

Embracing Seasonal and Festive Themes:

The concept of "Bookstagrammer-Created Book Tags" embraces seasonal and festive themes. Bookstagrammers may design tags inspired by holidays, seasonal reads, or even bookish resolutions for the New Year. The tags become a reflection of the joy and excitement of literary celebrations.

Incorporating Visual Creativity:

"Bookstagrammer-Created Book Tags" may incorporate visual creativity into the tags. Bookstagrammers may use aesthetically pleasing graphics, images, or illustrations to enhance the visual appeal of the tags. The tags become a blend of literary and visual artistry.

IN CONCLUSION:

"Bookstagrammer-Created Book Tags" on bookstagram offer a delightful and interactive concept. By devising creative sets of bookish questions or prompts, bookstagrammers invite their followers to participate in engaging bookish discussions and foster a sense of community among readers. The tags encourage creativity, personal expression, and exploration of diverse book themes and genres. They lead to the discovery of hidden literary gems and recommendations while promoting reading diversity and inclusivity. As followers immerse themselves in the world of "Bookstagrammer-Created Book Tags," they celebrate the joy of books and connect with fellow book lovers within the captivating world of bookstagram.

FIFTY-FOUR
BOOKISH THIS OR THAT:
A CAPTIVATING JOURNEY THROUGH EDITIONS AND COVERS

THE CONCEPT EXPLAINED:

Presenting Choices Between Book Editions or Covers:

"Bookish This or That" challenges on bookstagram are engaging and interactive posts or stories where bookstagrammers present followers with choices between different editions or covers of the same book. The bookstagrammer introduces the concept, explaining that the challenges celebrate the visual appeal of books.

Inviting Followers to Choose Their Preferences:

The essence of "Bookish This or That" challenges lies in inviting followers to choose their preferences between the presented options. Bookstagrammers may ask questions like "Do you prefer the classic hardcover or the modern paperback edition?" or "Which cover design captures your attention more?" The challenges become an invitation to participate in bookish debates.

Celebrating Diverse Book Designs:

The concept of "Bookish This or That" challenges celebrates the diverse book designs available in the publishing world. As followers encounter different editions or covers, they gain insight into the various artistic choices that go into presenting a book to readers. The challenges become a tribute to the creativity of book designers.

Fostering Lively Bookish Discussions:

"Bookish This or That" challenges foster lively bookish discussions among followers. As participants share their preferences and reasons for their choices, they engage in friendly debates and learn about different cover design elements. The challenges become a platform for spirited bookish exchanges.

Uncovering Bookish Preferences:

The concept of "Bookish This or That" challenges uncovers followers' bookish preferences. As readers choose between editions or covers, they reveal their visual tastes and inclinations when it comes to book design. The challenges become a window into readers' bookish personalities.

Discovering Visual Storytelling:

"Bookish This or That" challenges help followers discover the power of visual storytelling in book design. As participants compare different covers, they recognize how cover art can convey themes, moods, and elements of the story. The challenges become an exploration of visual language in literature.

Promoting Appreciation for Book Aesthetics:

The concept of "Bookish This or That" challenges promotes appreciation for book aesthetics. As participants immerse themselves in the beauty of different editions or covers, they develop an eye for the artistic appeal of books. The challenges become a celebration of the visual allure of literature.

Encouraging Exploration of Book Collections:

"Bookish This or That" challenges encourage exploration of book collections. As participants encounter different editions, they may be inspired to expand their bookshelves with unique and visually appealing editions. The challenges become an invitation to curate bookish treasures.

Sparking Bookish Wishlists:

The concept of "Bookish This or That" challenges sparks bookish wishlists among followers. As readers come across covers they love, they may add these editions to their list of must-have books. The challenges become a source of bookish desires.

Incorporating Author Insights:

"Bookish This or That" challenges may incorporate author insights into cover preferences. Bookstagrammers may share authors' thoughts on cover designs and the visual representation of their stories. The challenges become a bridge between authors and readers.

IN CONCLUSION:

"Bookish This or That" challenges on bookstagram offer a delightful and interactive concept. By presenting choices between different editions or covers of the same book, these challenges invite followers to participate in bookish debates and uncover their visual book preferences. They celebrate the diverse and captivating artistry of book design while fostering lively bookish discussions and promoting appreciation for book aesthetics. As followers immerse themselves in the world of "Bookish This or That" challenges, they embark on a captivating journey through editions and covers, discovering the beauty of literature through the lens of visual storytelling within the captivating world of bookstagram.

FIFTY-FIVE
THEMED BOOK CURATION:
A JOURNEY THROUGH EMOTIONS AND FEELINGS IN LITERATURE

THE CONCEPT EXPLAINED:

Curating Books Based on Emotions or Feelings:

"Themed Book Curation" challenges on bookstagram involve bookstagrammers curating book lists or recommendations centered around specific emotions or feelings. For example, they may create lists like "Books that capture the essence of love," "Novels that evoke a sense of wonder and awe," or "Stories that explore the depths of grief." The bookstagrammer introduces the concept, explaining that these themed curation lists aim to evoke emotions and foster literary connections.

Invoking Emotion and Empathy:

The essence of "Themed Book Curation" lies in invoking emotions and evoking empathy among followers. As readers explore the books recommended for a specific emotion, they may find themselves drawn into the characters' experiences and emotions. The curation lists become a bridge to emotional connections with fictional worlds.

Celebrating the Depth of Human Emotions:

The concept of "Themed Book Curation" celebrates the depth and complexity of human emotions. Through books that explore joy, sorrow, fear, hope, and everything in between, readers gain a deeper understanding of the myriad emotions that shape the human experience. The curation lists become a tribute to the emotional tapestry of literature.

Empowering Emotional Self-Expression:

"Themed Book Curation" challenges empower emotional self-expression among followers. As readers encounter books that resonate with their own emotions, they may find solace, validation, or a sense of catharsis through literature. The curation lists become a canvas for emotional exploration and expression.

Creating a Sense of Connection:

The concept of "Themed Book Curation" creates a sense of connection within the bookstagram community. As followers discover books that touch on shared emotions, they realize that they are not alone in their feelings and experiences. The curation lists become a source of comfort and camaraderie.

Fostering Empathy and Understanding:

"Themed Book Curation" challenges foster empathy and understanding among readers. As participants immerse themselves in books that depict diverse emotional journeys, they gain insights into the human condition and the complexities of emotions. The curation lists become a catalyst for empathy and compassion.

Encouraging Emotional Resonance with Books:

The concept of "Themed Book Curation" encourages emotional resonance with books. As readers find books that evoke specific emotions, they may discover new favorites and deepen their connection with literature. The curation lists become a gateway to emotional connections with stories.

Exploring Emotional Themes Across Genres:

"Themed Book Curation" challenges encourage the exploration of emotional themes across genres and literary styles. Bookstagrammers may curate lists that span classic literature, contemporary fiction, fantasy, romance, and non-fiction, offering diverse perspectives on emotions. The curation lists become a celebration of emotional diversity in literature.

Inspiring Thoughtful Reading Choices:

The concept of "Themed Book Curation" inspires thoughtful reading choices among followers. As readers encounter books curated for specific emotions, they may become more intentional in selecting books that align with their emotional interests. The curation lists become a source of literary inspiration.

Incorporating Personal Book Recommendations:

"Themed Book Curation" challenges may incorporate personal book recommendations from bookstagrammers. As they share books that deeply touched their emotions, they invite followers to discover the emotional resonance of these stories. The curation lists become a glimpse into bookstagrammers' emotional connections with literature.

IN CONCLUSION:

"Themed Book Curation" based on different emotions or feelings on bookstagram offers a captivating and evocative concept. By curating book lists centered around specific emotions, these challenges invite followers on an emotional journey through the pages of literature. They celebrate the power of storytelling in evoking empathy, connection, and understanding among readers while empowering emotional self-expression and fostering a sense of community. As followers explore the diverse range of emotions depicted in books, "Themed Book Curation" becomes a celebration of the emotional tapestry of literature, offering a gateway to explore the depths of human feelings within the captivating world of bookstagram.

FIFTY-SIX
BOOKISH AMBIENCE:
CREATING SERENE READING SESSIONS WITH RELAXING BACKGROUND MUSIC

THE CONCEPT EXPLAINED:

Creating Serene Reading Spaces:

"Bookish Ambience" videos on bookstagram are serene and enchanting videos with relaxing background music and soothing visuals. The bookstagrammer curates these videos to create a serene reading space for followers. The concept is introduced, explaining that "Bookish Ambience" videos aim to provide a tranquil environment for reading.

Enhancing the Reading Experience:

The essence of "Bookish Ambience" lies in enhancing the reading experience for followers. As readers watch these videos, they are enveloped in a calming atmosphere that complements the joy of reading. The videos become a complement to the reading journey.

Choosing Relaxing Background Music:

The concept of "Bookish Ambience" videos involves carefully selecting relaxing background music that sets the right tone for reading. The music may feature soft instrumental melodies or gentle nature sounds. The videos become an auditory treat for book lovers.

Incorporating Soothing Visuals:

"Bookish Ambience" challenges may incorporate soothing visuals like flickering candle flames, falling raindrops, or gentle ocean waves. The visuals are designed to create a serene and peaceful ambiance. The videos become a feast for the eyes and soul.

Fostering Focus and Concentration:

The concept of "Bookish Ambience" videos fosters focus and concentration among readers. As followers immerse themselves in the calming atmosphere, they can better concentrate on their reading. The videos become a tool for enhanced reading sessions.

Providing a Retreat from Distractions:

"Bookish Ambience" challenges provide a retreat from distractions. As readers watch these videos, they can escape the noise and distractions of everyday life, entering a tranquil oasis for reading. The videos become a sanctuary for peaceful reading moments.

Creating a Sense of Calm and Relaxation:

The concept of "Bookish Ambience" videos creates a sense of calm and relaxation among followers. The serene music and visuals inspire a feeling of tranquility, promoting a peaceful state of mind. The videos become a source of emotional rejuvenation.

Encouraging Mindful Reading:

"Bookish Ambience" challenges encourage mindful reading practices. As followers engage with the soothing videos, they are encouraged to be present in the moment and fully immersed in their reading experiences. The videos become a gateway to mindful literary journeys.

Inspiring Reading Rituals:

The concept of "Bookish Ambience" videos inspires followers to create reading rituals. As they incorporate these videos into their reading routines, they may find comfort and solace in the consistent ambiance. The videos become a part of treasured reading traditions.

Promoting Reading as Self-Care:

"Bookish Ambience" challenges promote reading as an act of self-care. As followers indulge in serene reading sessions, they embrace the importance of dedicating time to nurture their minds and souls through literature. The videos become a reminder of the nourishing power of reading.

IN CONCLUSION:

"Bookish Ambience" videos on bookstagram offer a serene and enchanting concept. By curating videos with relaxing background music and soothing visuals, these challenges create a tranquil environment for reading sessions. They enhance the reading experience, foster focus and concentration, and provide a retreat from distractions. As followers immerse themselves in the calming ambiance of "Bookish Ambience" videos, they find solace and rejuvenation in the world of literature, turning reading into an act of self-care and emotional replenishment within the captivating world of bookstagram.

FIFTY-SEVEN
BOOKSTAGRAMMER'S BOOKSHELF TOURS:

A JOURNEY THROUGH LITERARY TREASURES AND PERSONAL FAVORITES

THE CONCEPT EXPLAINED:

Virtual Exploration of Bookshelves:

"Bookstagrammer's Bookshelf Tours" on bookstagram are immersive and captivating videos or posts where bookstagrammers take their followers on a virtual exploration of their bookshelves.

The bookstagrammer introduces the concept, explaining that the tours offer an intimate look into their personal literary collections.

Showcasing Book Treasures:

The essence of "Bookstagrammer's Bookshelf Tours" lies in showcasing book treasures. As followers view the bookshelves, they discover a diverse array of titles, genres, and editions that make up the bookstagrammer's collection. The tours become a treasure trove of literary delights.

Sharing Favorite Books with Explanations:

The concept of "Bookstagrammer's Bookshelf Tours" involves the bookstagrammer sharing their favorite books with heartfelt explanations. As they highlight specific titles, they explain what makes these books special to them, whether it's the writing style, the themes, or personal connections. The tours become a celebration of beloved literary gems.

Offering a Glimpse into Personal Literary Tastes:

"Bookstagrammer's Bookshelf Tours" offer a glimpse into the personal literary tastes of the bookstagrammer. As they discuss their favorite books, followers learn about the genres and themes that resonate with the bookstagrammer. The tours become an intimate look into the bookstagrammer's reading preferences.

Inspiring Reading Recommendations:

The concept of "Bookstagrammer's Bookshelf Tours" inspires reading recommendations among followers. As they discover the bookstagrammer's favorite books, they may find new titles to add to their own reading lists. The tours become a source of literary inspiration.

Connecting with Fellow Book Lovers:

"Bookstagrammer's Bookshelf Tours" foster connections with fellow book lovers. As followers comment on shared favorites or express curiosity about certain books, they engage in bookish discussions with the bookstagrammer and other followers. The tours become a platform for literary conversations.

Unveiling Literary Treasures:

The concept of "Bookstagrammer's Bookshelf Tours" unveils literary treasures that followers might not have encountered otherwise. As they see unique editions or lesser-known titles on the bookshelves, they expand their literary horizons. The tours become a journey of literary discovery.

Adding a Personal Touch:

"Bookstagrammer's Bookshelf Tours" add a personal touch to the bookstagrammer's online presence. As they share their favorite books and the stories behind them, they build authentic connections with their followers. The tours become a reflection of the bookstagrammer's literary journey.

Creating a Sense of Community:

The concept of "Bookstagrammer's Bookshelf Tours" creates a sense of community among book lovers. As followers engage with the tour and express their thoughts, they become part of a shared literary experience. The tours become a celebration of bookish camaraderie.

Promoting Appreciation for Physical Books:

"Bookstagrammer's Bookshelf Tours" challenges promote appreciation for physical books. As followers see the bookstagrammer's collection, they may be reminded of the joy of owning and displaying physical copies of beloved books. The tours become a tribute to the tangible beauty of literature.

IN CONCLUSION:

"Bookstagrammer's Bookshelf Tours" on bookstagram offer an immersive and captivating concept. By taking their followers on a virtual journey through their bookshelves and sharing explanations of their favorite books, bookstagrammers create a source of inspiration, connection, and discovery for fellow book lovers. These tours unveil literary treasures, foster community, and promote appreciation for physical books. As followers immerse themselves in the world of "Bookstagrammer's Bookshelf Tours," they celebrate the joy of literature and the personal connections that books create within the captivating world of bookstagram.

FIFTY-EIGHT
COLLABORATIVE WRITING CHALLENGES:
EMBARKING ON COLLECTIVE STORYTELLING ADVENTURES

THE CONCEPT EXPLAINED:

Inviting Followers to Join the Writing Adventure:

"Collaborative Writing Challenges" on bookstagram are exciting and interactive challenges initiated by bookstagrammers. The bookstagrammer introduces the concept, inviting followers to join a unique writing adventure. The challenges are designed to celebrate creativity and literary collaboration.

Contributing to a Shared Story:

The essence of "Collaborative Writing Challenges" lies in followers contributing to a shared story. Each participant adds their own portion to the story, continuing the narrative based on the contributions of others. The challenges become a tapestry of diverse voices and ideas.

Building Upon the Creativity of Others:

The concept of "Collaborative Writing Challenges" encourages participants to build upon the creativity of others. As each writer continues the story, they embrace the existing plot twists and character developments while adding their unique twists. The challenges become a celebration of collective creativity.

Fostering Imagination and Writing Skills:

"Collaborative Writing Challenges" challenges foster imagination and writing skills among participants. As writers delve into the shared story, they explore new worlds, characters, and conflicts, honing their storytelling abilities. The challenges become a platform for literary growth.

Creating a Sense of Literary Community:

The concept of "Collaborative Writing Challenges" creates a sense of literary community among followers. As participants read and build upon each other's contributions, they become part of a shared storytelling experience. The challenges become a space for literary camaraderie.

Encouraging Engagement and Participation:

"Collaborative Writing Challenges" challenges encourage engagement and participation among followers. As participants contribute to the story, they become invested in its progression and eagerly await the next additions. The challenges become a platform for active involvement.

Embracing Diverse Writing Styles and Voices:

The concept of "Collaborative Writing Challenges" embraces diverse writing styles and voices. Participants come from various backgrounds, and their unique contributions add depth and variety to the narrative. The challenges become a tapestry of literary expressions.

Unleashing Unpredictable Plot Developments:

"Collaborative Writing Challenges" challenges unleash unpredictable plot developments. As participants add their twists to the story, the narrative takes unexpected turns, keeping everyone intrigued. The challenges become a thrilling adventure in storytelling.

Creating a Story of Collective Inspiration:

The concept of "Collaborative Writing Challenges" creates a story of collective inspiration. The final narrative reflects the collaboration of minds, ideas, and imaginations from different corners of the bookstagram community. The challenges become a testament to the power of collective creativity.

Embodying the Joy of Writing Together:

"Collaborative Writing Challenges" challenges embody the joy of writing together. As participants immerse themselves in the shared story, they experience the excitement of co-creating a tale with like-minded individuals. The challenges become a celebration of literary togetherness.

IN CONCLUSION:

"Collaborative Writing Challenges" on bookstagram offer a thrilling and interactive concept. By inviting followers to contribute to a shared story, bookstagrammers create a platform for literary collaboration, imagination, and creativity. These challenges foster engagement, build literary community, and celebrate diverse writing styles and voices. As participants embark on collective storytelling adventures, they experience the joy of writing together, creating a tapestry of imaginative narratives within the captivating world of bookstagram. "Collaborative Writing Challenges" become a testament to the power of collective inspiration and the boundless possibilities of collaborative storytelling.

FIFTY-NINE
BOOKSTAGRAMMER TRUTH OR DARE:

A WHIMSICAL JOURNEY INTO LITERARY ADVENTURES

THE CONCEPT EXPLAINED:

Embracing the Classic Truth or Dare Game:

"Bookstagrammer Truth or Dare" challenges on bookstagram are inspired by the classic truth or dare game, where participants take turns choosing between revealing a truth or performing a dare. The bookstagrammer introduces the concept, explaining that the game will have a book-themed twist.

Infusing Bookish Elements:

The essence of "Bookstagrammer Truth or Dare" lies in infusing bookish elements into the game. The truth questions and dares revolve around books, reading habits, literary preferences, and imaginative book-themed challenges. The challenges become a celebration of all things bookish.

Answering Book-Themed Truth Questions:

The concept of "Bookstagrammer Truth or Dare" challenges involves answering book-themed truth questions. Participants are asked about their favorite genres, memorable book characters, most cherished reading moments, and literary guilty pleasures. The challenges become a glimpse into participants' bookish lives.

Performing Book-Themed Dares:

"Bookstagrammer Truth or Dare" challenges include performing book-themed dares. Participants may be dared to recreate a scene from their favorite book, create book-inspired artwork, or write a short story featuring beloved characters. The challenges become a creative exploration of bookish whimsy.

Fostering Engagement and Interaction:

The concept of "Bookstagrammer Truth or Dare" challenges fosters engagement and interaction among followers. As participants share their truth answers and perform dares, they create a lively and entertaining bookish exchange. The challenges become a platform for bookish camaraderie.

Celebrating Bookish Creativity:

"Bookstagrammer Truth or Dare" challenges celebrate bookish creativity. As participants take on dares that involve artistic expressions, writing, or imaginative play, they unleash their creativity within a literary context. The challenges become a tribute to the boundless creativity of book lovers.

Inspiring Book Recommendations:

The concept of "Bookstagrammer Truth or Dare" challenges inspires book recommendations. As participants share their favorite books or characters in response to truth questions, they introduce fellow followers to new and exciting reads. The challenges become a source of literary discoveries.

Creating a Playful Atmosphere:

"Bookstagrammer Truth or Dare" challenges create a playful and lighthearted atmosphere. The book-themed dares and questions infuse joy and laughter into the bookstagram community, fostering a sense of fun and adventure. The challenges become a delightful escape into the world of books.

Encouraging Bookish Challenges:

The concept of "Bookstagrammer Truth or Dare" challenges encourages bookish challenges among participants. As they take on dares related to books, readers step out of their comfort zones and embrace new literary adventures. The challenges become a catalyst for bookish exploration.

Building Bookish Bonds:

"Bookstagrammer Truth or Dare" challenges build bookish bonds among followers. As participants engage in the playful game, they forge connections with fellow book lovers and discover shared literary interests. The challenges become a celebration of bookish friendships.

IN CONCLUSION:

"Bookstagrammer Truth or Dare" challenges on bookstagram offer a playful and whimsical concept. By infusing the classic truth or dare game with bookish elements, bookstagrammers create an interactive platform for followers to embark on literary adventures. These challenges foster engagement, creativity, and bookish exploration, inspiring book recommendations and building bookish bonds. As participants embrace the joy of "Bookstagrammer Truth or Dare" challenges, they discover the delight of combining the magic of reading with lighthearted fun, creating a delightful and entertaining bookish journey within the captivating world of bookstagram.

SIXTY
BOOKISH DISCUSSIONS ON CONTROVERSIAL TOPICS WITHIN LITERATURE:

NAVIGATING COMPLEX THEMES AND PERSPECTIVES

THE CONCEPT EXPLAINED:

Exploring Challenging Themes:

"Bookish Discussions on Controversial Topics" on bookstagram are thought-provoking conversations that delve into challenging themes portrayed in literature. The discussions may revolve around sensitive subjects like racism, mental health, violence, sexuality, politics, and more. The bookstagrammer introduces the concept, emphasizing the importance of engaging with such topics thoughtfully.

Recognizing the Power of Literature:

The essence of "Bookish Discussions on Controversial Topics" lies in recognizing the power of literature to illuminate complex social and ethical issues. Books often serve as mirrors to society, reflecting both its beauty and its flaws. The discussions become an exploration of the profound impact of literature on readers.

Encouraging Diverse Viewpoints:

The concept of "Bookish Discussions on Controversial Topics" encourages participants to share diverse viewpoints. By inviting bookstagrammers to express their thoughts, feelings, and interpretations, the discussions become enriched with multiple perspectives. The discussions become an inclusive space for open dialogue.

Promoting Empathy and Understanding:

"Bookish Discussions on Controversial Topics" challenges promote empathy and understanding. As participants engage with differing viewpoints, they develop a deeper understanding of others' experiences and perspectives. The discussions become a catalyst for compassion and tolerance.

Navigating Complex Ethical Dilemmas:

The concept of "Bookish Discussions on Controversial Topics" involves navigating complex ethical dilemmas presented in literature. Participants may grapple with moral questions and conflicting ideologies portrayed in the books they read. The discussions become an exploration of ethical and philosophical considerations.

Fostering Critical Thinking:

"Bookish Discussions on Controversial Topics" challenges foster critical thinking skills. Participants are encouraged to analyze the intricacies of the presented themes and form well-reasoned arguments based on evidence from the texts. The discussions become a platform for intellectual growth.

Examining Social Relevance:

The concept of "Bookish Discussions on Controversial Topics" involves examining the social relevance of literary themes. Participants consider how these themes reflect real-world issues and influence cultural perceptions. The discussions become an exploration of literature's role in shaping societal consciousness.

Respecting Differing Opinions:

"Bookish Discussions on Controversial Topics" challenges emphasize the importance of respecting differing opinions. Participants engage in constructive conversations while acknowledging that disagreements are a natural part of meaningful discussions. The discussions become a testament to civil discourse.

Promoting Inclusivity and Diversity:

The concept of "Bookish Discussions on Controversial Topics" promotes inclusivity and diversity. Participants from various backgrounds and cultures share their perspectives, enriching the discussions with a broad range of insights. The discussions become a celebration of diverse voices.

Inspiring Further Reading and Learning:

"Bookish Discussions on Controversial Topics" challenges inspire further reading and learning. As participants explore challenging themes in books, they may seek out additional literature and research to deepen their understanding. The discussions become a stepping stone for continuous learning.

IN CONCLUSION:

"Bookish Discussions on Controversial Topics" on bookstagram offer a thought-provoking and essential concept. By engaging in meaningful conversations about complex themes and ethical dilemmas presented in literature, readers and bookstagrammers navigate challenging subjects with empathy, understanding, and critical thinking. These discussions promote inclusivity, respect for differing opinions, and an appreciation for the power of literature to shed light on societal issues. As participants embrace the opportunity to explore diverse viewpoints and examine the social relevance of literary themes, they contribute to a broader and more empathetic understanding of the world, making "Bookish Discussions on Controversial Topics" an intellectually enriching and transformative journey within the captivating world of literature and bookstagram.

SIXTY-ONE
INTERACTIVE BOOK CHARACTER QUIZZES:
UNVEILING LITERARY COUNTERPARTS IN AN ENGAGING JOURNEY

THE CONCEPT EXPLAINED:

Embarking on a Character Exploration:

"Interactive Book Character Quizzes" on bookstagram are captivating and interactive quizzes designed to help followers find their literary counterparts. Participants answer a series of questions that assess their personality traits, preferences, and values. The bookstagrammer introduces the concept, explaining the adventure that awaits participants.

Discovering Literary Counterparts:

The essence of "Interactive Book Character Quizzes" lies in discovering literary counterparts – fictional characters whose attributes align with participants' responses. Each quiz result reveals a character that shares common traits with the participant. The quizzes become a journey of self-discovery through literature.

Creating a Connection with Beloved Characters:

The concept of "Interactive Book Character Quizzes" fosters a connection with beloved characters from literature. As participants receive their quiz results, they experience a sense of affinity with the characters, relating to their experiences and personalities. The quizzes become a celebration of literary connections.

Enhancing Engagement and Interactivity:

"Interactive Book Character Quizzes" challenges enhance engagement and interactivity on bookstagram. As participants eagerly respond to the quiz questions, they become actively involved in the quest to find their literary counterparts. The quizzes become a playful and exciting bookish adventure.

Embracing the Magic of Imagination:

The concept of "Interactive Book Character Quizzes" embraces the magic of imagination. Participants imagine themselves within the worlds of beloved characters, exploring the fictional universes crafted by talented authors. The quizzes become a tribute to the boundless realms of imagination.

Reflecting on Personal Identity:

"Interactive Book Character Quizzes" challenges encourage participants to reflect on their personal identity. As they explore the traits and qualities that align them with specific characters, they gain insights into their own selves. The quizzes become a mirror to self-discovery.

Inspiring Further Reading:

The concept of "Interactive Book Character Quizzes" inspires further reading. Participants who find their literary counterparts may feel drawn to explore the books featuring those characters to delve deeper into their narratives. The quizzes become a gateway to literary exploration.

Connecting with Other Book Lovers:

"Interactive Book Character Quizzes" challenges create connections among book lovers. As participants share their quiz results and engage in conversations about their literary counterparts, they foster a sense of camaraderie with fellow bookstagrammers. The quizzes become a platform for bookish bonding.

Encouraging a Love for Literature:

The concept of "Interactive Book Character Quizzes" encourages a love for literature. As participants immerse themselves in the enchanting worlds of fictional characters, they cultivate a deeper appreciation for the transformative power of books. The quizzes become a celebration of literary enchantment.

Embracing the Diversity of Characters:

"Interactive Book Character Quizzes" challenges embrace the diversity of characters in literature. Participants may find themselves matched with characters from various genres and backgrounds, celebrating the rich tapestry of fictional personalities. The quizzes become a tribute to the vast array of literary personas.

IN CONCLUSION:

"Interactive Book Character Quizzes" on bookstagram offer a captivating and playful concept. By creating interactive quizzes for followers to discover their literary counterparts, bookstagrammers foster a connection with beloved characters and celebrate the profound impact of books on personal identity and imagination. These quizzes become a journey of self-discovery through literature, inspiring further reading and connecting book lovers with fellow enthusiasts. As participants embark on the adventure of finding their literary counterparts, they embrace the magic of imagination and gain insights into their own selves. "Interactive Book Character Quizzes" become a delightful and transformative exploration of the enchanting world of literature within the captivating realm of bookstagram.

SIXTY-TWO
"BOOKISH QUOTES" CALLIGRAPHY OR TYPOGRAPHY CHALLENGES:

CELEBRATING THE BEAUTY OF WORDS IN ARTISTIC CREATIONS

THE CONCEPT EXPLAINED:

Infusing Words with Artistic Flair:

"Bookish Quotes" calligraphy or typography challenges on bookstagram are artistic endeavors that infuse beloved book quotes with creative flair. Participants are tasked with transforming the written words of famous authors into visually captivating masterpieces using calligraphy or typography techniques. The bookstagrammer introduces the concept, setting the stage for a celebration of literary beauty through art.

Celebrating Beloved Book Quotes:

The essence of "Bookish Quotes" challenges lies in celebrating beloved book quotes that have touched the hearts of readers. Participants choose their favorite quotes from literature, emphasizing the words that resonate with them on a personal level. The challenges become a tribute to the power of words in shaping emotions and perspectives.

Unleashing Artistic Expressions:

The concept of "Bookish Quotes" challenges encourages participants to unleash their artistic expressions. Calligraphy enthusiasts utilize penmanship skills to create elegant lettering, while typography artists experiment with digital or traditional methods to design visually striking quotes. The challenges become a canvas for artistic ingenuity and creativity.

Emphasizing Visual Aesthetics:

"Bookish Quotes" calligraphy or typography challenges emphasize the visual aesthetics of words. Participants focus on font styles, layouts, colors, and embellishments to enhance the visual impact of the quotes. The challenges become a celebration of the artistry in language.

Merging Art and Literature:

The concept of "Bookish Quotes" challenges merges the worlds of art and literature. As participants transform book quotes into visual artworks, they explore the dynamic relationship between language and visual representation. The challenges become an amalgamation of literary and artistic expression.

Inspiring Reflection and Appreciation:

"Bookish Quotes" calligraphy or typography challenges inspire reflection and appreciation for the beauty of words. Participants engage with the quotes on a deeper level as they recreate them, savoring the meaning and significance behind the chosen words. The challenges become a moment of literary contemplation.

Fostering a Bookish Community:

The concept of "Bookish Quotes" challenges fosters a bookish community on bookstagram. As participants share their creations and engage in discussions about the quotes, they bond over their shared love for literature and art. The challenges become a platform for bookish camaraderie.

Encouraging Skill Development:

"Bookish Quotes" calligraphy or typography challenges encourage skill development among participants. As artists experiment with lettering techniques or typography software, they hone their artistic abilities and explore new horizons of expression. The challenges become a journey of artistic growth.

Sparking Inspiration:

The concept of "Bookish Quotes" challenges sparks inspiration for both creators and admirers. Participants draw inspiration from the quotes they choose, and their artistic creations, in turn, inspire others to appreciate the beauty of words and artistry. The challenges become a catalyst for creative inspiration.

Showcasing Bookstagram Talent:

"Bookish Quotes" challenges showcase the diverse talent within the bookstagram community. Participants marvel at the skill and creativity of fellow bookstagrammers' artworks, fostering mutual admiration and support. The challenges become a celebration of bookstagram artistry.

IN CONCLUSION:

"Bookish Quotes" calligraphy or typography challenges on bookstagram offer a captivating and creative concept. By inviting followers to transform beloved book quotes into visually captivating masterpieces, bookstagrammers celebrate the beauty of words and the artistry of expression. These challenges become a tribute to the profound impact of literature, inspiring reflection, and appreciation for the power of language. As participants unleash their artistic expressions, they merge the worlds of art and literature, creating a bookish community that celebrates talent and creative inspiration. "Bookish Quotes" challenges become an inspiring and visually enchanting journey within the captivating world of literature and bookstagram, where words come alive in artistic creations that touch the hearts of readers and artists alike.

SIXTY-THREE
A "BEST BOOKSTAGRAMMERS TO FOLLOW" LIST:

A CURATED COLLECTION OF LITERARY GEMS

THE CONCEPT EXPLAINED:

Curating a Personalized Collection:

A "Best Bookstagrammers to Follow" list on bookstagram is a curated collection of accounts that hold a special place in the heart of the bookstagrammer. The list typically features a select number of bookstagram accounts that the bookstagrammer admires, finds inspiring, or resonates with on a personal level. The bookstagrammer introduces the concept, emphasizing that the list is subjective and based on their individual preferences.

Celebrating Bookstagram Community:

The essence of a "Best Bookstagrammers to Follow" list lies in celebrating the bookstagram community and its diverse talents. The list includes accounts that excel in various aspects, such as book photography, thoughtful book reviews, creative bookish content, engaging captions, and inspiring book recommendations. The list becomes a tribute to the collective creativity and love for literature on bookstagram.

Fostering Bookish Camaraderie:

The concept of a "Best Bookstagrammers to Follow" list fosters bookish camaraderie among bookstagrammers. As the bookstagrammer shares their favorite accounts, they promote a sense of appreciation and support within the community. The list becomes a platform for celebrating fellow book lovers.

Inspiring Book Discoveries:

A "Best Bookstagrammers to Follow" list inspires book discoveries among followers. As the bookstagrammer introduces their favorite accounts, followers may explore these profiles, discovering new book recommendations, diverse perspectives, and captivating bookish content. The list becomes a gateway to literary exploration.

Recognizing Talented Bookstagrammers:

The concept of a "Best Bookstagrammers to Follow" list recognizes talented individuals within the bookstagram community. By featuring these accounts, the bookstagrammer acknowledges the dedication and creativity displayed by fellow book lovers. The list becomes a celebration of bookstagram artistry.

Building a Sense of Trust:

A "Best Bookstagrammers to Follow" list builds a sense of trust among followers. As the bookstagrammer shares their favorite accounts, they implicitly endorse the quality of content and authenticity of these profiles. The list becomes a reflection of the bookstagrammer's personal values and preferences.

Creating a Resourceful Guide:

The concept of a "Best Bookstagrammers to Follow" list creates a resourceful guide for followers seeking engaging and inspiring book-related content. As the bookstagrammer provides descriptions and insights about each account, followers gain a deeper understanding of the featured profiles. The list becomes a valuable reference for finding like-minded bookstagrammers.

Emphasizing Inclusivity and Diversity:

A "Best Bookstagrammers to Follow" list emphasizes inclusivity and diversity. The bookstagrammer may include accounts that represent various genres, perspectives, and cultural backgrounds, promoting a well-rounded and inclusive bookstagram experience. The list becomes a celebration of diverse voices within the community.

Encouraging Positive Bookish Engagement:

The concept of a "Best Bookstagrammers to Follow" list encourages positive bookish engagement. As followers explore the featured accounts and engage with their content, they contribute to a supportive and uplifting bookstagram community. The list becomes a catalyst for positive interactions.

IN CONCLUSION:

A "Best Bookstagrammers to Follow" list on bookstagram offers a thoughtful and celebratory concept. By curating a personalized collection of favorite accounts, bookstagrammers celebrate the diverse talents and contributions within the community. These lists foster bookish camaraderie, inspire book discoveries, and promote positive bookish engagement. As followers explore the featured accounts, they gain insights into different perspectives, creative content, and diverse voices within the bookstagram community. Ultimately, a "Best Bookstagrammers to Follow" list becomes a valuable and resourceful guide, connecting book lovers and celebrating the enchanting world of literature within the captivating realm of bookstagram.

SIXTY-FOUR
WEEKLY BOOKSTAGRAM SHOUTOUTS:

CELEBRATING OUTSTANDING FOLLOWERS AND ACCOUNTS IN THE LITERARY COMMUNITY

THE CONCEPT EXPLAINED:

Acknowledging Bookstagram Community:

"Weekly Bookstagram Shoutouts" on bookstagram are dedicated posts that acknowledge and appreciate outstanding followers or accounts within the community. The bookstagrammer chooses a specific day each week to feature these individuals or profiles. The concept is introduced as a way to express gratitude and celebrate the bookstagram community.

Recognizing Creativity and Contributions:

The essence of "Weekly Bookstagram Shoutouts" lies in recognizing the creativity and contributions of fellow book lovers. The shoutouts may feature accounts that excel in various aspects, such as exceptional book photography, engaging book reviews, captivating book recommendations, thought-provoking discussions, or inspiring book-related content. The shoutouts become a tribute to the collective creativity and passion for literature on bookstagram.

Fostering Bookish Camaraderie:

The concept of "Weekly Bookstagram Shoutouts" fosters bookish camaraderie within the community. As the bookstagrammer highlights outstanding followers or accounts, they promote a sense of appreciation and support among bookstagrammers. The shoutouts become a platform for celebrating the achievements and efforts of fellow book lovers.

Encouraging Positive Interactions:

"Weekly Bookstagram Shoutouts" challenges encourage positive interactions among followers. When featured accounts receive a shoutout, they often express gratitude in the comments section, leading to uplifting and supportive exchanges. The shoutouts become a catalyst for positive bookish engagement.

Spreading Literary Inspiration:

The concept of "Weekly Bookstagram Shoutouts" spreads literary inspiration throughout the community. When exceptional accounts are recognized, they may inspire other bookstagrammers to explore new ideas, experiment with creative content, and engage more actively with their followers. The shoutouts become a source of encouragement and motivation for bookstagram creativity.

Building a Supportive Community:

"Weekly Bookstagram Shoutouts" challenges contribute to building a supportive and close-knit bookstagram community. As accounts are featured, followers from different profiles come together to celebrate the recognized individuals. The shoutouts become a platform for fostering connections and friendships among book lovers.

Creating a Sense of Appreciation:

The concept of "Weekly Bookstagram Shoutouts" creates a sense of appreciation among followers. As outstanding accounts are featured, they feel acknowledged and valued for their efforts, encouraging them to continue sharing their passion for books. The shoutouts become a testament to the impact of active and engaged bookstagrammers.

Promoting Discoverability:

"Weekly Bookstagram Shoutouts" challenges promote discoverability among followers. As accounts are featured, their unique content and contributions are highlighted, leading to increased visibility and potential growth in followers. The shoutouts become a platform for exploring new bookstagram accounts and perspectives.

Encouraging Community Interaction:

The concept of "Weekly Bookstagram Shoutouts" encourages community interaction. Followers often engage with featured accounts, leaving encouraging comments and connecting with like-minded book lovers. The shoutouts become a bridge for bookish conversations and mutual support.

IN CONCLUSION:

"Weekly Bookstagram Shoutouts" on bookstagram offer a heartwarming and uplifting concept. By dedicating weekly posts to celebrate outstanding followers or accounts, bookstagrammers acknowledge and appreciate the creativity, engagement, and contributions of fellow book lovers.

These shoutouts foster bookish camaraderie, encourage positive interactions, and spread literary inspiration throughout the community. As featured accounts receive recognition, they feel appreciated and valued, contributing to the growth of a supportive and close-knit bookstagram community. "Weekly Bookstagram Shoutouts" become a platform for exploring new accounts, fostering bookish connections, and celebrating the diverse talents and passions within the captivating world of literature on bookstagram.

SIXTY-FIVE
BOOKISH MINDFULNESS EXERCISES:
UNWINDING THROUGH LITERARY ESCAPES

THE CONCEPT EXPLAINED:

Mindfulness and Literary Escape:

"Bookish Mindfulness Exercises" on bookstagram blend the practice of mindfulness with the captivating world of books and literature. The bookstagrammer guides their followers through a series of relaxing exercises that encourage participants to focus on the present moment, embrace their emotions, and immerse themselves in the enchantment of literary escape. The concept is introduced as a way to promote relaxation and self-awareness through the magic of storytelling.

Centering on Literary Themes:

The essence of "Bookish Mindfulness Exercises" lies in centering the exercises around literary themes. The bookstagrammer may choose books known for their calming and introspective qualities or select passages that inspire tranquility and self-reflection. The exercises become a tribute to the therapeutic power of literature.

Guided Meditation for Relaxation:

The concept of "Bookish Mindfulness Exercises" includes guided meditation for relaxation. The bookstagrammer gently leads participants through calming visualizations and encourages them to release tension, breathe deeply, and embrace a sense of inner calm. The exercises become a haven of tranquility amidst the hustle and bustle of daily life.

Encouraging Presence and Awareness:

"Bookish Mindfulness Exercises" challenges encourage presence and awareness. Participants are guided to observe their thoughts and emotions without judgment, fostering self-awareness and acceptance. The exercises become a journey of self-discovery and emotional clarity.

Embracing the Magic of Literary Imagery:

The concept of "Bookish Mindfulness Exercises" embraces the magic of literary imagery. Participants may be asked to visualize themselves within the enchanting worlds of beloved books, experiencing the sights, sounds, and emotions depicted in the stories. The exercises become a celebration of the boundless realms of imagination.

Fostering Gratitude through Books:

"Bookish Mindfulness Exercises" challenges foster gratitude through books. The bookstagrammer may prompt participants to reflect on the books that have left a lasting impact on their lives, inspiring gratitude for the wisdom, comfort, and joy found within literature. The exercises become a reminder of the blessings that books bring.

Inspiring Emotional Release:

The concept of "Bookish Mindfulness Exercises" inspires emotional release. Participants may find solace and healing through guided meditations that allow them to process and release pent-up emotions. The exercises become a space for emotional catharsis and healing.

Promoting Stress Relief and Well-being:

"Bookish Mindfulness Exercises" challenges promote stress relief and overall well-being. As participants engage in mindfulness practices centered around books, they experience a sense of relaxation, peace, and rejuvenation. The exercises become a balm for the mind, body, and soul.

Creating a Safe and Inclusive Space:

The concept of "Bookish Mindfulness Exercises" creates a safe and inclusive space for participants. The bookstagrammer emphasizes that the exercises are open to all, irrespective of their experience with mindfulness or their familiarity with the featured books. The exercises become a nurturing space for self-care and self-compassion.

IN CONCLUSION:

"Bookish Mindfulness Exercises" on bookstagram offer a soul-soothing and transformative concept. By guiding followers through mindfulness practices centered around the themes of books and literary escape, bookstagrammers create a haven of relaxation, stress relief, and introspection within the bookstagram community. These exercises celebrate the therapeutic power of literature, fostering self-awareness, emotional release, and gratitude through the magic of storytelling. As participants immerse themselves in the enchanting worlds of beloved books, they embrace the calming presence of the present moment and find solace in the boundless realms of imagination. "Bookish Mindfulness Exercises" become a heartwarming and nurturing journey, where mindfulness and literature intertwine to create a haven of tranquility and well-being within the captivating realm of bookstagram.

SIXTY-SIX
"GUESS THE GENRE" CHALLENGES:
UNVEILING THE LITERARY MYSTERIES

THE CONCEPT EXPLAINED:

Unveiling Literary Mysteries:

"Guess the Genre" challenges on bookstagram are captivating games that unveil literary mysteries. The bookstagrammer introduces the concept as an opportunity for followers to test their literary knowledge, explore new genres, and engage in friendly bookish competitions. The challenges become an enticing blend of creativity and intellectual curiosity.

Presenting Intriguing Book Descriptions:

The essence of "Guess the Genre" challenges lies in presenting intriguing book descriptions. The bookstagrammer crafts concise and captivating summaries that highlight key elements of the plot, characters, or themes without explicitly revealing the genre. The challenges become a showcase of the power of bookish storytelling.

Exercising Literary Detective Skills:

The concept of "Guess the Genre" challenges exercises participants' literary detective skills. As followers receive the book descriptions, they analyze the clues, draw upon their reading experiences, and venture educated guesses about the genre. The challenges become a stimulating exercise in critical thinking and literary analysis.

Fostering Genre Exploration:

"Guess the Genre" challenges foster genre exploration among participants. As they encounter diverse book descriptions, followers may be encouraged to step outside their comfort zones and explore genres they might not have considered before. The challenges become a gateway to literary diversity and breadth of reading experiences.

Engaging in Friendly Competitions:

The concept of "Guess the Genre" challenges encourages friendly competitions within the bookstagram community. Followers eagerly participate, sharing their guesses in the comments section, and engaging in lively discussions about the featured books. The challenges become a celebration of bookish camaraderie and knowledge sharing.

Sparking Curiosity and Interest:

"Guess the Genre" challenges spark curiosity and interest in featured books. As followers encounter intriguing summaries, they become intrigued by the mysteries concealed within the books' genres, motivating them to explore and read further. The challenges become a source of inspiration for literary discoveries.

Promoting Interaction with Literature:

The concept of "Guess the Genre" challenges promotes active interaction with literature. Participants may research, discuss, and explore the books in their quest to uncover the genre. The challenges become an immersive and participatory bookish experience.

Showcasing the Versatility of Genres:

"Guess the Genre" challenges showcase the versatility of genres in literature. As followers encounter a wide range of book descriptions, they witness how genres can encompass a diverse array of themes, tones, and narratives. The challenges become a celebration of the richness of literary genres.

Creating a Supportive Learning Environment:

The concept of "Guess the Genre" challenges creates a supportive learning environment. Followers may share their insights and learn from one another's literary knowledge, fostering a sense of community and intellectual growth. The challenges become a space for mutual support and bookish discoveries.

IN CONCLUSION:

"Guess the Genre" challenges on bookstagram offer an enthralling and interactive concept. By presenting followers with intriguing book descriptions and inviting them to guess the genre, bookstagrammers create a literary guessing game that tests literary knowledge, fosters genre exploration, and promotes friendly bookish competitions. These challenges become a showcase of the power of storytelling, engaging participants' critical thinking skills and sparking curiosity about featured books. As participants immerse themselves in the world of literary sleuthing, they celebrate the versatility and richness of genres, uncovering the mysteries concealed within the captivating world of literature on bookstagram. "Guess the Genre" challenges become a delightful and intellectually stimulating journey, where literature enthusiasts engage in friendly competitions, share insights, and celebrate the enchanting world of books within the captivating realm of bookstagram.

SIXTY-SEVEN
VIRTUAL BOOKISH FIELD TRIPS:

UNCOVERING LITERARY TREASURES FROM AFAR

THE CONCEPT EXPLAINED:

Journeying to Literary Destinations:

"Virtual Bookish Field Trips" on bookstagram offer a unique opportunity to journey to literary destinations from afar. The bookstagrammer introduces the concept as a way to explore the rich heritage of books, literature, and culture without physically leaving one's home. The field trips become a gateway to literary adventures and cultural explorations.

Immersive Virtual Tours:

The essence of "Virtual Bookish Field Trips" lies in providing immersive virtual tours. The bookstagrammer uses multimedia elements such as photos, videos, and live-streaming to transport followers to fascinating museums, historic libraries, charming bookstores, or places with literary significance. The field trips become a captivating blend of storytelling and visual splendor.

Uncovering Literary Treasures:

The concept of "Virtual Bookish Field Trips" involves uncovering literary treasures. As followers embark on these virtual tours, they discover rare manuscripts, timeless classics, original book covers, and artifacts related to famous authors and literary movements. The field trips become a celebration of the literary legacy and cultural heritage.

Offering Historical Anecdotes:

"Virtual Bookish Field Trips" challenges offer historical anecdotes and behind-the-scenes insights. The bookstagrammer shares fascinating stories about the featured museums or places, shedding light on their connection to literature and the creative geniuses who shaped them. The field trips become a journey through time and literary history.

Promoting Literary Learning:

The concept of "Virtual Bookish Field Trips" promotes literary learning among participants. As followers encounter literary artifacts and cultural gems, they gain new perspectives on the impact of literature on society and the world. The field trips become an enriching educational experience.

Cultural and Artistic Appreciation:

"Virtual Bookish Field Trips" challenges foster cultural and artistic appreciation. Participants encounter diverse forms of artistic expression, from book illustrations to architectural marvels, showcasing the enduring beauty of books and literature. The field trips become a tribute to the convergence of art and literature.

Connecting with Literary Communities:

The concept of "Virtual Bookish Field Trips" connects followers with literary communities around the world. As participants explore these virtual tours, they interact with fellow book lovers, sharing their impressions, thoughts, and literary insights. The field trips become a platform for global literary connections.

Accessible and Inclusive Experiences:

"Virtual Bookish Field Trips" challenges offer accessible and inclusive experiences. The bookstagrammer emphasizes that anyone can join these virtual tours, regardless of their location or physical ability. The field trips become a celebration of inclusivity and diversity within the bookstagram community.

Encouraging Cultural Exchange:

The concept of "Virtual Bookish Field Trips" encourages cultural exchange. As followers discover literary treasures from different parts of the world, they gain a deeper appreciation for the diverse literary traditions and narratives that enrich the global literary landscape. The field trips become a celebration of cultural diversity and shared humanity.

IN CONCLUSION:

"Virtual Bookish Field Trips" on bookstagram offer an innovative and immersive concept. By leading followers on virtual tours to museums, libraries, bookstores, or places related to books and literature, bookstagrammers provide a transformative and educational experience. These field trips uncover literary treasures, offer historical anecdotes, and promote cultural and artistic appreciation. Participants journey through time, exploring the literary legacy and cultural heritage that shaped the world of literature. As followers engage in these virtual tours, they connect with literary communities, foster global literary connections, and celebrate the rich tapestry of cultural diversity within the captivating realm of bookstagram. "Virtual Bookish Field Trips" become a magical and enlightening journey, where book lovers embark on literary adventures and uncover cultural gems from the comfort of their screens.

SIXTY-EIGHT
"BOOKISH RECOMMEND ME" POSTS:

A PERSONALIZED HAVEN FOR LITERARY SEEKERS

THE CONCEPT EXPLAINED:

Personalized Book Recommendations:

"Bookish Recommend Me" posts on bookstagram are dedicated spaces for personalized book recommendations. The bookstagrammer introduces the concept as a way for followers to seek guidance in discovering their next literary adventure or finding books that resonate with their unique reading preferences. The posts become a testament to the power of individualized reading experiences.

Welcoming Literary Seekers:

The essence of "Bookish Recommend Me" posts lies in welcoming literary seekers with open arms. The bookstagrammer emphasizes that all followers are invited to request recommendations, whether they are seasoned book lovers or new to the world of reading. The posts become a nurturing space for readers of all backgrounds.

Thoughtful and Tailored Responses:

The concept of "Bookish Recommend Me" posts involves providing thoughtful and tailored responses to each request. The bookstagrammer takes the time to understand the follower's preferences, genres of interest, and preferred reading experience before suggesting books. The posts become a showcase of the bookstagrammer's dedication to their followers' literary needs.

Fostering Meaningful Interactions:

"Bookish Recommend Me" challenges foster meaningful interactions within the bookstagram community. As followers request recommendations and receive responses, they engage in bookish discussions, share their thoughts on recommended books, and express gratitude for the personalized suggestions. The posts become a catalyst for literary conversations and connections.

Igniting the Spark of Discovery:

The concept of "Bookish Recommend Me" posts ignites the spark of discovery in book lovers. As followers receive personalized recommendations, they are inspired to explore new authors, genres, and literary voices they might not have encountered otherwise. The posts become a source of literary adventures and growth.

Curating a Diverse Range of Books:

"Bookish Recommend Me" posts curate a diverse range of books for different tastes. The bookstagrammer suggests books from various genres, including contemporary fiction, classic literature, non-fiction, fantasy, romance, and more, ensuring that every follower finds a recommendation that resonates with them. The posts become a celebration of literary diversity and inclusivity.

Building a Trusted Bookish Resource:

The concept of "Bookish Recommend Me" posts builds a trusted bookish resource within the bookstagram community. As followers receive personalized and well-researched recommendations, they come to rely on the bookstagrammer's expertise as a go-to source for discovering new reads. The posts become a treasured literary guide.

Encouraging Bookish Engagement:

"Bookish Recommend Me" challenges encourage bookish engagement. As followers request recommendations, they actively participate in the bookstagrammer's posts, creating a sense of community and involvement. The posts become a bridge for book lovers to share their literary journeys.

Supporting Diverse Reading Experiences:

The concept of "Bookish Recommend Me" posts supports diverse reading experiences. The bookstagrammer acknowledges that every reader is unique, and their preferences and interests vary widely, ensuring that each recommendation is tailored to the individual. The posts become a testament to the beauty of individual reading paths.

IN CONCLUSION:

"Bookish Recommend Me" posts on bookstagram offer a personalized and welcoming concept. By dedicating posts for followers to request personalized book recommendations, bookstagrammers create a haven for literary seekers. These posts provide thoughtful and tailored responses, fostering meaningful interactions and igniting the spark of literary discovery. As followers receive personalized book recommendations, they explore new literary voices, genres, and perspectives, celebrating the diversity and inclusivity of reading experiences. "Bookish Recommend Me" posts become a trusted and treasured bookish resource, a bridge for book lovers to share their literary journeys, and a testament to the power of individualized reading experiences within the captivating realm of bookstagram.

SIXTY-NINE
THEMED READING CHALLENGES:
EMBARKING ON LITERARY ADVENTURES

THE CONCEPT EXPLAINED:

Curating Themed Reading Experiences:

"Themed Reading Challenges" on bookstagram offer curated reading experiences centered around specific themes or criteria. The bookstagrammer introduces the concept as an opportunity for followers to expand their reading horizons, explore new genres, or delve into books they might not have considered before. The challenges become a celebration of the diversity and richness of literature.

Specific Criteria for Book Choices:

The essence of "Themed Reading Challenges" lies in providing specific criteria for book choices. The bookstagrammer sets guidelines such as reading books from a particular genre, by a certain author, based on a specific theme, or with a particular setting. The challenges become a roadmap for literary exploration and discovery.

Fostering a Sense of Adventure:

The concept of "Themed Reading Challenges" fosters a sense of adventure in the bookstagram community. As followers take on the challenge, they embrace the excitement of embarking on a literary journey that aligns with the specified theme or criteria. The challenges become an invitation to embark on literary quests.

Encouraging Diverse Literary Experiences:

"Themed Reading Challenges" challenges encourage diverse literary experiences. The bookstagrammer may set criteria that encompass a range of genres, time periods, or cultural perspectives, ensuring that participants encounter a wide array of storytelling styles. The challenges become a celebration of literary diversity and inclusivity.

Discovering Hidden Gems:

The concept of "Themed Reading Challenges" involves discovering hidden literary gems. As followers explore books that align with the specified theme or criteria, they may encounter lesser-known works or indie authors that capture their hearts. The challenges become a treasure hunt for literary treasures.

Building a Community of Readers:

"Themed Reading Challenges" challenges build a community of readers within the bookstagram community. Participants share their progress, thoughts, and book recommendations, creating a supportive and interactive space. The challenges become a platform for bookish camaraderie and connections.

Igniting the Joy of Reading:

The concept of "Themed Reading Challenges" ignites the joy of reading among followers. As participants immerse themselves in books that resonate with the specified theme, they experience the sheer delight of storytelling and the power of words. The challenges become a source of literary joy and inspiration.

Promoting Goal-Oriented Reading:

"Themed Reading Challenges" challenges promote goal-oriented reading. Participants set targets for themselves, striving to read a certain number of books that align with the specified criteria within a given time frame. The challenges become a pathway for achieving reading goals and expanding literary accomplishments.

Embracing Bookish Conversations:

The concept of "Themed Reading Challenges" embraces bookish conversations. As followers discuss the books they read, exchange thoughts on the themes, and recommend additional titles, they contribute to a vibrant and dynamic literary discourse. The challenges become a hub of literary discussions and insights.

IN CONCLUSION:

"Themed Reading Challenges" on bookstagram offer an enthralling and interactive concept. By creating challenges with specific criteria for book choices, bookstagrammers curate reading experiences that celebrate the diversity of literature, foster a sense of adventure, and encourage diverse literary exploration. These challenges become a roadmap for literary discovery, a treasure hunt for hidden literary gems, and a platform for building a community of readers within the bookstagram community. As followers embark on these themed challenges, they ignite the joy of reading, set goal-oriented reading targets, and embrace bookish conversations that enrich their literary experiences. "Themed Reading Challenges" become a celebration of the power of storytelling, a testament to the beauty of literary diversity, and a testament to the boundless possibilities of literary adventures within the captivating realm of bookstagram.

SEVENTY
"BOOKISH MYTHBUSTERS":
UNVEILING THE TRUTHS BEHIND LITERARY LEGENDS

THE CONCEPT EXPLAINED:

Unveiling Literary Truths:

"Bookish Mythbusters" posts on bookstagram offer a quest to unveil the truths behind common book-related myths and misconceptions. The bookstagrammer introduces the concept as an opportunity for followers to gain clarity on popular literary beliefs, ensuring that readers can make informed judgments about the books they read. The posts become a journey of intellectual exploration and discovery.

Debunking Misconceptions:

The essence of "Bookish Mythbusters" lies in debunking misconceptions surrounding books and literature. The bookstagrammer takes on popular myths, urban legends, or widely-held beliefs related to authors, book genres, literary history, or reading habits. The posts become a reliable source of accurate information and literary insights.

Fact-Based Research and Analysis:

The concept of "Bookish Mythbusters" involves fact-based research and analysis. The bookstagrammer delves into literary history, explores reputable sources, and consults experts to ensure that the posts provide well-substantiated information. The posts become a showcase of thorough and meticulous investigation.

Fostering Informed Discussions:

"Bookish Mythbusters" challenges foster informed discussions within the bookstagram community. As followers engage with the posts, they share their own perspectives, experiences, and knowledge, contributing to a dynamic and intellectually stimulating discourse. The posts become a platform for bookish conversations and exchange of ideas.

Promoting Critical Thinking:

The concept of "Bookish Mythbusters" promotes critical thinking among followers. As readers encounter the truths behind common literary myths, they are encouraged to question assumptions, challenge preconceived notions, and approach literature with a discerning mindset. The posts become an exercise in intellectual curiosity and analytical reasoning.

Correcting Misinformation:

"Bookish Mythbusters" challenges correct misinformation that might have spread within the bookstagram community or beyond. By addressing common misconceptions head-on, the bookstagrammer ensures that readers have access to accurate and reliable information. The posts become a valuable resource for book lovers seeking truth amidst the noise of myths.

Empowering Readers with Knowledge:

The concept of "Bookish Mythbusters" empowers readers with knowledge about the books they love. As followers gain insights into literary history, authorial intent, or the origins of popular beliefs, they deepen their appreciation for literature and storytelling. The posts become a beacon of enlightenment and empowerment for book enthusiasts.

Celebrating Literary Complexity:

"Bookish Mythbusters" challenges celebrate the complexity of literature and the multi-faceted nature of literary legends. As myths are debunked, readers come to understand that books are often products of diverse influences, interpretations, and cultural contexts. The posts become a celebration of the richness and depth of literary artistry.

Creating a Trusted Literary Resource:

The concept of "Bookish Mythbusters" creates a trusted literary resource within the bookstagram community. As followers encounter accurate and well-researched information, they come to rely on the bookstagrammer's expertise as a reliable source of literary knowledge. The posts become a beacon of reliability and credibility in the world of books.

IN CONCLUSION:

"Bookish Mythbusters" posts on bookstagram offer a fascinating and enlightening concept. By debunking common book-related myths or misconceptions, bookstagrammers unveil the truths behind popular literary beliefs, foster informed discussions, and promote critical thinking among followers. These posts become a valuable resource for book lovers seeking accurate information and knowledge about the books they cherish. As followers engage with "Bookish Mythbusters" challenges, they celebrate the complexity and richness of literature, deepen their understanding of storytelling, and gain a deeper appreciation for the diverse influences that shape literary legends. "Bookish Mythbusters" become a beacon of intellectual exploration, a platform for bookish conversations, and a trusted source of reliable information within the captivating realm of bookstagram.

SEVENTY-ONE

COLLABORATIVE BOOK FAN-FICTION PROJECTS:

UNITING LITERARY IMAGINATIONS

THE CONCEPT EXPLAINED:

Embracing Literary Creativity:

"Collaborative Book Fan-Fiction Projects" on bookstagram offer an invitation to embrace literary creativity. The bookstagrammer introduces the concept as a unique opportunity for followers to unleash their imaginations and contribute to the world of storytelling through fan fiction. The projects become a celebration of the boundless creativity of literature enthusiasts.

Uniting Literary Imaginations:

The essence of "Collaborative Book Fan-Fiction Projects" lies in uniting literary imaginations. The bookstagrammer sets the stage for collaborative storytelling, where followers come together to collectively craft narratives, share ideas, and build upon each other's contributions. The projects become a manifestation of the collective power of storytelling.

Expanding Beloved Book Universes:

The concept of "Collaborative Book Fan-Fiction Projects" involves expanding beloved book universes. As co-authors, followers have the opportunity to build upon the worlds created by their favorite authors, adding depth and richness to the existing narratives. The projects become an extension of cherished literary realms.

Exploring Alternative Plotlines:

"Collaborative Book Fan-Fiction Projects" challenges explore alternative plotlines. Co-authors delve into "what if" scenarios, reimagining pivotal moments in the original stories or crafting new adventures for characters beyond the confines of the published works. The projects become a journey of literary exploration and storytelling freedom.

Diving into Character Perspectives:

The concept of "Collaborative Book Fan-Fiction Projects" involves diving into character perspectives. Co-authors have the opportunity to delve into the minds and hearts of beloved characters, providing insight into their thoughts, emotions, and motivations. The projects become an intimate exploration of character development and complexity.

Fostering Collaborative Creativity:

"Collaborative Book Fan-Fiction Projects" challenges foster collaborative creativity within the bookstagram community. As co-authors share their ideas, feedback, and contributions, they engage in a creative dialogue that fosters camaraderie and friendship. The projects become a platform for literary bonding and shared passion.

Supporting Safe and Inclusive Spaces:

The concept of "Collaborative Book Fan-Fiction Projects" supports safe and inclusive spaces for creative expression. The bookstagrammer emphasizes that all followers are welcome to participate, regardless of their writing experience or background. The projects become a testament to the diverse voices and perspectives within the bookstagram community.

Encouraging Feedback and Encouragement:

"Collaborative Book Fan-Fiction Projects" challenges encourage feedback and encouragement among co-authors. As participants share their chapters or contributions, they receive supportive feedback from fellow writers, fostering a nurturing and constructive environment. The projects become a space for writers to grow and improve their craft.

Celebrating the Joy of Writing:

The concept of "Collaborative Book Fan-Fiction Projects" celebrates the joy of writing. As co-authors immerse themselves in the creative process, they rediscover the magic of storytelling and the pleasure of crafting words. The projects become a celebration of the written word and the beauty of storytelling.

IN CONCLUSION:

"Collaborative Book Fan-Fiction Projects" on bookstagram offer an exhilarating and interactive concept. By initiating fan-fiction projects where followers become co-authors, bookstagrammers unite literary imaginations, expand beloved book universes, and explore alternative plotlines. These projects become a journey of literary exploration, where co-authors dive into character perspectives and collectively craft narratives that celebrate the joy of writing and the boundless creativity of storytelling. As followers engage in these collaborative projects, they bond with fellow book enthusiasts, embrace the power of creative collaboration, and celebrate the diversity of voices within the bookstagram community. "Collaborative Book Fan-Fiction Projects" become a testament to the magic of fan fiction, a platform for literary exploration, and a celebration of the shared passion for storytelling within the captivating realm of bookstagram.

SEVENTY-TWO
BOOK-INSPIRED HOME DECOR:
RANSFORMING SPACES WITH LITERARY MAGIC

THE CONCEPT EXPLAINED:

Infusing Literary Magic into Home Spaces:

"Book-Inspired Home Decor Ideas and DIY Projects" on bookstagram offer a charming opportunity to infuse literary magic into home spaces. The bookstagrammer introduces the concept as a creative journey of transforming living spaces into literary sanctuaries. The posts become a celebration of the deep connection between books and our personal spaces.

Showcasing Imaginative Decor:

The essence of "Book-Inspired Home Decor Ideas and DIY Projects" lies in showcasing imaginative decor inspired by books. The bookstagrammer shares curated decor elements, furniture, and accessories that evoke the essence of beloved literary worlds. The posts become a gallery of artistic and imaginative bookish decor.

Reflecting Personal Bookish Passions:

The concept of "Book-Inspired Home Decor Ideas and DIY Projects" involves reflecting personal bookish passions within living spaces. The bookstagrammer emphasizes that every book lover's home decor can be a reflection of their favorite books, genres, and literary characters. The posts become a celebration of individual literary journeys and preferences.

Curating Themed Room Designs:

"Book-Inspired Home Decor Ideas and DIY Projects" challenges curate themed room designs inspired by specific books or literary genres. The bookstagrammer presents ideas for transforming bedrooms, living rooms, home libraries, and other spaces into havens dedicated to the magic of literature. The posts become a treasure trove of creative ideas for thematic room makeovers.

Sharing DIY Projects and Tutorials:

The concept of "Book-Inspired Home Decor Ideas and DIY Projects" involves sharing do-it-yourself projects and tutorials. The bookstagrammer guides followers through crafting bookish decor elements, customizing furniture, and creating literary-inspired artwork. The posts become a source of inspiration and guidance for book lovers eager to embark on creative DIY ventures.

Creating Literary Nooks and Corners:

"Book-Inspired Home Decor Ideas and DIY Projects" challenges encourage creating literary nooks and corners within home spaces. The bookstagrammer showcases ways to design cozy reading corners, bookshelves, and reading nooks that invite readers to lose themselves in the magic of books. The posts become an invitation to create serene and inspiring reading spaces.

Exploring Vintage and Antique Charm:

The concept of "Book-Inspired Home Decor Ideas and DIY Projects" involves exploring vintage and antique charm in decor. The bookstagrammer highlights decor elements such as vintage book covers, antique bookshelves, and old-world furnishings that add timeless elegance to home spaces. The posts become a celebration of the enduring allure of vintage books and decor.

Expressing Personal Creativity:

"Book-Inspired Home Decor Ideas and DIY Projects" challenges encourage expressing personal creativity through decor. The bookstagrammer invites followers to customize decor elements, incorporate favorite book quotes into artwork, and use bookish fabrics and patterns in home decor. The posts become a canvas for personal artistic expression and literary love.

IN CONCLUSION:

"Book-Inspired Home Decor Ideas and DIY Projects" on bookstagram offer an enchanting and imaginative concept. By sharing delightful ways to infuse literary magic into home spaces through inspired decor and do-it-yourself projects, bookstagrammers celebrate the profound impact of books on our lives and reflect the unique personalities and passions of book lovers. These posts become a gallery of artistic and imaginative bookish decor, a treasure trove of creative ideas for themed room designs, and a source of inspiration and guidance for crafting literary-inspired decor elements. As followers embark on the journey of creating literary nooks and corners within their homes, they express personal creativity, explore vintage charm, and transform their living spaces into havens dedicated to the magic of literature. "Book-Inspired Home Decor Ideas and DIY Projects" become a celebration of the enduring allure of books in our lives, a canvas for personal artistic expression, and a reflection of the beautiful marriage between literature and home decor within the captivating realm of bookstagram.

SEVENTY-THREE
"BOOKISH CONFESSIONS":
EMBRACING READING HABITS AND QUIRKS

THE CONCEPT EXPLAINED:

A Peek into the Reading Life:

"Bookish Confessions" on bookstagram offer followers a delightful peek into the reading lives of their favorite bookstagrammers. The bookstagrammer introduces the concept as a candid and authentic sharing of personal reading habits, quirks, and experiences. The posts become a window into the intimate relationship between readers and books.

Creating Relatable and Inclusive Content:

The essence of "Bookish Confessions" lies in creating relatable and inclusive content. The bookstagrammer emphasizes that everyone's reading journey is unique, and quirks and habits are part of what makes each reader special. The posts become a celebration of the diverse reading experiences within the bookstagram community.

Fostering Connection and Empathy:

The concept of "Bookish Confessions" fosters connection and empathy among followers. As bookstagrammers share their reading quirks and habits, readers are encouraged to embrace their own idiosyncrasies and connect with others who share similar experiences. The posts become a platform for book lovers to bond over shared reading traits.

Laughing at Ourselves:

"Bookish Confessions" challenges involve a lighthearted approach to self-awareness. The bookstagrammer shares humorous anecdotes and quirks, inviting followers to laugh along and find humor in their own reading habits. The posts become a source of joy and laughter within the bookstagram community.

Embracing Bookish Peculiarities:

The concept of "Bookish Confessions" involves embracing bookish peculiarities without judgment. The bookstagrammer encourages followers to celebrate their reading quirks and see them as endearing aspects of their book-loving identities. The posts become a celebration of the delightful and unique aspects of each reader's relationship with books.

Exploring Reading Rituals:

"Bookish Confessions" challenges explore reading rituals and habits that shape the reading experience. The bookstagrammer may share details about favorite reading spots, comfort reads, bookmark preferences, or book sniffing habits. The posts become an exploration of the little rituals that add magic to the act of reading.

Revealing Guilty Pleasures:

The concept of "Bookish Confessions" involves revealing guilty pleasures in reading. The bookstagrammer shares guilty pleasure reads, hidden book-buying habits, or guilty delights in particular book tropes. The posts become a space to revel in guilty pleasures and find acceptance within the book-loving community.

Encouraging Self-Reflection:

"Bookish Confessions" challenges encourage self-reflection among followers. The bookstagrammer may pose questions or prompts that prompt readers to reflect on their own reading habits and quirks. The posts become an opportunity for personal growth and self-discovery as readers examine their reading preferences.

Empowering Authenticity:

The concept of "Bookish Confessions" empowers authenticity within the bookstagram community. The bookstagrammer emphasizes that there are no right or wrong ways to love books, and each reader's journey is valid and worth celebrating. The posts become a celebration of bookish individuality and the beauty of diverse reading experiences.

IN CONCLUSION:

"Bookish Confessions" posts on bookstagram offer an endearing and relatable concept. By sharing personal reading habits, quirks, and idiosyncrasies, bookstagrammers create a warm and inviting space for followers to connect, relate, and embrace the joys and peculiarities of being book lovers. These posts become a celebration of diverse reading experiences, a platform for self-awareness and self-reflection, and a source of joy and laughter within the bookstagram community. As followers laugh at their own bookish quirks and discover shared reading traits, they celebrate the unique aspects of their relationship with books and find acceptance and empathy within the captivating realm of bookstagram. "Bookish Confessions" become a celebration of authenticity, a window into the intimate bond between readers and books, and a reflection of the delightful and cherished nuances of being book lovers within the enchanting world of bookstagram.

SEVENTY-FOUR
"BOOKSTAGRAMMER TRIVIA":
UNVEILING THE ENCHANTING JOURNEY

THE CONCEPT EXPLAINED:

Personalizing the Bookstagram Experience:

"Bookstagrammer Trivia" on bookstagram offers an opportunity for followers to get to know the person behind the bookish photos. The bookstagrammer introduces the concept as a journey of personalization, sharing intriguing facts and stories that offer a glimpse into their life, interests, and growth as a bookstagrammer. The posts become a celebration of the diverse personalities within the bookstagram community.

Fostering Deeper Connections:

The essence of "Bookstagrammer Trivia" lies in fostering deeper connections with followers. As the bookstagrammer shares personal stories and experiences, followers gain insights into the journey behind the carefully curated bookstagram feed. The posts become a bridge that brings bookstagrammers and followers closer together.

Showcasing Milestones and Achievements:

The concept of "Bookstagrammer Trivia" involves showcasing significant milestones and achievements in the bookstagram journey. The bookstagrammer may share memorable interactions with authors, collaborations, or moments of recognition within the bookstagram community. The posts become a celebration of the bookstagrammer's growth and accomplishments.

Sharing Bookish Experiences:

"Bookstagrammer Trivia" challenges share bookish experiences that have shaped the bookstagrammer's journey. The bookstagrammer may talk about favorite books, transformative reads, or the inception of their love for literature. The posts become a testament to the transformative power of books in the bookstagrammer's life.

Revealing Bookstagram Insights:

The concept of "Bookstagrammer Trivia" involves revealing insights into the bookstagrammer's creative process. The bookstagrammer may share their favorite photography techniques, creative challenges, or tips for managing a bookstagram account. The posts become a source of inspiration and guidance for fellow bookstagrammers.

Embracing Bookish Idiosyncrasies:

"Bookstagrammer Trivia" challenges embrace bookish idiosyncrasies and quirks. The bookstagrammer may confess to unusual book organizing habits, favorite reading spots, or unique rituals associated with bookstagramming. The posts become a celebration of the delightful and eccentric aspects of being a book lover.

Narrating Memorable Moments:

The concept of "Bookstagrammer Trivia" involves narrating memorable moments that have shaped the bookstagrammer's journey. The bookstagrammer may share heartwarming interactions with followers, experiences at book events, or touching encounters with fellow book lovers. The posts become a reflection of the meaningful connections and friendships formed through bookstagram.

Unveiling Challenges and Growth:

"Bookstagrammer Trivia" challenges unveil challenges and growth within the bookstagram journey. The bookstagrammer may talk about overcoming creative slumps, navigating content creation, or finding their authentic voice on bookstagram. The posts become a testament to resilience and personal development.

Expressing Gratitude to Followers:

The concept of "Bookstagrammer Trivia" involves expressing gratitude to followers for their support and presence on the bookstagram journey. The bookstagrammer may share heartfelt anecdotes about the positive impact of the bookstagram community on their life. The posts become an expression of appreciation and connection with followers.

IN CONCLUSION:

"Bookstagrammer Trivia" posts on bookstagram offer an engaging and enlightening concept. By sharing intriguing facts, personal stories, and behind-the-scenes anecdotes about their bookstagram journey, bookstagrammers foster deeper connections with followers, celebrate their growth and accomplishments, and embrace the delightful nuances of being book lovers. These posts become a reflection of the transformative power of books, a celebration of meaningful connections and friendships, and a source of inspiration and guidance for fellow bookstagrammers. As followers engage with "Bookstagrammer Trivia" challenges, they gain insights into the person behind the bookish photos, experience gratitude and connection, and celebrate the enchanting journey of being part of the captivating realm of bookstagram. "Bookstagrammer Trivia" becomes a bridge that unites bookstagrammers and followers, a celebration of personal growth and passion for literature, and a testament to the beautiful connections that bloom within the enchanting world of bookstagram.

SEVENTY-FIVE
VIRTUAL WRITING WORKSHOPS AND CREATIVE WRITING CHALLENGES:
NURTURING LITERARY CREATIVITY

THE CONCEPT EXPLAINED:

Encouraging Creative Expression:

"Virtual Writing Workshops and Creative Writing Challenges" on bookstagram create a safe and supportive environment for followers to express their creativity through writing. The bookstagrammer introduces the concept as a space where literary imagination and storytelling take flight. The workshops and challenges become a celebration of the power of words and storytelling.

Virtual Writing Workshops:

The essence of "Virtual Writing Workshops" lies in bookstagrammers hosting interactive sessions focused on various aspects of creative writing. These workshops may explore character development, plot construction, world-building, dialogue writing, and other essential elements of storytelling. The workshops become an opportunity for followers to learn and refine their writing skills in a collaborative and nurturing environment.

Creative Writing Challenges:

The concept of "Creative Writing Challenges" involves bookstagrammers presenting writing prompts or themes for followers to craft their own short stories, poems, or flash fiction. These challenges may have specific word limits, genres, or themes to inspire creativity. The challenges become an invitation for followers to unleash their creativity and explore new literary terrains.

Feedback and Community Support:

"Virtual Writing Workshops and Creative Writing Challenges" emphasize the value of feedback and community support. The bookstagrammer encourages participants to share their writing with each other and offer constructive feedback and encouragement. The workshops and challenges become a platform for growth and connection as writers support and inspire one another.

Celebrating Diverse Voices:

The concept of "Virtual Writing Workshops and Creative Writing Challenges" celebrates the diverse voices and perspectives within the bookstagram community. The bookstagrammer emphasizes the importance of inclusivity and representation in storytelling. The workshops and challenges become a celebration of the richness of cultural and individual identities.

Inspiring Literary Exploration:

"Virtual Writing Workshops and Creative Writing Challenges" inspire followers to explore different genres, writing styles, and themes. The bookstagrammer may offer reading recommendations and resources to spark literary exploration. The workshops and challenges become a gateway to discovering new literary horizons.

Guidance from Writing Experts:

The concept of "Virtual Writing Workshops and Creative Writing Challenges" involves collaboration with writing experts or authors who may lead some of the workshops or provide guidance and tips for participants. The workshops become an opportunity for followers to learn from experienced writers and gain insights into the craft of storytelling.

Building a Creative Community:

"Virtual Writing Workshops and Creative Writing Challenges" foster a sense of community among participants. The bookstagrammer encourages followers to engage with each other's work, exchange ideas, and celebrate each other's achievements. The workshops and challenges become a platform for building lasting connections with fellow writers.

Celebrating Progress and Growth:

The concept of "Virtual Writing Workshops and Creative Writing Challenges" celebrates the progress and growth of participants in their writing journey. The bookstagrammer may highlight success stories and accomplishments of writers who have participated in past challenges or workshops. The workshops become a testament to the power of practice and perseverance in honing writing skills.

IN CONCLUSION:

"Virtual Writing Workshops and Creative Writing Challenges" on bookstagram offer a nurturing and empowering concept. By hosting interactive sessions that encourage creative expression through writing, bookstagrammers provide followers with a virtual space to explore and enhance their storytelling skills. These workshops and challenges become a celebration of the diverse voices and stories within the bookstagram community, a platform for growth and connection, and an inspiration for literary exploration. As participants engage with writing prompts, receive feedback, and support each other's creative endeavors, they build a vibrant creative community that celebrates the power of words and storytelling. "Virtual Writing Workshops and Creative Writing Challenges" become a celebration of literary passion and imagination within the enchanting world of bookstagram, nurturing the seeds of creativity and inspiring a new generation of storytellers.

SEVENTY-SIX
"BEHIND THE BOOK" FEATURES:
UNVEILING THE PUBLISHING PROCESS

THE CONCEPT EXPLAINED:

Peeking into the Creative Cauldron:

"Behind the Book" features on bookstagram invite followers to peek into the creative cauldron where stories are forged. The bookstagrammer introduces the concept as a unique opportunity to explore the birth of a book and witness the craftsmanship that brings it to life. The features become a celebration of the artistry and passion of authors, editors, and publishing professionals.

Navigating the Writing Process:

The essence of "Behind the Book" lies in unraveling the writing process of an author. The bookstagrammer may interview authors or share anecdotes about their writing journey, from the spark of an idea to the completion of a manuscript. The features become a testament to the dedication and resilience required to create compelling narratives.

Connecting with Authors:

The concept of "Behind the Book" involves fostering a deeper connection between authors and their readers. The bookstagrammer may encourage followers to submit questions for authors, creating a virtual dialogue between the creator and the audience. The features become a platform for authors to engage with their readers and vice versa.

Revealing the Editing Journey:

"Behind the Book" features delve into the intricate editing process that refines and polishes a manuscript. The bookstagrammer may collaborate with editors or share insights from authors about the revision process. The features become a celebration of the collaborative effort that transforms drafts into masterpieces.

Unveiling Cover Design:

The concept of "Behind the Book" includes showcasing cover design and illustration. The bookstagrammer may interview cover artists or reveal early drafts and concepts that shaped the final cover. The features become a visual journey into the artistry that captures a book's essence.

Understanding Book Production:

"Behind the Book" features explore the fascinating world of book production and manufacturing. The bookstagrammer may offer insights into printing processes, paper selection, and bookbinding. The features become an appreciation of the craftsmanship that transforms words into tangible works of art.

Navigating the Publishing Industry:

The concept of "Behind the Book" involves navigating the intricate landscape of the publishing industry. The bookstagrammer may interview literary agents, publishers, and other industry professionals to shed light on the process of bringing a book to market. The features become an educational journey for aspiring authors and book lovers alike.

Celebrating Book Launches:

"Behind the Book" features celebrate the excitement and anticipation surrounding book launches. The bookstagrammer may share glimpses of book launch events, author signings, and release day celebrations. The features become a virtual toast to the birth of new stories.

Exploring Book Promotion:

The concept of "Behind the Book" involves exploring book promotion and marketing efforts. The bookstagrammer may collaborate with publicists or authors to share insights into book tours, social media campaigns, and promotional strategies. The features become an acknowledgment of the work that introduces books to their readers.

Showcasing Author Interviews:

"Behind the Book" features may include interviews with authors about their experiences throughout the publishing journey. The bookstagrammer may inquire about their inspiration, challenges, and advice for aspiring writers. The features become a source of inspiration and wisdom for aspiring authors.

IN CONCLUSION:

"Behind the Book" features on bookstagram offer an enlightening and captivating concept. By providing followers with an exclusive glimpse into the creative and intricate journey of a book from conception to publication, these features become a celebration of the artistry, dedication, and collaboration that shape beloved stories. They foster a deeper connection between authors and readers, offer a visual journey into cover design and book production, and unveil the mysteries of the publishing industry. As followers explore the writing process, editing journey, and book promotion efforts, they gain insights into the craftsmanship that brings literature to life. "Behind the Book" features become a celebration of storytelling, a platform for author-reader engagement, and a treasure trove of knowledge and inspiration for book lovers and aspiring authors within the captivating world of bookstagram.

SEVENTY-SEVEN
BOOKSTAGRAMMER-HOSTED WRITING CONTESTS:
FOSTERING LITERARY CREATIVITY WITH BOOKISH THEMES

THE CONCEPT EXPLAINED:

Inviting Literary Exploration:

"Bookstagrammer-Hosted Writing Contests" on bookstagram extend a warm invitation to literary exploration. The bookstagrammer introduces the concept as a creative journey where followers can venture into bookish realms, weaving their stories around beloved characters, worlds, or literary genres. The contests become a celebration of imagination and the power of storytelling.

Bookish Themes and Prompts:

The essence of these contests lies in the bookish themes and prompts chosen by the bookstagrammer. The themes may revolve around favorite books, literary genres, iconic characters, or alternative endings to well-loved tales. The contests become a canvas for writers to express their passion for literature in unique and imaginative ways.

Celebrating Diverse Writing Styles:

The concept of "Bookstagrammer-Hosted Writing Contests" celebrates the diversity of writing styles and voices within the bookstagram community. Writers are encouraged to embrace their individuality and interpret the bookish themes in their distinctive ways. The contests become a tapestry of literary artistry, woven with individual flair and creativity.

Fostering a Writing Community:

The contests foster a vibrant writing community within the bookstagram platform. Participants engage with each other's work, exchange feedback, and form connections over their shared passion for storytelling. The contests become a collaborative space where writers support and inspire one another.

Providing a Platform for Aspiring Writers:

The concept of "Bookstagrammer-Hosted Writing Contests" provides aspiring writers with a platform to showcase their talent and gain recognition. Participants have the opportunity to share their work with a broader audience, including fellow book lovers, authors, and potential literary agents. The contests become a stepping stone for emerging writers on their literary journey.

Inspiring Literary Confidence:

"Bookstagrammer-Hosted Writing Contests" inspire writers to embrace their craft and boost their literary confidence. By participating in themed challenges, writers can explore new genres, experiment with styles, and overcome creative blocks. The contests become a source of encouragement and growth in the writing process.

Celebrating Literary Winners:

The contests culminate in the celebration of literary winners who emerge from a pool of talented participants. The bookstagrammer may showcase the winning entries and acknowledge outstanding creativity, storytelling, and interpretation of the bookish themes. The contests become a stage to applaud the literary achievements of participants.

Engaging with Writing Experts:

The concept of "Bookstagrammer-Hosted Writing Contests" may involve collaborations with writing experts, authors, or editors who provide guidance, feedback, or serve as contest judges. Their expertise and insights enhance the writing experience for participants. The contests become a valuable learning opportunity for writers to receive professional feedback.

Sparking Literary Dialogue:

"Bookstagrammer-Hosted Writing Contests" spark literary dialogue as followers engage with the bookish themes and explore alternative narratives. Participants may discuss their writing process, inspirations, and love for books within the contest community. The contests become a celebration of the connections between literature, imagination, and creativity.

IN CONCLUSION:

"Bookstagrammer-Hosted Writing Contests" on bookstagram offer an inspiring and engaging concept. By organizing creative writing contests centered around bookish themes, bookstagrammers provide a platform for followers to embark on literary explorations, showcase their writing talent, and celebrate the magic of storytelling. These contests foster a sense of community, inspire literary confidence, and celebrate the diverse voices and writing styles within the bookstagram community. As participants engage with bookish prompts, form connections with fellow writers, and share their love for literature, they become part of a vibrant creative community that celebrates the beauty and power of words. "Bookstagrammer-Hosted Writing Contests" become a celebration of literary imagination and expression, a stage to acknowledge and applaud outstanding creativity, and a nurturing ground for aspiring writers within the enchanting world of bookstagram.

SEVENTY-EIGHT "BOOKISH TIME CAPSULE" CHALLENGES:

PRESERVING LITERARY MEMORIES AND TREASURES

THE CONCEPT EXPLAINED:

A Journey Down Memory Lane:

"Bookish Time Capsule" challenges on bookstagram take followers on a journey down memory lane. The booksta-grammer introduces the concept as an opportunity to revisit cherished moments, relive beloved stories, and cele-brate the impact of books on one's life. The challenges become a celebration of the enduring love for literature and the memories it creates.

Sharing Literary Treasures:

The essence of these challenges lies in followers sharing items that hold sentimental value and are connected to books. These treasures may include well-worn copies of favorite books, bookish mementos from book events or signings, or gifts received from fellow book lovers. The challenges become a virtual showcase of the special bonds between readers and their literary treasures.

Nostalgic Memories:

The concept of "Bookish Time Capsule" involves followers sharing nostalgic memories associated with books. These memories may include the first book that ignited a passion for reading, a book that provided solace during difficult times, or a literary quote that resonates deeply. The challenges become a celebration of the profound emotional connections books forge in people's lives.

Creating Virtual Time Capsules:

"Bookish Time Capsule" challenges encourage followers to create virtual time capsules on their profiles or share their items and memories using specific hashtags. The bookstagrammer may provide prompts or themes to guide the entries. The challenges become a tapestry of cherished memories and literary appreciation shared within the bookstagram community.

Building a Bookish Community:

The concept of "Bookish Time Capsule" fosters a sense of community among participants. As followers engage with each other's entries, they discover shared experiences and a deep appreciation for the impact of books. The challenges become a platform for book lovers to bond over their shared love for literature.

Embracing Diversity of Literary Treasures:

"Bookish Time Capsule" challenges celebrate the diversity of literary treasures that hold significance for different readers. Participants are encouraged to share items and memories that represent their unique bookish journeys. The challenges become an acknowledgment of the beauty and individuality of each reader's literary experiences.

Inspiring Creativity and Reflection:

The concept of "Bookish Time Capsule" challenges inspires followers to reflect on their literary journeys and get creative in presenting their entries. Participants may craft visually appealing displays or heartfelt captions to accompany their submissions. The challenges become a celebration of creativity, nostalgia, and literary expression.

Preserving Literary Legacies:

"Bookish Time Capsule" challenges emphasize the importance of preserving literary legacies for future generations. Participants are encouraged to consider the significance of their bookish items and memories in the context of their personal histories. The challenges become a collective effort to preserve and celebrate the enduring impact of literature.

Building Emotional Connections:

The concept of "Bookish Time Capsule" challenges fosters emotional connections between followers, authors, and books. Participants may share their entries with authors or publishers, creating a sense of shared appreciation and gratitude. The challenges become a bridge between readers and the creators who have touched their lives through literature.

IN CONCLUSION:

"Bookish Time Capsule" challenges on bookstagram offer a nostalgic and heartwarming concept. By inviting followers to share their literary treasures and cherished memories, bookstagrammers create virtual time capsules that celebrate the enduring impact of books on people's lives. These challenges foster a sense of connection, inspire creativity and reflection, and embrace the diverse and unique experiences of each reader's bookish journey. As participants share their items and memories, they build a bookish community that celebrates the magic of literature and preserves its legacy for future generations. "Bookish Time Capsule" challenges become a celebration of the sentimental ties between readers and their favorite books, a platform for emotional connections and shared memories, and a heartwarming tribute to the enduring power of storytelling within the enchanting world of bookstagram.

SEVENTY-NINE
BOOKISH FASHION BATTLES:
A STYLISH SHOWDOWN OF LITERARY-INSPIRED OUTFITS

THE CONCEPT EXPLAINED:

Unleashing Literary Style:

"Bookish Fashion Battles" on bookstagram unleash the creativity of participants to blend literature and fashion. The bookstagrammer introduces the concept as a delightful opportunity to express one's love for books through personal style. The battles become a celebration of the unique connection between literature and fashion.

Book-Inspired Fashion Challenges:

The essence of these battles lies in the book-inspired fashion challenges set by the bookstagrammer. Participants may be asked to create outfits inspired by specific books, characters, genres, or literary settings. The battles become a canvas for participants to showcase their sartorial interpretations of beloved literary elements.

Embracing Literary Characters:

The concept of "Bookish Fashion Battles" encourages participants to embrace their favorite literary characters in their outfit choices. Participants may dress up as iconic characters, reimagine modern interpretations of classic figures, or combine elements from multiple books to create unique ensembles. The battles become a stylish homage to the fictional characters that have left an indelible mark on readers' hearts.

Celebrating Book Settings and Themes:

Beyond characters, the battles celebrate the enchanting worlds and themes woven throughout literature. Participants may draw inspiration from book settings such as Hogwarts or Narnia, or showcase their love for specific genres like fantasy, romance, or dystopia. The battles become a visual celebration of the diverse and immersive worlds that books transport readers to.

Voting for the Best Outfit:

In "Bookish Fashion Battles," followers are invited to vote on the best book-inspired outfit among the participants. The bookstagrammer may set up polls or use interactive features to enable voting. The battles become a democratic and engaging process where the bookstagram community determines the most captivating literary fashion choices.

Fostering a Fashionable Community:

The concept of "Bookish Fashion Battles" fosters a fashionable community within the bookstagram platform. Participants engage with each other's outfits, share styling tips, and exchange admiration for each other's creativity. The battles become a stylish showcase of camaraderie and mutual appreciation among book lovers.

Inspiring Creativity and Individuality:

"Bookish Fashion Battles" inspire participants to embrace their creativity and individuality in expressing their love for literature through fashion. Participants are encouraged to interpret bookish themes in their unique and personal ways. The battles become a celebration of the diverse and imaginative expressions of literary-inspired style.

A Platform for Bookish Style Exploration:

The concept of "Bookish Fashion Battles" provides a platform for participants to explore and experiment with book-inspired style. Participants may discover new books or characters through fashion research, leading to further literary exploration. The battles become an exciting gateway to discovering new literary worlds and characters.

Blurring the Lines Between Fiction and Reality:

"Bookish Fashion Battles" blur the lines between fiction and reality as participants bring fictional worlds and characters to life through their outfits. The bookstagrammer may encourage participants to share their outfit stories or how they channeled a character's essence. The battles become a celebration of the magical intersection between books and everyday life.

IN CONCLUSION:

"Bookish Fashion Battles" on bookstagram offer a stylish and engaging concept. By hosting creative fashion battles where followers showcase their best book-inspired outfits, bookstagrammers unleash the power of personal style in celebrating literature. These battles spark imagination, foster a sense of community, and inspire participants to embrace the magical connection between books and fashion. As participants dress up as beloved characters, reimagine enchanting worlds, and showcase their literary-inspired style, they become part of a fashionable community that celebrates the creative fusion of literature and personal expression. "Bookish Fashion Battles" become a canvas for participants to share their love for books through sartorial storytelling, a platform for camaraderie and admiration among book lovers, and a vibrant showcase of imaginative fashion within the enchanting world of bookstagram.

EIGHTY
BOOKISH DISCUSSIONS ON SOCIAL AND CULTURAL ISSUES DEPICTED IN LITERATURE:
EXPLORING THE IMPACT OF STORIES ON SOCIETY

THE CONCEPT EXPLAINED:

Exploring Literary Themes with Depth:

"Bookish Discussions on Social and Cultural Issues" invite followers to explore literary works beyond their surface narratives. The bookstagrammer introduces the concept as a journey into the deeper layers of stories, where themes of social justice, equality, diversity, and identity are dissected and analyzed. The discussions become a celebration of literature's capacity to engage readers in profound explorations of humanity.

Spotlighting Cultural and Social Representations:

The essence of these discussions lies in spotlighting the cultural and social representations found in literature. Participants may analyze how authors portray gender, race, ethnicity, sexuality, mental health, socio-economic disparities, and other crucial issues. The discussions become a platform to appreciate diverse perspectives and foster understanding of complex human experiences.

Recognizing Literature as a Mirror of Society:

The concept of "Bookish Discussions on Social and Cultural Issues" acknowledges literature as a mirror of society. Literary works often reflect the prevailing social norms, challenges, and triumphs of their time. The discussions become a realization of the dynamic relationship between literature and the societies in which it is created.

Promoting Empathy and Understanding:

These discussions encourage participants to empathize with the experiences of characters from diverse backgrounds. By stepping into the shoes of fictional personas, readers gain insights into the lives of others and foster understanding and compassion. The discussions become a celebration of the transformative power of literature in building empathy and bridges of understanding.

Analyzing Impact on Readers:

The concept involves analyzing the impact of literary representations on readers' perspectives. Bookstagrammers may explore how reading about social and cultural issues shapes readers' awareness, attitudes, and actions in real life. The discussions become a reflection of literature's potential to inspire positive change and critical self-reflection.

Fostering Inclusive Dialogues:

"Bookish Discussions on Social and Cultural Issues" foster inclusive dialogues within the bookstagram community. Participants from diverse backgrounds come together to share their thoughts, experiences, and insights on the themes discussed. The discussions become a celebration of the collective wisdom and diversity of voices within the bookstagram platform.

Challenging Stereotypes and Prejudices:

The concept of these discussions challenges stereotypes and prejudices perpetuated by literature. By engaging in thoughtful conversations, participants critically assess harmful narratives and seek to break down biases. The discussions become a catalyst for positive change and dispelling harmful stereotypes.

*Recognizing Literature's Role in Social Movements:***

These discussions recognize literature's historical role in driving social movements. Literary works have often played a pivotal role in advocating for human rights, civil liberties, and social justice. The discussions become a celebration of literature's enduring influence on societal progress.

Inspiring Responsible Reading and Literary Criticism:

The concept encourages responsible reading and literary criticism. Participants are urged to engage with literature critically, recognizing both its strengths and limitations in addressing social and cultural issues. The discussions become a testament to the power of informed and thoughtful reading.

Nurturing a Community of Thoughtful Readers:

"Bookish Discussions on Social and Cultural Issues" nurture a community of thoughtful readers who appreciate literature's potential to shape minds and hearts. Participants engage in respectful exchanges of ideas, sparking new perspectives and expanding their understanding of the world. The discussions become a celebration of intellectual curiosity, empathy, and open-mindedness within the bookstagram community.

IN CONCLUSION:

"Bookish Discussions on Social and Cultural Issues Depicted in Literature" on bookstagram offer an enlightening and thought-provoking concept. By initiating meaningful conversations about the portrayal of social and cultural issues in literary works, bookstagrammers create spaces for critical thinking, empathy, and understanding. These discussions spotlight diverse perspectives, challenge stereotypes, and celebrate the transformative power of literature in shaping perceptions and driving social change. As participants engage in inclusive dialogues, explore the impact of literature on readers, and foster responsible reading practices, they become part of a community that celebrates literature's capacity to inspire positive change and promote a more compassionate and equitable world. "Bookish Discussions on Social and Cultural Issues" become a celebration of literature's ability to ignite conversations that enrich minds and hearts, and a testament to the profound impact of stories on society within the captivating world of bookstagram.

EIGHTY-ONE
"GUESS THE AUTHOR" QUIZZES:

UNRAVELING LITERARY GENIUS THROUGH QUOTES

THE CONCEPT EXPLAINED:

Celebrating Literary Voices:

"Guess the Author" quizzes invite followers to embark on a journey to recognize the distinct voices of various writers. The bookstagrammer introduces the concept as a delightful exploration of literary genius, where participants get to test their knowledge and appreciation of authors' unique writing styles. The quizzes become a celebration of the diversity and brilliance of literary voices across genres and eras.

Identifying Iconic Quotes:

The essence of these quizzes lies in selecting iconic quotes from renowned literary works. Participants are presented with quotes that capture the essence of the authors' storytelling and philosophical musings. The quizzes become a showcase of timeless words that have left indelible marks on the literary landscape.

Discovering Literary Themes and Styles:

The concept of "Guess the Author" quizzes encourages participants to discover literary themes and writing styles associated with different authors. From poetic elegance to satirical wit, participants explore the nuances of authors' storytelling techniques. The quizzes become an appreciation of the multifaceted world of literature and the myriad ways writers convey their visions.

Promoting Literary Exploration:

These quizzes promote literary exploration as participants encounter quotes from diverse genres and literary traditions. Participants may encounter quotes from classic literature, modern bestsellers, or works from lesser-known writers. The quizzes become a gateway to discovering new literary treasures and expanding one's reading horizons.

Stimulating Intellectual Curiosity:

The concept involves stimulating intellectual curiosity as participants ponder over the possible authors behind each quote. The bookstagrammer may provide hints or contextual information to guide participants in their guessing process. The quizzes become a delightful exercise in literary detective work, encouraging participants to dive into the minds behind the words.

Fostering Community Engagement:

"Guess the Author" quizzes foster engagement and community participation within the bookstagram platform. Followers interact with each other, share their guesses, and engage in friendly competitions to test their literary knowledge. The quizzes become a celebration of the sense of camaraderie and shared passion for literature within the bookstagram community.

Honoring Literary Legacy:

The concept of these quizzes honors the literary legacy of writers whose words continue to resonate with readers across generations. Participants may encounter quotes from classic authors like Shakespeare, Jane Austen, or Mark Twain, as well as contemporary voices like Chimamanda Ngozi Adichie, Neil Gaiman, or Haruki Murakami. The quizzes become a tribute to the enduring impact of literary icons on the literary world.

Encouraging Research and Learning:

These quizzes encourage participants to delve into the works and biographies of authors as they seek to uncover the correct answers. Participants may take this opportunity to learn more about the authors' lives and literary contributions. The quizzes become a gateway to scholarly pursuits and expanding one's literary knowledge.

Creating Interactive Literary Fun:

The concept involves creating interactive and entertaining literary fun for followers. The bookstagrammer may turn the quizzes into a series or incorporate additional elements like polls or interactive stories.

The quizzes become a source of enjoyment and amusement for book lovers seeking to test their literary acumen.

IN CONCLUSION:

"Guess the Author" quizzes on bookstagram offer an engaging and intellectually stimulating concept. By crafting quizzes that challenge followers to identify the authors behind iconic quotes, bookstagrammers celebrate the brilliance of literary voices across genres and eras. These quizzes spark curiosity, promote literary exploration, and foster community engagement among book lovers as they unravel the minds behind timeless words. As participants immerse themselves in literary detective work, they celebrate the enduring legacy of writers who have left an indelible mark on the literary world. "Guess the Author" quizzes become a delightful celebration of literary genius, a gateway to discovering new literary treasures, and a testament to the captivating power of words within the enchanting world of bookstagram.

EIGHTY-TWO
"BOOKISH THROWBACK" POSTS:
REVISITING CHILDHOOD FAVORITES AND NOSTALGIC READS

THE CONCEPT EXPLAINED:

A Trip Down Memory Lane:

"Bookish Throwback" posts invite followers on a delightful trip down memory lane. The bookstagrammer introduces the concept as a heartwarming journey back to the books that once captivated their young hearts and ignited their love for reading. The posts become a celebration of the lasting influence of childhood favorites on the bookstagrammer's reading journey.

Sharing Nostalgic Reads:

The essence of these posts lies in sharing books that evoke nostalgia and fond memories. The bookstagrammer may display tattered and well-loved copies of childhood favorites, showcasing the wear and tear that bears witness to countless readings. The posts become a tribute to the books that have accompanied the bookstagrammer throughout the years.

Reconnecting with Beloved Characters:

The concept of "Bookish Throwback" posts encourages the bookstagrammer to reconnect with beloved characters from childhood reads. Whether it's revisiting the magical world of Harry Potter, following Anne Shirley's adventures in Green Gables, or solving mysteries with Nancy Drew, the posts evoke cherished memories of fictional friends. The posts become a celebration of the enduring bond between readers and the characters who have touched their hearts.

Fostering a Sense of Community:

These posts foster a sense of community among followers who may share similar reading experiences. As the bookstagrammer reminisces about beloved books, followers engage in conversations about their own childhood favorites, creating a shared space of nostalgia and connection. The posts become a celebration of the shared joy and camaraderie among book lovers.

Celebrating Timeless Stories:

The concept involves celebrating timeless stories that continue to resonate with readers across generations. The bookstagrammer may share classic children's literature, picture books, or young adult novels that have stood the test of time. The posts become a tribute to the enduring power of storytelling and its ability to transcend age and time.

Encouraging Intergenerational Conversations:

These posts encourage intergenerational conversations as followers of different ages come together to reminisce about their own childhood favorites. Older followers may rediscover books they cherished in their youth, while younger readers may discover new titles to add to their reading lists. The posts become a celebration of the bridge between generations built by beloved stories.

Inspiring Reading Diversity:

The concept of "Bookish Throwback" posts inspires reading diversity as the bookstagrammer revisits a range of genres, themes, and authors from their past. By sharing a variety of childhood favorites, the bookstagrammer encourages followers to explore a diverse array of books. The posts become a gateway to discovering new and varied reading experiences.

A Source of Warmth and Comfort:

These posts offer warmth and comfort to followers as they share in the nostalgia and joy of revisiting childhood favorites. The bookstagrammer's personal anecdotes and reflections create a cozy and inviting atmosphere, inviting followers to reminisce about their own reading journeys. The posts become a source of solace and reassurance in the power of literature to touch our hearts.

IN CONCLUSION:

"Bookish Throwback" posts on bookstagram offer a heart-warming and nostalgic concept. By sharing old childhood favorites and revisiting nostalgic reads, bookstagrammers take followers on a journey down memory lane. These posts evoke feelings of nostalgia, foster connections through shared reading experiences, and celebrate the enduring impact of books on our lives. As the bookstagrammer reconnects with beloved characters and stories, followers engage in intergenerational conversations, and reading diversity is celebrated, a sense of community and camaraderie emerges within the bookstagram platform. "Bookish Throwback" posts become a tribute to the timeless stories that have touched our hearts, a celebration of the enduring power of literature to create lasting memories, and a comforting reminder of the warmth and joy found in the world of books within the enchanting realm of bookstagram.

EIGHTY-THREE
BOOKSTAGRAMMER-CURATED SPOTIFY PLAYLISTS:

ENHANCING READING MOODS THROUGH MELODIES

THE CONCEPT EXPLAINED:

A Symphony of Words and Melodies:

"Bookstagrammer-Curated Spotify Playlists" invite followers to immerse themselves in a symphony of words and melodies. The bookstagrammer introduces the concept as a harmonious union of literature and music, where playlists are carefully crafted to complement the themes and atmospheres of various books. The playlists become a celebration of the transformative power of combining the arts.

Enhancing Reading Moods:

The essence of these playlists lies in enhancing reading moods through carefully selected music. Bookstagrammers create playlists that align with different emotional tones, genres, and settings of books, enhancing the reader's experience. The playlists become a guide to navigating the emotions and ambiance of literary worlds.

Setting the Literary Stage:

The concept of "Bookstagrammer-Curated Spotify Playlists" involves setting the literary stage for readers. Bookstagrammers may introduce playlists for specific genres like fantasy, romance, mystery, or historical fiction, as well as playlists tailored to different emotions like excitement, contemplation, or tranquility. The playlists become an invitation to embark on unique literary adventures.

Fostering Immersive Experiences:

These playlists foster immersive reading experiences by creating an ambient backdrop for the reader's imagination to flourish. The bookstagrammer selects tracks that evoke the desired mood and blend seamlessly with the book's narrative. The playlists become a catalyst for total immersion in the world of books.

Curation as an Art Form:

The concept involves curating playlists as an art form. Bookstagrammers carefully select tracks based on lyrics, instrumentals, and emotions, creating a cohesive and evocative musical journey that complements the reading material. The playlists become a showcase of the bookstagrammer's artistic sensibility.

Exploring Literary Themes Through Music:

These playlists explore literary themes through music, enhancing the reader's understanding of the book's nuances and emotions. Bookstagrammers may incorporate songs with lyrics that resonate with the book's themes or instrumentals that evoke the story's ambiance. The playlists become a celebration of the connections between literature and music.

Catering to Different Tastes:

The concept of "Bookstagrammer-Curated Spotify Playlists" caters to diverse musical tastes. The bookstagrammer may include a wide range of genres, from classical and instrumental to pop, rock, or electronic, ensuring there is something for everyone. The playlists become a reflection of the bookstagrammer's commitment to inclusivity and diverse artistic expressions.

Encouraging Personalization:

These playlists encourage personalization as followers create their own reading soundtracks based on the bookstagrammer's inspiration. Readers can add or remove tracks, tailoring the playlist to their preferences and the specific book they are reading. The playlists become a celebration of individuality and creative expression.

Elevating the Reading Experience:

The concept involves elevating the reading experience to a multisensory level. By engaging with both literature and music, readers find a deeper connection to the stories and characters, amplifying the emotional impact of the book. The playlists become a testament to the transformative potential of the arts.

IN CONCLUSION:

"Bookstagrammer-Curated Spotify Playlists" on bookstagram offer a delightful and immersive concept. By combining the power of music with the pleasure of reading, bookstagrammers enhance reading moods, set the literary stage, and foster immersive reading experiences. These playlists cater to diverse tastes, explore literary themes through music, and encourage personalization, inviting readers to embark on unique literary journeys. The concept celebrates the artistic curation of playlists, elevates the reading experience to a multisensory level, and creates a harmonious union of words and melodies within the enchanting realm of bookstagram. As followers immerse themselves in these musical reading experiences, they celebrate the transformative power of combining the arts and the joy of getting lost in the world of books with a perfectly curated soundtrack to accompany them on their literary adventures.

EIGHTY-FOUR
BOOK-THEMED VIRTUAL ESCAPE ROOMS:

UNRAVELING LITERARY ENIGMAS AND PUZZLES

THE CONCEPT EXPLAINED:

An Adventure into Literary Realms:

"Book-Themed Virtual Escape Rooms" invite followers on an adventure into the captivating realms of their favorite books. The bookstagrammer introduces the concept as an interactive and exciting way to immerse oneself in the stories, characters, and mysteries of literature. The escape rooms become a celebration of the magic of books and the power of imagination.

Unraveling Literary Enigmas:

The essence of these escape rooms lies in unraveling literary enigmas. Bookstagrammers craft puzzles, riddles, and challenges inspired by the themes, settings, and plotlines of well-known books, requiring participants to exercise their critical thinking and problem-solving skills. The escape rooms become a test of intellectual prowess and a tribute to the intricacies of literature.

Engaging with Beloved Characters:

The concept of "Book-Themed Virtual Escape Rooms" involves engaging with beloved characters in new and exciting ways. Participants may find themselves teaming up with the protagonists to overcome obstacles or assisting their favorite fictional detectives in solving mysteries. The escape rooms become an opportunity to step into the shoes of beloved literary figures.

Interactive Literary Exploration:

These escape rooms encourage interactive literary exploration as participants uncover hidden clues, discover secret passages, and explore the immersive world of their chosen book. The bookstagrammer may incorporate multimedia elements like audio clips or visual cues to enhance the experience. The escape rooms become a gateway to experiencing literature in a dynamic and interactive manner.

A Challenge for Book Lovers:

The concept involves crafting challenges that cater to book lovers' passions and knowledge. Participants may encounter puzzles that test their familiarity with plot twists, literary quotes, or character motivations, creating a sense of camaraderie among fellow book enthusiasts. The escape rooms become a celebration of the shared love for literature within the bookstagram community.

Immersive Atmospheres:

These escape rooms strive to create immersive atmospheres that transport participants to the heart of their favorite literary worlds. The bookstagrammer may design virtual environments that mirror the settings of the books, from mysterious castles to magical forests or bustling cityscapes. The escape rooms become a testament to the power of literature to transport readers to new realms.

Collaborative Adventures:

The concept of "Book-Themed Virtual Escape Rooms" fosters collaborative adventures among participants. Bookstagrammers may encourage followers to form teams and work together to overcome challenges, fostering a sense of teamwork and camaraderie. The escape rooms become a celebration of the joy of shared reading experiences and collective problem-solving.

A Journey of Discovery:

These escape rooms offer a journey of discovery as participants uncover hidden layers of their favorite books and encounter lesser-known facets of the stories. The bookstagrammer may include Easter eggs or references to lesser-known works by the same author, encouraging participants to explore beyond the familiar. The escape rooms become a celebration of the depth and richness of literary worlds.

A Platform for Creativity:

The concept involves creating a platform for creativity, allowing bookstagrammers to craft unique and original escape room experiences tailored to their favorite books. From classic literature to contemporary bestsellers, the possibilities are endless. The escape rooms become a showcase of the bookstagrammer's creativity and love for literature.

IN CONCLUSION:

"Book-Themed Virtual Escape Rooms" on bookstagram offer an ingenious and immersive concept. By blending the thrill of escape room challenges with the enchantment of literature, bookstagrammers engage followers in interactive and intellectually stimulating adventures. These escape rooms become an opportunity to unravel literary enigmas, engage with beloved characters, and explore immersive literary worlds. As participants work collaboratively, tap into their knowledge of literature, and embark on a journey of discovery, they celebrate the magic of books and the joy of shared reading experiences within the captivating realm of bookstagram. The concept of "Book-Themed Virtual Escape Rooms" becomes a tribute to the power of literature to inspire creativity, imagination, and intellectual engagement, offering book lovers an unforgettable and immersive literary escape within the enchanting world of books.

EIGHTY-FIVE
INTERACTIVE STORYTELLING:
CO-CREATING LITERARY ADVENTURES ONE WORD AT A TIME

THE CONCEPT EXPLAINED:

A Literary Journey of Words:

"Interactive Storytelling" invites followers on a delightful and spontaneous literary journey of words. The booksta-grammer introduces the concept as a collaborative story-telling experience, where each participant contributes a single word to craft a cohesive narrative. The sessions become a celebration of the creativity and imagination that emerge from collective storytelling.

Collective Creativity Unleashed:

The essence of this concept lies in unleashing collective creativity. As each participant adds their word, they become an active co-creator of the story, building upon the ideas of others and shaping the direction of the narrative. The sessions become a testament to the power of shared creativity and the synergy of diverse voices.

Fostering a Sense of Community:

These storytelling sessions foster a sense of community and camaraderie among followers. Participants join together in an immersive storytelling adventure, irrespective of their backgrounds or locations, connecting through the shared experience of crafting a story together. The sessions become a source of shared joy and engagement within the bookstagram community.

Spontaneity and Surprise:

The concept of "Interactive Storytelling" thrives on spontaneity and surprise. As the bookstagrammer initiates the storytelling session, participants eagerly anticipate the next word contributed by others, leading to unexpected twists and turns in the narrative. The sessions become a delightful journey of surprises and serendipity.

Filling the Blank Canvas:

These storytelling sessions offer a blank canvas waiting to be filled with creativity. Each word added by a participant paints a new stroke on the canvas, gradually forming a vivid and imaginative picture. The sessions become an unfolding masterpiece of collective storytelling.

Embracing Limitations:

The concept involves embracing the limitations of one word contributions. Participants must carefully select their words to fit seamlessly into the narrative, sparking their creativity and enhancing the cohesion of the story. The sessions become a testament to the art of storytelling within the constraints of limited input.

Experiencing Creative Flow:

These storytelling sessions offer an opportunity to experience creative flow. As participants immerse themselves in the collaborative process, they become deeply engaged in the story's development, experiencing the joy of creative expression. The sessions become a celebration of the transformative power of storytelling on both writers and readers.

Fostering Playful Imagination:

The concept of "Interactive Storytelling" fosters playful imagination. Participants may explore different genres, settings, and characters, allowing their minds to wander and weave a tapestry of ideas. The sessions become an invitation to play with language and explore the endless possibilities of storytelling.

Celebrating Inclusivity:

These storytelling sessions celebrate inclusivity as participants from diverse backgrounds, ages, and perspectives come together to contribute to the narrative. The co-creation of the story fosters an environment of acceptance and openness. The sessions become a platform for diverse voices to be heard and celebrated.

IN CONCLUSION:

"Interactive Storytelling" on bookstagram offers a captivating and participatory concept that celebrates the power of collective creativity and the joy of collaborative storytelling. As followers co-create a unique and imaginative narrative one word at a time, they embark on a literary journey of surprises and spontaneous creativity. These sessions foster a sense of community and inclusivity, bringing participants from different backgrounds together in a playful exploration of language and storytelling. The concept of "Interactive Storytelling" becomes a testament to the transformative power of words, the magic of storytelling, and the joy of shared creativity within the enchanting realm of bookstagram. As participants join hands in crafting a narrative that is greater than the sum of its parts, they celebrate the power of imagination, the beauty of collective storytelling, and the sense of connection that emerges from creating literary adventures together.

EIGHTY-SIX
BOOKISH BUCKET LIST:
INSPIRING READING ADVENTURES AND ACHIEVING GOALS

THE CONCEPT EXPLAINED:

A Literary Journey of Exploration:

"Bookish Bucket List" challenges invite followers on a literary journey of exploration and discovery. The bookstagrammer introduces the concept as an opportunity to set personalized reading goals and embark on unique literary adventures. The challenges become a celebration of the joy of reading and the thrill of exploring new literary territories.

Personalized Reading Goals:

The essence of these challenges lies in setting personalized reading goals tailored to each follower's preferences, interests, and reading habits. Bookstagrammers may curate a diverse range of goals, including reading specific genres, exploring new authors, completing classic novels, or delving into literary themes. The challenges become a testament to the individuality of reading experiences and the diversity of literary interests.

A Sense of Accomplishment:

The concept of "Bookish Bucket List" challenges encourages followers to experience a sense of accomplishment as they check off each goal they achieve. Participants can share their progress with the bookstagrammer and the community, celebrating their literary conquests. The challenges become a source of pride and joy for followers as they complete their reading goals.

Encouraging Reading Diversity:

These challenges promote reading diversity and exploration of different literary landscapes. Bookstagrammers may include prompts that encourage participants to read books from diverse cultures, authors of various backgrounds, or books in different formats. The challenges become a celebration of the richness and inclusivity of literature.

Exploring Uncharted Literary Worlds:

The concept involves encouraging followers to step outside their comfort zones and explore uncharted literary worlds. Bookstagrammers may curate reading goals that challenge participants to read books they might not have considered before. The challenges become an invitation to broaden horizons and discover hidden literary gems.

Fostering a Sense of Community:

These challenges foster a sense of community and camaraderie among followers. Participants can share their experiences, recommendations, and accomplishments with each other, creating a supportive and inspiring space for shared reading adventures. The challenges become a platform for connecting with fellow book lovers and exchanging literary insights.

Reading as an Adventure:

The concept of "Bookish Bucket List" challenges encourages followers to view reading as an adventure. Each goal becomes a new quest to embark upon, with books serving as gateways to exciting and imaginative worlds. The challenges become a celebration of the magic and escapism that literature offers.

Embracing a Growth Mindset:

These challenges promote a growth mindset towards reading and learning. Participants are encouraged to set ambitious goals, attempt genres they are unfamiliar with, and embrace challenges that push the boundaries of their reading comfort zones. The challenges become an opportunity for personal growth and continuous learning through literature.

Celebrating the Joy of Reading:

The essence of "Bookish Bucket List" challenges lies in celebrating the joy of reading and the power of books to enrich our lives. Participants are encouraged to cherish the time spent with books, savor the beauty of language, and find solace, inspiration, and connection in the stories they encounter. The challenges become a testament to the transformative power of literature and its ability to touch hearts and minds.

IN CONCLUSION:

"Bookish Bucket List" challenges on bookstagram offer an exciting and motivating concept that celebrates the joy of reading and encourages followers to achieve their personalized literary goals. By curating reading challenges that encompass diverse genres, authors, and themes, bookstagrammers inspire their followers to embark on unique literary adventures and explore the wonders of literature. These challenges foster a sense of accomplishment, personal growth, and a deeper appreciation for the magic of reading. The concept of "Bookish Bucket List" challenges becomes a celebration of the diverse and wondrous world of books, the joy of shared reading experiences within the bookstagram community, and the limitless potential for exploration and discovery that literature offers. As participants set and achieve their reading goals, they celebrate the power of books to ignite curiosity, inspire imagination, and open new doors of knowledge and understanding.

EIGHTY-SEVEN
VIRTUAL BOOKISH SCAVENGER HUNTS:

VIRTUAL BOOKISH SCAVENGER HUNTS:

THE CONCEPT EXPLAINED:

A Digital Literary Adventure:

"Virtual Bookish Scavenger Hunts" invite followers on a captivating and interactive digital literary adventure. The bookstagrammer introduces the concept as a thrilling quest, where participants must search for clues hidden within their posts and stories. The hunts become a celebration of the magic of books, the joy of exploration, and the power of storytelling in the digital age.

Unraveling Hidden Clues:

The essence of these virtual hunts lies in unraveling hidden clues. Bookstagrammers craft clever and imaginative clues, often inspired by beloved literary works, requiring participants to exercise their critical thinking and problem-solving skills. The hunts become a test of intellectual prowess and a tribute to the intricacies of literature.

Engaging with the Bookstagrammer's Storytelling:

These scavenger hunts encourage active engagement with the bookstagrammer's storytelling. As participants navigate through posts and stories, they discover a carefully woven narrative that guides them on their quest. The hunts become a testament to the power of storytelling to captivate and inspire readers.

Interactive and Community-Building:

The concept of "Virtual Bookish Scavenger Hunts" fosters interactivity and community-building within the bookstagram community. Participants often come together to share their discoveries, exchange ideas, and collaborate in solving challenges. The hunts become a platform for fostering connections and camaraderie among fellow book enthusiasts.

Encouraging Exploration of Bookstagram Profiles:

These virtual hunts encourage participants to explore bookstagram profiles in-depth, diving into past posts and stories to unearth hidden clues. Bookstagrammers may design hunts that prompt participants to revisit and engage with older content, rediscovering past literary gems. The hunts become an opportunity to rediscover and appreciate the diverse range of literary content shared by bookstagrammers.

Fostering Creativity in Clue Design:

The concept involves fostering creativity in clue design. Bookstagrammers may use various forms of wordplay, visual cues, and storytelling techniques to create clever and intriguing clues that challenge participants' minds. The hunts become a showcase of the bookstagrammer's creativity in crafting engaging and interactive experiences for their followers.

Creating a Sense of Excitement and Mystery:

These scavenger hunts create a sense of excitement and mystery as participants progress through the clues, not knowing what hidden surprises they might encounter next. The bookstagrammer may incorporate multimedia elements like images or videos to enhance the immersive experience. The hunts become an immersive journey into the unknown realms of literature.

Inclusivity and Accessible Participation:

The concept of "Virtual Bookish Scavenger Hunts" embraces inclusivity, ensuring that all followers can participate regardless of their location. Virtual hunts provide accessible opportunities for book enthusiasts from around the world to join in the literary adventure. The hunts become a celebration of the global reach and inclusivity of the bookstagram community.

Rewarding Discoveries:

These virtual hunts offer rewards and prizes for successful participants. Bookstagrammers may acknowledge and celebrate the achievements of participants who solve all the clues, creating a sense of accomplishment and gratification. The hunts become a celebration of the participants' efforts and dedication in unraveling the literary mysteries.

IN CONCLUSION:

"Virtual Bookish Scavenger Hunts" on bookstagram offer an innovative and immersive concept that celebrates the joy of reading, the power of storytelling, and the thrill of exploration. By blending the excitement of scavenger hunts with the enchantment of books, bookstagrammers engage their followers in interactive and intellectually stimulating challenges. These hunts become an opportunity to unravel hidden literary clues, navigate through digital storytelling, and foster a sense of camaraderie within the bookstagram community. The concept of "Virtual Bookish Scavenger Hunts" becomes a celebration of the creativity of bookstagrammers in crafting engaging experiences for their followers, the inclusivity of the bookstagram community, and the joy of shared literary adventures in the digital age. As participants embark on their quests, they celebrate the magic of books, the wonders of digital exploration, and the endless possibilities that storytelling offers within the captivating realm of bookstagram.

EIGHTY-EIGHT
COLLABORATIVE BOOK CHARACTER DREAM CASTING:

BRINGING LITERARY WORLDS TO LIFE WITH FOLLOWERS' IMAGINATION

THE CONCEPT EXPLAINED:

Casting Literary Characters:

"Collaborative Book Character Dream Casting" invites followers to cast their favorite book characters as if they were to be portrayed in film or TV adaptations. The bookstagrammer introduces the concept by sharing a character from a beloved book and inviting followers to suggest actors they envision in that role. The sessions become a celebration of the love for literature and the joy of envisioning characters in new ways.

Engaging Imagination and Creativity:

The essence of these collaborative sessions lies in engaging the imagination and creativity of followers. As participants suggest actors for various characters, they bring their own interpretation of the literary persona to the forefront. The sessions become an exploration of diverse perspectives and visions for beloved characters.

Embracing Diverse Interpretations:

These casting discussions embrace diverse interpretations of book characters. Each participant may envision a character differently based on their individual reading experience, cultural background, and personal preferences. The sessions become a platform for celebrating the richness and complexity of literary characters.

Fostering Community Interaction:

The concept of "Collaborative Book Character Dream Casting" fosters community interaction within the bookstagram space. Participants eagerly share their casting ideas, sparking conversations, and engaging in friendly debates about the best actors to embody iconic literary roles. The sessions become a source of connection and camaraderie among followers.

Interactive Fan Engagement:

These collaborative sessions offer interactive fan engagement with literary works. Followers become active participants in bringing books to life, contributing to the collective experience of exploring characters beyond the written page. The sessions become a celebration of the interactive and immersive nature of bookstagram.

Exploring Book-to-Screen Transitions:

The concept involves exploring the transition of characters from the written page to the screen. By envisioning actors in specific roles, participants delve into the potential of adapting books into visual media. The sessions become an opportunity to contemplate the magic of storytelling in different forms.

Inspiring Artistic Visualizations:

These collaborative discussions inspire artistic visualizations of beloved book characters. Bookstagrammers may use images or graphics to represent the suggested actors, creating a captivating visual feast for participants. The sessions become a celebration of the intersection of literature and visual art.

Discovering New Perspectives:

The concept of "Collaborative Book Character Dream Casting" encourages followers to discover new perspectives on characters. As participants encounter casting ideas different from their own, they gain fresh insights into the complexities of literary personas. The sessions become an opportunity for personal growth and expanded horizons in literary appreciation.

Casting Across Genres and Eras:

These casting discussions transcend genres and eras. Participants may suggest actors from various film and television industries or even consider historical figures for characters set in different time periods. The sessions become an exploration of cross-cultural and cross-temporal imaginings.

Appreciating Actors and Characters Alike:

The concept involves appreciating both actors and characters alike. As participants suggest actors for characters they love, they celebrate the talent of performers and the allure of beloved literary personas. The sessions become a tribute to the artistry of actors and authors alike.

IN CONCLUSION:

"Collaborative Book Character Dream Casting" on bookstagram offers a delightful and interactive concept that celebrates the magic of books and the power of imagination. By inviting followers to suggest actors for beloved book characters, bookstagrammers engage their community in lively discussions and explorations of literary personas. These casting sessions become a celebration of diversity, creativity, and interactive fan engagement within the bookstagram space. The concept of "Collaborative Book Character Dream Casting" fosters a sense of community and camaraderie, bringing followers together to envision characters beyond the written page and into the realm of visual storytelling. As participants share their casting suggestions and engage in friendly debates, they celebrate the joy of collaborative storytelling, the richness of literary characters, and the limitless possibilities of bookstagram's imaginative space.

EIGHTY-NINE
BOOKSTAGRAMMER-HOSTED LIVE READATHONS:
FOSTERING A COMMUNITY OF READING AND CONNECTION

THE CONCEPT EXPLAINED:

Reading Together in Real-Time:

"Bookstagrammer-Hosted Live Readathons" invite followers to read together in real-time with the bookstagrammer. The concept involves scheduling a specific date and time for the readathon, during which the bookstagrammer shares their reading progress live with the audience. The readathons become a celebration of the joy of reading and the power of shared literary experiences.

Interactive Audience Participation:

The essence of these live readathons lies in interactive audience participation. As the bookstagrammer reads, followers can join in by reading the same book, discussing plot developments, sharing reactions, and engaging in real-time conversations through comments or live chat. The readathons become an opportunity for followers to actively engage with the bookstagrammer and each other.

Building a Reading Community:

These readathons build a reading community within the bookstagram space. By gathering readers together for a shared literary experience, the bookstagrammer fosters a sense of camaraderie and belonging among followers who may not have known each other otherwise. The readathons become a platform for connecting book enthusiasts and creating meaningful relationships.

Inspiring Reading Enthusiasm:

The concept of "Bookstagrammer-Hosted Live Readathons" inspires reading enthusiasm among followers. As participants witness the bookstagrammer's passion for the written word and engage in discussions with fellow readers, they are encouraged to prioritize reading in their own lives. The readathons become a celebration of the transformative power of books.

Encouraging Mindful Reading:

These live readathons encourage mindful reading practices. Participants can savor each chapter and immerse themselves fully in the book, as the bookstagrammer shares their thoughts and reactions in real-time. The readathons become an opportunity to experience books with heightened mindfulness and appreciation.

Exploring Diverse Literary Genres:

The concept involves exploring diverse literary genres through readathons. The bookstagrammer may host readathons featuring different genres, enabling participants to discover new and diverse literary worlds. The readathons become an exploration of the vast landscape of literature.

A Sense of Accomplishment:

These readathons provide participants with a sense of accomplishment as they progress through the book alongside the bookstagrammer. Followers can celebrate each milestone and discuss their reading achievements. The readathons become a celebration of individual reading accomplishments and growth.

Sparking Thoughtful Discussions:

The interactive nature of live readathons sparks thoughtful discussions and debates about plot twists, character arcs, and deeper themes within the book. The readathons become a space for intellectual exchange and critical analysis of literature.

Creating Memorable Reading Experiences:

The concept involves creating memorable reading experiences that participants cherish. Live readathons often leave a lasting impact on followers, making them feel connected to the bookstagrammer and the reading community. The readathons become cherished memories of shared literary journeys.

Building Author and Book Awareness:

These readathons contribute to building author and book awareness. By featuring specific books during the readathon, the bookstagrammer can introduce lesser-known authors and promote diverse literature. The readathons become a platform for supporting authors and celebrating the literary world.

IN CONCLUSION:

"Bookstagrammer-Hosted Live Readathons" on bookstagram offer an engaging and communal concept that celebrates the joy of reading and the power of shared literary experiences. By reading together in real-time and encouraging audience participation, bookstagrammers create a sense of community, inspire reading enthusiasm, and foster meaningful connections among followers. These readathons become a celebration of the transformative power of books, the diversity of literature, and the magic of shared reading adventures. As participants engage in real-time discussions and celebrate reading accomplishments, they experience the joy of reading together and build lasting memories of literary camaraderie. The concept of "Bookstagrammer-Hosted Live Readathons" becomes a testament to the connective power of storytelling and the cherished bonds formed within the bookstagram community.

NINETY
BOOKISH UNSOLVED MYSTERIES:
UNRAVELING THE ENIGMATIC THREADS OF LITERATURE

THE CONCEPT EXPLAINED:

Unraveling Literary Puzzles:

"Bookish Unsolved Mysteries" posts invite followers to embark on a journey of unraveling literary puzzles. The bookstagrammer introduces the concept by selecting a book or series and highlighting specific aspects of the narrative that remain unanswered or mysterious. The posts become a celebration of the intricacies and nuances of storytelling.

Engaging Critical Thinking:

The essence of these posts lies in engaging critical thinking and analytical skills. As followers delve into the enigmatic elements of the book, they consider various theories and possibilities, discussing potential explanations for the unanswered questions. The posts become an opportunity for intellectual exploration and interpretation.

Inspiring Discussion and Debate:

These posts inspire lively discussions and debates among followers. As participants share their interpretations and theories, they engage in friendly debates and exchange insights, exploring the book from diverse perspectives. The posts become a platform for fostering interactive and thought-provoking conversations.

Delving into Character Motivations:

The concept involves delving into character motivations and intentions that may have been left ambiguous in the narrative. Followers ponder the underlying reasons behind characters' actions, contemplating the nuances of their choices and decisions. The posts become an exploration of the intricacies of character development.

Exploring Symbolism and Allegory:

These posts encourage exploration of symbolism and allegory present in the book. Followers analyze recurring themes, metaphors, and symbols, seeking deeper meanings within the narrative. The posts become a celebration of the literary craftsmanship and depth of storytelling.

Celebrating Authorial Intent:

The concept involves celebrating authorial intent and creative choices. While exploring unsolved mysteries, participants consider how the author's deliberate decisions contribute to the overall impact of the narrative.The posts become an acknowledgment of the author's artistry and storytelling prowess.

Promoting Textual Analysis:

These posts promote textual analysis and close reading. Followers may revisit passages or chapters to extract clues and hints that shed light on the mysteries of the book. The posts become an opportunity for exploring the intricacies of language and narrative structure.

Encouraging Fan Theories:

The concept of "Bookish Unsolved Mysteries" encourages the development of fan theories. Followers share their imaginative interpretations and speculate on potential resolutions to the mysteries. The posts become a tribute to the creativity and passion of book enthusiasts.

Acknowledging Narrative Complexity:

These posts acknowledge the complexity of narratives and the beauty of unresolved elements. Followers embrace the uncertainty and recognize that some mysteries may intentionally remain open-ended to provoke thought and leave room for interpretation. The posts become an appreciation of the enigmatic allure of storytelling.

Intriguing Readers for New Discoveries:

The concept involves intriguing readers to seek out new discoveries. As followers engage with "Bookish Unsolved Mysteries" posts, they may be inspired to reread the book or explore related works to gain deeper insights into the narrative. The posts become a gateway to ongoing literary exploration.

Strengthening Literary Appreciation:

These posts strengthen literary appreciation by highlighting the complexities of narratives. Followers gain a deeper understanding of the layers and depths within books, enhancing their appreciation for the art of storytelling. The posts become a celebration of the multifaceted nature of literature.

IN CONCLUSION:

"Bookish Unsolved Mysteries" posts on bookstagram offer a captivating and intellectually stimulating concept that celebrates the mysteries and complexities of storytelling. By exploring unanswered questions and enigmatic elements in books, bookstagrammers engage their followers in thought-provoking discussions, inspiring critical analysis, and fostering curiosity. These posts become a testament to the power of literature to provoke thought, spark imagination, and ignite curiosity within the bookstagram community. As followers ponder character motivations, analyze symbolism, and share fan theories, they celebrate the artistry of authors and the enigmatic allure of storytelling. The concept of "Bookish Unsolved Mysteries" becomes an invitation to embrace the beauty of unanswered questions and find joy in the ongoing exploration of the vast landscape of literature.

NINETY-ONE
THEMED BOOK-INSPIRED WORKOUTS:

FUSING LITERARY PASSION WITH FITNESS

THE CONCEPT EXPLAINED:

Merging Literary Passions and Fitness:

"Themed Book-Inspired Workouts" invite followers to merge their love for books with their passion for fitness. The bookstagrammer introduces the concept by selecting a specific book or literary theme as inspiration for the workout routine. The workouts become a celebration of the intersection of literary worlds and physical well-being.

Engaging Creative Imagination:

The essence of these themed workouts lies in engaging creative imagination. As the bookstagrammer designs fitness routines inspired by the essence of the book, followers are encouraged to visualize the characters, settings, and themes while exercising. The workouts become an opportunity for immersive and imaginative fitness experiences.

Infusing Fun and Motivation:

These themed workouts infuse fun and motivation into fitness routines. By incorporating elements from beloved books, the workouts become more enjoyable and provide followers with an added incentive to engage in physical activity. The workouts become a source of joy and enthusiasm in fitness pursuits.

Catering to Diverse Fitness Levels:

The concept of "Themed Book-Inspired Workouts" caters to diverse fitness levels. The bookstagrammer may design routines that suit beginners, intermediate, and advanced fitness enthusiasts, ensuring inclusivity for all followers. The workouts become accessible to individuals with varying fitness capabilities.

Promoting Active Living and Well-Being:

These themed workouts promote active living and well-being. By encouraging followers to incorporate physical activity into their daily lives, the bookstagrammer fosters a culture of health and self-care within the bookstagram community. The workouts become a celebration of holistic wellness and balanced living.

Highlighting Literary Themes:

The concept involves highlighting literary themes in the workout routines. Followers may experience workouts that reflect the adventurous spirit of a fantasy novel, the determination of a protagonist, or the calming ambiance of a serene setting. The workouts become a celebration of the diversity of literary themes.

Embodying Book Characters:

These themed workouts offer followers the opportunity to embody book characters during exercise. Whether mimicking the strength and agility of a beloved hero or channeling the grace of a fictional dancer, participants can feel a deeper connection to the literary worlds they adore. The workouts become a tribute to the embodiment of literary personas.

Creating Community Participation:

The concept encourages community participation in the themed workouts. Followers may share their experiences, progress, and adaptations of the routines, fostering a supportive and motivational environment. The workouts become a platform for encouraging shared fitness journeys.

Inspiring Book Discussions:

These themed workouts inspire book discussions among followers. As participants engage in the workouts, they may reflect on the book that inspired the routine, sharing thoughts and insights with other bookstagram community members. The workouts become an opportunity for book enthusiasts to connect over shared literary experiences.

Encouraging Regular Exercise:

The concept of "Themed Book-Inspired Workouts" encourages regular exercise and physical activity. By providing fresh and exciting routines based on different books, the bookstagrammer inspires followers to incorporate fitness into their daily routines. The workouts become a source of motivation for consistent exercise habits.

IN CONCLUSION:

"Themed Book-Inspired Workouts" on bookstagram offer a unique and creative concept that celebrates the fusion of literary passions with fitness. By designing routines inspired by beloved books or literary themes, bookstagrammers engage followers in immersive and imaginative fitness experiences. These workouts become a celebration of the diverse literary worlds and characters, inspiring a deeper connection to books and promoting holistic wellness within the bookstagram community. As participants embody book characters during exercise and share their progress, the themed workouts foster a supportive and motivational environment. The concept of "Themed Book-Inspired Workouts" becomes a testament to the power of literature to inspire and enrich all aspects of life, including physical well-being. Through these workouts, book enthusiasts embark on literary fitness journeys, finding joy and motivation in the delightful fusion of books and exercise.

NINETY-TWO
BOOKSTAGRAMMER-HOSTED DIGITAL BOOK FAIRS:

EMBRACING THE LITERARY WORLD IN A VIRTUAL REALM

THE CONCEPT EXPLAINED:

Bringing Book Fairs to the Digital World:

"Bookstagrammer-Hosted Digital Book Fairs" bring the charm and excitement of traditional book fairs to the digital realm. The bookstagrammer acts as the host, curating a virtual space that captures the essence of a bustling book fair. The digital book fairs become a celebration of the literary world in an accessible and engaging format.

Virtual Booths and Exhibitors:

The concept involves setting up virtual booths representing authors, publishers, and bookish businesses. Each booth showcases the work of authors and book-related products, allowing followers to explore an array of literary delights. The virtual booths become a hub of literary exploration and discovery.

Interactive Author Interviews:

These digital book fairs feature interactive author interviews and Q&A sessions. The bookstagrammer invites authors to participate in live interviews, where followers can learn about the authors' inspirations, writing processes, and upcoming projects. The author interviews become a fascinating opportunity for followers to connect with their favorite writers.

Spotlight on New Releases:

The concept involves spotlighting new book releases from various authors and publishers. The bookstagrammer may dedicate specific segments of the fair to introduce followers to exciting new titles, generating anticipation and interest among readers. The spotlight on new releases becomes a celebration of literary innovation and creativity.

Book Recommendations and Reviews:

These digital book fairs offer book recommendations and reviews from the bookstagrammer and participating authors. Followers can access insightful recommendations and reviews that guide them in their literary journeys. The book recommendations become a valuable resource for readers seeking their next favorite book.

Virtual Book Signings:

The concept may include virtual book signings, where authors sign digital bookplates or personalized messages for followers. These virtual signings allow book enthusiasts to obtain signed copies of their favorite books without geographical limitations. The virtual book signings become a cherished memento of the digital book fair experience.

Engaging Bookish Activities:

These digital book fairs may feature engaging bookish activities, such as book-themed quizzes, games, and challenges. These activities encourage followers to immerse themselves further in the world of books and authors. The bookish activities become a source of enjoyment and entertainment for participants.

Collaborations with Bookish Brands:

The concept involves collaborations with bookish brands and businesses to showcase book-related merchandise and products. Followers can explore a diverse range of book-inspired items, such as bookish candles, bookmarks, and art prints. The collaborations become a celebration of the creativity and artistry of bookish businesses.

Access to Exclusive Content:

These digital book fairs may offer access to exclusive content, such as sneak peeks of upcoming book releases, cover reveals, and behind-the-scenes insights from authors. The exclusive content becomes a delightful treat for book enthusiasts, offering a glimpse into the literary world.

Connecting the Bookstagram Community:

The concept fosters connection and community among bookstagrammers and followers. As participants explore the virtual book fair, they may engage in discussions, share their favorite finds, and celebrate their love for books together. The digital book fairs become a gathering place for book enthusiasts to bond over their shared passion.

IN CONCLUSION:

"Bookstagrammer-Hosted Digital Book Fairs" offer an exciting and innovative concept that embraces the literary world in a virtual landscape. By curating virtual booths, featuring interactive author interviews, and spotlighting new releases, bookstagrammers create engaging and immersive book fair experiences for followers. These digital events become a celebration of the literary universe, offering a treasure trove of bookish wonders for exploration and discovery. As followers engage in bookish activities, connect with authors, and explore book-related merchandise, the digital book fairs foster a sense of community and camaraderie among book enthusiasts. The concept of "Bookstagrammer-Hosted Digital Book Fairs" becomes a testament to the adaptability and creativity of the bookstagram community, as it recreates the magic of traditional book fairs in the digital age, opening doors to endless literary adventures for book enthusiasts worldwide.

NINETY-THREE
BOOKISH CONFESSIONS:
EMBRACING LITERARY VULNERABILITY AND SHARED SECRETS

THE CONCEPT EXPLAINED:

A Safe Haven for Bookish Revelations:

"Bookish Confessions" provide followers with a safe and inviting space to share their book-related habits, quirks, and guilty pleasures. The bookstagrammer introduces the concept by inviting followers to participate in sharing their "bookish confessions." The posts become a celebration of literary vulnerability and the beauty of shared experiences.

Embracing Diversity in Reading Habits:

The essence of "Bookish Confessions" lies in embracing the diversity of reading habits. Followers from various backgrounds and experiences come together to share their unique bookish preferences, providing insights into the broad spectrum of reading tastes. The posts become a celebration of the individuality and diversity within the bookstagram community.

Fostering Connection through Shared Secrets:

These confessions foster connection and camaraderie among book enthusiasts. As followers read and respond to each other's confessions, they find comfort and validation in knowing they are not alone in their bookish habits and secrets. The posts become a source of connection and understanding within the bookstagram community.

Laughing at Bookish Guilty Pleasures:

The concept involves laughing at bookish guilty pleasures and realizing that many readers share similar "guilty" joys. Followers may confess to enjoying particular book genres or tropes that they might hesitate to admit openly. The posts become a tribute to the joy and pleasure of reading, regardless of individual preferences.

Sharing Reading Rituals and Quirks:

These confessions also involve sharing reading rituals and quirks that followers may have developed over time. From unique reading positions to peculiar bookmark choices, the bookish confessions offer glimpses into the idiosyncrasies of book lovers. The posts become an appreciation of the little joys and habits that make reading special for each individual.

Discovering Relatable Experiences:

The concept of "Bookish Confessions" encourages followers to discover relatable experiences shared by others. As they read confessions, they may nod in agreement or share their own stories in response. The posts become a celebration of the common ground among book lovers.

Encouraging Self-Reflection and Growth:

These confessions encourage self-reflection and self-awareness among followers. Participants may explore their reading preferences and habits, leading to a deeper understanding of their relationship with books. The posts become an opportunity for personal growth and exploration within the realm of reading.

Normalizing "Unpopular" Opinions:

The concept involves normalizing "unpopular" bookish opinions and preferences. Followers may confess to not enjoying a popular book or having a different perspective on a beloved character, creating an environment where diverse opinions are embraced. The posts become a celebration of individual tastes and perspectives in the literary world.

Celebrating the Love for Reading:

These confessions celebrate the universal love for reading that unites the bookstagram community. Regardless of the specific confessions shared, the underlying theme is the passion for books and literature. The posts become an ode to the timeless allure of reading.

Building a Supportive Bookstagram Community:

The concept of "Bookish Confessions" contributes to building a supportive bookstagram community. By encouraging vulnerability and non-judgmental sharing, bookstagrammers foster an inclusive and welcoming space for book lovers to connect. The posts become a testament to the strong bonds formed through a shared love for books.

IN CONCLUSION:

"Bookish Confessions" on bookstagram offer a heart-warming and engaging concept that embraces literary vulnerability and shared secrets. By providing a safe space for followers to share their bookish habits, guilty pleasures, and reading quirks, bookstagrammers foster connection, understanding, and camaraderie within the community. These confessions become a celebration of the diversity and individuality within the bookstagram world, highlighting the universal joy of reading that unites book enthusiasts worldwide. As followers laugh at their bookish guilty pleasures, share reading rituals, and normalize diverse book opinions, they form strong bonds and discover relatable experiences that bring them closer together. The concept of "Bookish Confessions" becomes a tribute to the beauty of shared vulnerability and the profound connections forged through the timeless magic of literature. Through these confessions, bookstagrammers inspire readers to embrace their unique bookish selves and find solace in the knowledge that they are part of a supportive and understanding community of fellow book lovers.

NINETY-FOUR
VIRTUAL BOOK-TO-FILM CLUB:
A CINEMATIC EXPLORATION OF BELOVED BOOKS

THE CONCEPT EXPLAINED:

Celebrating the Convergence of Literature and Film:

The Virtual Book-to-Film Club celebrates the convergence of literature and film, two powerful forms of storytelling. The bookstagrammer introduces the concept by selecting a popular book that has been adapted into a film. The club becomes a celebration of the dynamic relationship between these two creative mediums.

Interactive Virtual Discussions:

The essence of the concept lies in hosting interactive virtual discussions. The bookstagrammer invites followers to join the discussion and share their thoughts on the adaptation, its faithfulness to the source material, and the impact of cinematic choices on their perception of the story. The discussions become a platform for diverse perspectives and insights.

Comparing Book and Film Interpretations:

These virtual discussions involve comparing the book and film interpretations of the story. Participants may explore how certain plot points, characters, or themes were adapted for the screen, leading to insightful analyses and discussions. The comparisons become an exploration of the creative choices behind adapting literature to film.

Creating a Sense of Community:

The concept fosters a sense of community among bookstagrammers and followers. As participants come together to discuss adaptations, they find camaraderie in their shared love for both books and movies. The club becomes a gathering place for enthusiasts of both mediums.

Discovering New Perspectives:

These discussions enable followers to discover new perspectives on the story through the film adaptation. Participants may gain fresh insights from others' observations and interpretations, enriching their understanding of the narrative. The discussions become a source of enlightenment and intellectual exchange.

Appreciating the Challenges of Adaptation:

The concept involves appreciating the challenges of adapting books to film. Participants may discuss the limitations of a visual medium compared to the written word and how directors and screenwriters approach these challenges. The discussions become an exploration of the art of adaptation.

Exploring Film Techniques and Cinematography:

These virtual discussions offer an opportunity to explore film techniques, cinematography, and visual storytelling. Participants may analyze the film's cinematographic choices and how they contribute to the overall mood and atmosphere of the adaptation. The discussions become an appreciation of the cinematic artistry involved in bringing stories to life on screen.

Encouraging Constructive Criticism:

The concept encourages constructive criticism of adaptations. While participants may express their preferences for certain aspects of the book or film, the discussions remain respectful and open to diverse viewpoints. The club becomes a space for thoughtful analysis and constructive feedback.

Highlighting Diverse Adaptations:

These discussions may highlight diverse adaptations, from faithful renditions to creative reinterpretations. Participants can explore adaptations that remain true to the source material and those that take artistic liberties. The club becomes an exploration of the vast spectrum of adaptation possibilities.

Inspiring New Reading and Viewing Experiences:

The concept inspires followers to seek out both the original literary works and the film adaptations. Participants may be encouraged to read the book if they watched the film first or vice versa, broadening their literary and cinematic horizons. The discussions become a catalyst for new reading and viewing experiences.

IN CONCLUSION:

The "Virtual Book-to-Film Club" on bookstagram offers an exciting and engaging concept that celebrates the convergence of literature and film. By hosting interactive discussions on adaptations of popular books, bookstagrammers provide a platform for followers to explore the world of cinematic storytelling. The club becomes a celebration of diverse perspectives, creative choices, and the challenges involved in adapting literature to film. Through thoughtful comparisons and respectful critiques, participants gain a deeper appreciation for both the original literary works and the film adaptations. The Virtual Book-to-Film Club fosters a sense of community among bookstagrammers and followers, where enthusiasts of both mediums come together to bond over their shared love for stories. As participants explore film techniques, cinematography, and the art of adaptation, they enrich their understanding of the dynamic relationship between literature and film. Ultimately, the "Virtual Book-to-Film Club" becomes a testament to the power of storytelling in all its forms, as bookstagrammers and followers embark on cinematic explorations of beloved books, discovering new perspectives and gaining a deeper appreciation for the diverse and multifaceted world of storytelling.

NINETY-FIVE
BOOKSTAGRAMMER'S "TO BE READ" (TBR) JAR CHALLENGE:
A SERENDIPITOUS READING ADVENTURE

THE CONCEPT EXPLAINED:

Inviting Book Recommendations from Followers:

The essence of the TBR Jar challenge lies in inviting book recommendations from followers. The bookstagrammer introduces the concept by announcing the challenge and encouraging followers to submit book titles they think would be interesting reads. The challenge becomes a celebration of the bookstagram community's diverse literary tastes.

Creating a TBR Jar:

After receiving book suggestions, the bookstagrammer compiles them into a TBR Jar – a container filled with the submitted book titles. The TBR Jar becomes a symbol of literary serendipity, where the next reading adventure awaits.

The Element of Surprise:

The beauty of the TBR Jar challenge lies in its element of surprise. The bookstagrammer randomly draws a book title from the jar without knowing what book will be selected next. The challenge becomes a delightful and suspenseful experience, akin to unwrapping a surprise gift.

Reading Diverse Genres and Authors:

The concept encourages reading diverse genres and authors. Since book suggestions come from a variety of followers with different tastes, the TBR Jar challenge leads to an eclectic reading list that spans various literary genres. The challenge becomes an exploration of literary diversity and discovery.

Embracing the Unexpected:

By embracing the unexpected book selections, the bookstagrammer embarks on a literary adventure they might not have chosen otherwise. This openness to unexpected reads broadens their reading horizons and introduces them to new authors and perspectives. The challenge becomes an embrace of the unexpected and a willingness to venture beyond comfort zones.

Fostering Community Engagement:

The TBR Jar challenge fosters community engagement and interaction. As followers submit book suggestions and anticipate which book will be drawn next, they become active participants in the reading journey. The challenge becomes a collaborative and interactive reading experience.

Encouraging Follow-up Discussions:

After reading each book, the bookstagrammer can share their thoughts and impressions with followers. This opens the door to follow-up discussions, where participants can exchange views on the chosen book and recommend more titles. The challenge becomes a catalyst for meaningful literary conversations.

Sparking Excitement and Curiosity:

The TBR Jar challenge sparks excitement and curiosity among followers, who eagerly await each draw to discover which book will be chosen. The suspenseful element adds an extra layer of thrill to the reading experience. The challenge becomes a source of excitement and anticipation within the bookstagram community.

Building Empathy and Connection:

As the bookstagrammer reads and shares their experiences with different books, they may find common ground with followers who have read the same titles. This shared literary experience fosters empathy and connection. The challenge becomes a bridge that connects book lovers through shared reading adventures.

Promoting Reader Diversity:

By involving followers in the book selection process, the TBR Jar challenge promotes reader diversity. Followers from various backgrounds and experiences contribute book suggestions, reflecting a wide range of perspectives and interests. The challenge becomes a tribute to the richness of reader diversity within the bookstagram community.

IN CONCLUSION:

The "To Be Read" (TBR) Jar challenge on bookstagram offers an exciting and interactive concept that celebrates the serendipity of literary adventures. By inviting followers to submit book suggestions and drawing titles randomly from a TBR Jar, bookstagrammers foster a sense of community, encourage diverse reading choices, and embark on a journey shaped by the collective imagination of their audience. The TBR Jar challenge becomes a celebration of literary diversity, as bookstagrammers explore a wide array of genres and authors based on their followers' recommendations. Embracing the element of surprise and openness to the unexpected, the challenge broadens the bookstagrammer's reading horizons and introduces them to new literary experiences. As the bookstagrammer shares their thoughts and experiences with followers, the challenge becomes a catalyst for engaging literary discussions within the bookstagram community. By promoting reader diversity and fostering community engagement, the TBR Jar challenge bridges the gap between bookstagrammers and their followers, creating a shared and immersive reading experience. Ultimately, the TBR Jar challenge becomes a testament to the power of literary serendipity, as bookstagrammers and their audience embark on a delightful reading adventure shaped by the collective love for books and the joy of shared storytelling.

NINETY-SIX
COLLABORATIVE BOOK PLAYLISTS:

A MUSICAL JOURNEY THROUGH LITERARY WORLDS AND CHARACTERS

THE CONCEPT EXPLAINED:

A Fusion of Music and Literature:

The essence of the concept lies in the fusion of music and literature. Bookstagrammers invite their followers to participate in creating playlists that embody the essence of different book worlds or characters. Each song selected represents a mood, theme, or emotion that resonates with the chosen literary universe. The playlists become a harmonious blend of literary and musical artistry.

Curating Playlists Together:

The process begins with the bookstagrammer announcing the collaborative playlist challenge, where followers are encouraged to submit song recommendations that align with specific books or characters. The bookstagrammer then compiles these recommendations into themed playlists, creating a collective work of art. The challenge becomes a celebration of shared creativity and artistic expression.

Emotional Journey through Literary Worlds:

As participants contribute songs that evoke the emotions and atmosphere of different book worlds, the collaborative playlists become an emotional journey through the pages of literature. Each song becomes a gateway into the unique setting, mood, and ambiance of the selected story. The playlists become a vessel for transporting participants to the heart of their favorite literary realms.

Understanding Characters on a Deeper Level:

The concept extends to collaborative character playlists, where followers contribute songs that capture the essence of beloved fictional personas. Each song is chosen to resonate with a character's personality, struggles, and growth throughout the narrative. The playlists become an exploration of the multifaceted personalities of fictional heroes and villains.

Fostering Community Connection:

As followers contribute to the playlists and listen to the collective musical creations, a sense of community connection is fostered. Participants engage in conversations about their musical choices and the emotions they associate with specific books or characters. The playlists become a source of bonding and camaraderie among bookstagrammers.

Enhancing Reading Experiences:

By immersing themselves in the collaborative playlists before, during, or after reading a book, participants enhance their reading experiences. The music heightens the emotional impact of the narrative, making the literary journey even more profound. The playlists become a companion that enriches the reading adventure.

Discovering New Music:

The collaborative nature of the playlists introduces participants to new music genres, artists, and songs. Followers may encounter music that perfectly complements the essence of a literary world, inspiring them to explore new musical horizons. The playlists become a gateway to musical discovery and exploration.

Exploring the Power of Emotional Connection:

The concept highlights the power of emotional connection between music and literature. Participants may discover that certain songs evoke memories of beloved stories or resonate deeply with their favorite characters, reinforcing the emotional impact of the books. The playlists become a testament to the enduring power of art to touch the soul.

An Ongoing Creative Journey:

The collaborative book playlists become an ongoing creative journey for both the bookstagrammer and their followers. As more book recommendations and song contributions flow in, the playlists continue to evolve and expand, reflecting the ever-growing literary interests of the community. The playlists become a living tribute to the dynamic and diverse world of literature.

A Tribute to Beloved Books and Characters:

Through their participation in the collaborative playlists, followers pay homage to the books and characters that have left a lasting impact on their lives. Each song becomes a heartfelt tribute to the literary creations that have captured their hearts. The playlists become a celebration of the enduring magic of literature.

IN CONCLUSION:

The concept of collaborative book playlists on bookstagram offers a captivating and immersive experience that combines the power of music and literature. By inviting followers to curate and contribute songs to playlists representing different book worlds and characters, bookstagrammers foster a sense of community connection and artistic expression. These playlists become emotional journeys through beloved literary realms, allowing participants to delve deeper into the essence of their favorite stories and characters. By understanding the profound emotional connection between music and literature, participants enrich their reading experiences and enhance the emotional impact of the narrative. The collaborative book playlists become a living tribute to the diverse and dynamic world of literature, a celebration of the enduring magic of storytelling, and a testament to the timeless connection between music and the written word. As the playlists continue to evolve and expand, they become a harmonious blend of literary and musical artistry, a true celebration of the vibrant and united bookstagram community.

NINETY-SEVEN
BOOKISH DEBATE CLUB:
A PLATFORM FOR ENGAGING LITERARY DISCUSSIONS

THE CONCEPT EXPLAINED:

Creating a Space for Thoughtful Discussions:

The essence of the Bookish Debate Club lies in creating a space for thoughtful and respectful discussions about controversial book topics. Bookstagrammers introduce the concept by announcing debate sessions or topics that are up for discussion. The club encourages participants to express their opinions openly and engage in constructive debates. The club becomes a haven for critical thinking and intellectual exploration within the bookstagram community.

Exploring Controversial Book Topics:

The Bookish Debate Club delves into controversial themes and topics found within literature. These topics could include moral dilemmas, ethical questions, contentious character decisions, or societal issues depicted in books. The club selects topics that prompt diverse and thought-provoking perspectives. The club becomes a catalyst for exploring the complexity and depth of literary narratives.

Fostering Respectful Discussions:

To ensure productive and respectful debates, the club establishes ground rules for communication and encourages participants to approach discussions with empathy and an open mind. All viewpoints are welcomed and encouraged, as long as they are expressed in a courteous manner. The club becomes a symbol of inclusivity and open dialogue.

Encouraging Diverse Perspectives:

The Bookish Debate Club embraces the diversity of perspectives within the bookstagram community. Participants come from various backgrounds, cultures, and experiences, enriching the discussions with their unique viewpoints. The club becomes a celebration of the richness of reader diversity.

Engaging in Healthy Debates:

Healthy and constructive debates fostered by the club provide an opportunity for participants to challenge their own beliefs, consider alternative viewpoints, and develop a deeper understanding of complex literary themes. Participants engage in discussions that encourage critical analysis and reflection. The club becomes a source of intellectual growth and introspection.

Strengthening Literary Appreciation:

Through debate and dialogue, participants gain a deeper appreciation for the complexity and intricacy of literature. Exploring controversial topics prompts readers to analyze characters, plotlines, and societal contexts with a more discerning eye. The club becomes a gateway to profound literary analysis and understanding.

Nurturing a Supportive Community:

The Bookish Debate Club fosters a supportive and empathetic community. Participants may find comfort in expressing their opinions and engaging in discussions, knowing that their views will be respected, and their voices will be heard. The club becomes a safe haven for exchanging ideas and thoughts without judgment.

Promoting Critical Thinking Skills:

By encouraging participants to present well-reasoned arguments and substantiate their viewpoints with evidence from the text, the club promotes critical thinking skills. Readers learn to approach literature with a more analytical mindset, enhancing their overall reading experience. The club becomes a catalyst for cultivating analytical and logical reasoning abilities.

Building Intellectual Confidence:

As participants engage in debates and articulate their viewpoints, they build intellectual confidence. Expressing opinions and engaging in thoughtful discussions contribute to a sense of empowerment and self-assurance. The club becomes a space where participants feel encouraged to express their ideas openly.

Fostering Lifelong Learning:

The Bookish Debate Club promotes lifelong learning and intellectual curiosity. Participants continually seek to expand their knowledge, engage with challenging ideas, and broaden their literary horizons. The club becomes a gateway to a lifetime of intellectual exploration.

IN CONCLUSION:

The Bookish Debate Club on bookstagram offers a dynamic and enlightening platform for discussing controversial book topics. By creating a space for thoughtful and respectful debates, the club encourages participants to explore diverse perspectives and engage in critical thinking. The club becomes a celebration of reader diversity, fostering empathy and understanding within the bookstagram community. Through healthy debates and intellectual discussions, participants gain a deeper appreciation for the complexity of literature and develop stronger critical thinking skills. The Bookish Debate Club nurtures a supportive and inclusive community where all viewpoints are welcomed and respected. Ultimately, the club becomes a vibrant symbol of intellectual curiosity, a testament to the power of literature to inspire meaningful discussions, and a cornerstone of the bookstagram community's commitment to fostering a love of reading and a deep appreciation for the power of words.

NINETY-EIGHT

BOOKSTAGRAMMER-HOSTED STORYTELLING SESSIONS:

REVIVING THE MAGIC OF CLASSIC FAIRYTALES AND MYTHS

THE CONCEPT EXPLAINED:

Rediscovering Classic Tales:

The essence of the concept lies in the bookstagrammer's passion for rediscovering classic fairytales and myths. Armed with a deep appreciation for these timeless stories, bookstagrammers embark on a journey to immerse themselves in the world of folklore, fairytales, and ancient myths. The sessions become an homage to the rich literary heritage of the past.

Modern-Day Storytelling:

The bookstagrammer takes on the role of a modern-day bard, inviting followers to join them in the virtual campfire of storytelling. The tales are not merely retold but infused with the storyteller's personal touch and flair. The sessions become an intimate and personalized storytelling experience.

Breathing New Life into Old Narratives:

Through their storytelling prowess, bookstagrammers breathe new life into old narratives, rekindling the allure and magic of these tales. The retellings offer fresh perspectives, drawing attention to the timeless themes and lessons that continue to resonate across generations. The sessions become a testament to the enduring power of storytelling.

Creating an Immersive Experience:

During the storytelling sessions, bookstagrammers set the stage for an immersive experience. They may create an ambiance by dimming the lights, lighting candles, or incorporating sound effects to enhance the storytelling atmosphere. The sessions become a mesmerizing escape into the world of imagination.

Connecting with Timeless Themes:

The tales chosen for the storytelling sessions often center around universal themes such as love, courage, sacrifice, and the battle between good and evil. Through these themes, the bookstagrammer seeks to strike a chord with the shared human experience. The sessions become a bridge between the past and the present.

Encouraging Participation and Interaction:

To make the storytelling sessions interactive, bookstagrammers may encourage followers to engage with the stories by asking questions, offering interpretations, or sharing their favorite parts of the tales. The sessions become a collaborative and participatory experience.

Promoting Literary Education:

The storytelling sessions serve as a platform for promoting literary education and cultural awareness. Bookstagrammers may provide historical context and insights into the origins and variations of the stories, fostering a deeper understanding of folklore and myths. The sessions become an educational exploration of the literary heritage.

Building a Sense of Community:

The storytelling sessions foster a sense of community among followers, as participants come together to listen, discuss, and revel in the magic of these classic tales. The shared experience strengthens bonds and creates lasting connections within the bookstagram community. The sessions become a celebration of shared literary passion.

Preserving Oral Tradition:

In embracing the role of storytellers, bookstagrammers play a part in preserving the age-old tradition of oral storytelling. As the tales are retold and passed down through digital platforms, the essence of storytelling is kept alive in the modern age. The sessions become a tribute to the enduring art of oral storytelling.

Fostering Creativity and Imagination:

The storytelling sessions ignite the fires of creativity and imagination within both the bookstagrammer and their followers. Listeners find themselves transported to far-off lands, mythical realms, and fantastical worlds. The sessions become a catalyst for igniting the imagination.

IN CONCLUSION:

The concept of "Bookstagrammer-Hosted Storytelling Sessions" encapsulates the magic and allure of classic fairytales and myths, brought to life in the modern age through the art of storytelling. As bookstagrammers immerse themselves in the world of folklore and ancient narratives, they rekindle the wonder and enchantment of these timeless stories. Through personalized and interactive retellings, the bookstagrammer invites their followers to rediscover the beauty and wisdom woven into these age-old tales. The sessions foster a sense of community, promote literary education, and preserve the oral tradition of storytelling. Ultimately, the storytelling sessions become a celebration of shared literary passion, a testament to the enduring power of storytelling, and a captivating journey into the realms of imagination and wonder. Through the Bookstagrammer-Hosted Storytelling Sessions, the bookstagram community rediscovers the allure of classic tales and finds themselves forever captivated by the enduring magic of storytelling.

NINETY-NINE
BOOKISH SKETCH-A-STORY:
UNLEASHING CREATIVITY THROUGH ILLUSTRATIONS

THE CONCEPT EXPLAINED:

Fusing Literature and Art:

The essence of the Bookish Sketch-a-Story challenge lies in the fusion of literature and art. Bookstagrammers encourage their followers to embrace their artistic talents by inviting them to illustrate scenes from books that have left a lasting impact on their imaginations. The challenge becomes a harmonious blend of two forms of creative expression.

Selecting Scenes from Favorite Books:

Participants in the challenge are free to choose scenes from any book that holds special significance to them. Whether it's a poignant moment, a thrilling climax, or a heart-warming encounter between characters, the challenge encourages diverse and captivating selections. The challenge becomes a diverse gallery of literary moments brought to life.

Encouraging Artistic Interpretation:

The Bookish Sketch-a-Story challenge celebrates individual artistic styles and interpretations. Each participant infuses their unique vision and creativity into the illustrations, resulting in a rich tapestry of diverse artistic expressions. The challenge becomes a testament to the beauty of artistic diversity.

Promoting Engagement and Interaction:

Throughout the challenge, bookstagrammers actively engage with their followers, offering words of encouragement and admiration for the illustrations. Participants, in turn, interact with each other, offering compliments, feedback, and support. The challenge becomes a collaborative and interactive artistic community.

Strengthening the Book-Reader Connection:

As participants delve into the process of illustrating scenes from books they love, they forge a deeper connection with the stories and characters. The act of visualizing and recreating these moments cements the emotional bond between the reader and the narrative. The challenge becomes an avenue for strengthening the reader-book relationship.

Fostering Creativity and Imagination:

The Bookish Sketch-a-Story challenge acts as a catalyst for nurturing creativity and imagination. Participants delve into the worlds of their favorite books, visualizing settings, characters, and emotions as they bring them to life on paper. The challenge becomes an inspiring journey of artistic exploration.

Exploring Visual Storytelling:

Through their illustrations, participants engage in visual storytelling. They encapsulate the essence of a book scene, conveying emotions, atmosphere, and the narrative's spirit through their art. The challenge becomes a celebration of the art of visual storytelling.

Providing Inspiration and Motivation:

The challenge motivates participants to challenge themselves artistically and explore new artistic techniques and styles. Seeing the creativity of fellow participants inspires them to push their artistic boundaries further. The challenge becomes a source of inspiration and artistic growth.

Celebrating the Joy of Creation:

The Bookish Sketch-a-Story challenge becomes a celebration of the joy of creation. Participants take delight in the process of bringing their favorite literary moments to life, basking in the satisfaction of their artistic achievements. The challenge becomes a joyful celebration of creativity and self-expression.

Building a Supportive Community:

Throughout the challenge, a supportive and encouraging community emerges. Participants cheer each other on, exchange tips, and celebrate each other's artistic triumphs. The challenge becomes a heartwarming showcase of a nurturing and positive community.

Preserving Literary Memories:

The Bookish Sketch-a-Story challenge acts as a means of preserving cherished literary memories. The illustrated scenes become tangible keepsakes that capture the essence of beloved books. The challenge becomes a tribute to the enduring impact of literature on our lives.

IN CONCLUSION:

The Bookish Sketch-a-Story challenge on bookstagram invites followers to embark on an artistic journey, bringing their favorite literary moments to life through illustrations. By fusing literature and art, the challenge celebrates creativity, individuality, and the power of storytelling. Participants delve into the worlds of their favorite books, forging a deeper connection with the narratives and characters. The challenge serves as a platform for exploring diverse artistic styles, visual storytelling, and creative expression. As participants engage with each other and their bookstagrammer hosts, a supportive and collaborative artistic community flourishes. Ultimately, the Bookish Sketch-a-Story challenge becomes a joyful celebration of creativity, a testament to the beauty of artistic diversity, and a showcase of the enduring impact of literature on the creative spirit. Through this challenge, bookstagrammers and their followers find themselves united in a shared love for art and literature, forever captivated by the magic of storytelling and the boundless possibilities of artistic expression.

ONE HUNDRED
BOOKISH ASMR VIDEOS:
A SERENE SYMPHONY OF READING AND WRITING

THE CONCEPT EXPLAINED:

The Magic of ASMR:

ASMR, known for inducing a tingling sensation or deep relaxation in some individuals, is harnessed as the foundation of Bookish ASMR Videos. The gentle sounds produced in these videos are carefully curated to evoke a sense of calm and comfort in the viewer. The videos become a delightful sensory experience for those seeking relaxation and tranquility.

Immersing in Reading and Writing Sounds:

Bookish ASMR Videos feature a rich tapestry of sounds related to reading and writing. From the soft turning of pages to the faint scratching of a pen on paper, each element is thoughtfully chosen to immerse viewers in the ambiance of literary pursuits. The videos become a symphony of bookish sounds, resonating with book lovers and writers.

Creating a Peaceful Ambiance:

The essence of Bookish ASMR Videos lies in their ability to create a peaceful ambiance that invites viewers to unwind and escape from the stresses of daily life. Whether one is an ardent reader, a writer seeking inspiration, or simply someone in need of tranquility, the videos offer a moment of solace. The videos become a sanctuary of calm in the midst of a busy world.

Enhancing the Reading Experience:

For book lovers, the gentle sounds of Bookish ASMR Videos enhance the reading experience, allowing them to sink deeper into the worlds of their favorite stories. The soft rustling of pages and the soothing whispers of book passages create an immersive atmosphere for literary exploration. The videos become an enchanting companion to the reading journey.

Inspiring Creative Writing:

Writers find inspiration in the rhythmic sounds of writing utensils on paper, reminiscent of the process of crafting words and stories. Bookish ASMR Videos serve as a muse for creative minds, encouraging them to embark on writing adventures. The videos become a catalyst for nurturing creativity and imagination.

A Meditative Retreat:

In the fast-paced digital age, Bookish ASMR Videos offer a meditative retreat, gently guiding viewers to a state of relaxation. The soft, repetitive sounds act as a lullaby, easing tension and promoting a sense of well-being. The videos become a moment of self-care and mindfulness.

Building a Sense of Connection:

The creators of Bookish ASMR Videos often engage with their audience, responding to comments and requests for specific bookish sounds. This interactive approach fosters a sense of connection and community among viewers. The videos become a shared experience that unites bookstagrammers in their love for literature and ASMR.

Celebrating the Beauty of Books:

Bookish ASMR Videos are a celebration of the physicality of books. The sounds of flipping pages, the rustle of covers, and the gentle handling of novels pay homage to the tangible beauty of printed works. The videos become a tribute to the allure of traditional book formats.

Encouraging Relaxation and Sleep:

The calming effects of Bookish ASMR Videos extend beyond the reading nook. Many viewers use these videos as part of their bedtime routine, relying on the soothing sounds to help them unwind and drift into a restful sleep. The videos become a bedtime companion, offering sweet dreams and peaceful slumber.

Supporting Focus and Concentration:

Bookish ASMR Videos can aid in focus and concentration, creating a background ambiance for studying or working on creative projects. The gentle sounds act as a buffer against distractions, allowing the mind to immerse itself in tasks at hand. The videos become a tool for boosting productivity and concentration.

IN CONCLUSION:

The concept of Bookish ASMR Videos on bookstagram offers a serene and immersive experience for bibliophiles, writers, and those seeking tranquility. By harnessing the soothing effects of ASMR and the gentle sounds of reading and writing, these videos transport viewers to a literary sanctuary of calm and creativity. Bookish ASMR Videos enhance the reading experience, inspire creative writing, and serve as a meditative retreat in the fast-paced digital world. They foster a sense of connection and community among bookstagrammers, celebrating the beauty of books and promoting relaxation and well-being. Through these gentle symphonies of sounds, bookstagrammers and their viewers find solace, comfort, and a shared love for literature and the art of ASMR. The Bookish ASMR Videos become a timeless embrace of serenity, inviting all to experience the enchanting union of reading, writing, and the soothing magic of ASMR.

Made in the USA
Monee, IL
04 November 2026

67387618R00233